IDENTITY IN THE SHADOW OF A GIANT

How the Rise of China Is Changing Taiwan

Scott Sigmund Gartner, Chin-Hao Huang, Yitan Li and Patrick James

First published in Great Britain in 2023 by

Bristol University Press
University of Bristol
1-9 Old Park Hill
Bristol
BS2 8BB
UK
t: +44 (0)117 334 6645
e: bup-info@bristol.ac.uk

Details of international sales and distribution partners are available at bristoluniversitypress.co.uk

© Bristol University Press 2023

British Library Cataloguing in Publication Data
A catalogue record for this book is available from the British Library

ISBN 978-1-5292-0987-7 hardcover
ISBN 978-1-5292-0988-4 paperback
ISBN 978-1-5292-0989-1 ePdf
ISBN 978-1-5292-0990-7 ePub

The right of Scott Sigmund Gartner, Chin-Hao Huang, Yitan Li and Patrick James to be identified as authors of this work has been asserted by them in accordance with the Copyright, Designs and Patents Act 1988.

All rights reserved: no part of this publication may be reproduced, stored in a retrieval system, or transmitted in any form or by any means, electronic, mechanical, photocopying, recording, or otherwise without the prior permission of Bristol University Press.

Every reasonable effort has been made to obtain permission to reproduce copyrighted material. If, however, anyone knows of an oversight, please contact the publisher.

The statements and opinions contained within this publication are solely those of the authors and not of the University of Bristol or Bristol University Press. The University of Bristol and Bristol University Press disclaim responsibility for any injury to persons or property resulting from any material published in this publication.

Bristol University Press works to counter discrimination on grounds of gender, race, disability, age and sexuality.

Cover design: Andrew Corbett
Front cover image: Getty/kecl

We would each like to dedicate this book to our families in appreciation for their amazing love and wonderful support.

Contents

List of Figures and Tables		vi
About the Authors		viii
Acknowledgements		xi
Preface		xiii
1	Identity in the Shadow of a Giant: How the Rise of China Is Changing Taiwan	1
2	Taiwan in Historical Perspective	21
3	The Problématique of Taiwanese Identity	43
4	Theorizing about Identity, Change in Capabilities and Dyadic Relations: An Approach Based on Analytic Eclecticism and Systemism	65
5	Elite Reflections	91
6	Popular Reflections (Survey I)	125
7	Factors Influencing Identifying Only as Taiwanese: A Layered Empirical Approach (Survey II)	155
8	A New Vision of Taiwanese Identity, the Rise of China, Cross-Strait Relations and the United States in Northeast Asia	181
Appendix A: Research Interview Questions		213
Appendix B: Survey Questions		215
Appendix C: Taiwan National Security Survey		221
References		229
Index		247

List of Figures and Tables

Figures

1.1	Changes in the Taiwanese/Chinese identity of Taiwanese	12
4.1	Functional relations in a social system	73
4.2	Cause and effect for Taiwanese identity, the rise of China, cross-Strait relations and US influence in Northeast Asia	79
6.1	Have you been to Mainland China in the past five years, excluding Hong Kong and Macao?	128
6.2	Do you think the standard of living is better in Taiwan or Mainland China now?	129
6.3	Do you think the standard of living will be better in Taiwan or Mainland China in ten years?	129
6.4	Is China's economic rise a threat or opportunity for Taiwan?	131
6.5	Do you think you should speak more native dialect or language, such as Taiwanese, Hakka or aboriginal language (November 2015)?	132
6.6	Do you wish the status of Taiwan and Mainland China to be unification, independence or status quo?	133
6.7	How would you describe the current status quo in the Taiwan Strait?	134
6.8	How would you describe cross-Strait relations?	134
6.9	Do you consider yourself Taiwanese, Chinese, both or other (November 2015)?	135
6.10	Cross-tabulation of identity and whether been to the Mainland	136
6.11	Do you agree that more Mainland tourists should be allowed to visit Taiwan?	138
6.12	Do you know what the '1992 Consensus' entails?	139

6.13	Of the two parts of the '1992 Consensus' – 'one China with different interpretations', which part do you agree with the most?	140
6.14	Is future political unification possible?	141
6.15	If cross-Strait clashes occur, how likely is it that the US will assist in defending Taiwan?	142
6.16	Do you agree or disagree that our culture is the traditional Chinese culture?	143
8.1	Cause and effect for Taiwanese identity, the rise of China, cross-Strait relations and US influence in Northeast Asia	185
8.2	Elaboration on the basis of further evidence	187

Tables

1.1	Ideation theoretical framework	15
4.1	Systemist notation	76
6.1	What was your main purpose to visit Mainland China?	128
6.2	What makes you think or feel you are Taiwanese?	137
7.1	Variables contributing to Taiwanese identity	159
7.2	Bivariate PRE values for *Identify Only as Taiwanese*	164
7.3	Layered PRE impact on *Identify Only as Taiwanese*	168
7.4	Multivariate analysis of *Identify Only as Taiwanese*	169
7.5	Ordered logit analysis of *Identity Choice*	171
7.6	Multivariate analysis of *Disapproval of President Tsai*	173

About the Authors

Scott Sigmund Gartner is Provost and Academic Dean of the United States Naval Postgraduate School, Monterey, California, where he also serves as Professor of Defense Analysis, having previously held the position as director of the Penn State School of International Affairs. Gartner's research focuses on great power conflict, international security, war and politics, counter-terrorism, conflict mediation and policy assessment. Gartner's publications include *Costly Calculations: A Theory of War, Casualties, and Politics, Strategic Assessment in War, International Conflict Mediation: New Approaches and Findings* and *The Historical Statistics of the United States*, in addition to articles in top journals in political science, sociology, international affairs, history, military intelligence, public policy, international negotiations and communications. His honours include the Jefferson award for the best government resource, the Reference and User Services Association Outstanding Reference Award, Booklist Editor's Choice Award, Library Journal Best Reference Award, History News Network Book of the Month and the American Political Science Association's best policy thesis award. He is past president of the International Studies Association (West). Gartner's op-ed columns have been published in *Huffington Post, USA Today, Christian Science Monitor, The Baltimore Sun*, and many other outlets. He holds a PhD and MA in political science from the University of Michigan, a BA in history and an MA in international relations from the University of Chicago.

Chin-Hao Huang is Assistant Professor of Political Science at Yale-NUS College. He specializes in international politics, with a focus on China's foreign policy, Southeast Asian politics and United States–China relations. He is the recipient of the Lee Kong Chian National University of Singapore–Stanford University Distinguished Fellowship on Contemporary Southeast Asia (2018–2019) and the American Political Science Association's Foreign Policy Section Best Paper Award (2014). He is the author or co-author of three books, and his work appears in *International Organization*, *The China Quarterly*, *The China Journal*, *Contemporary Southeast Asia* and *International Peacekeeping*, and in edited volumes. He has testified on China's foreign affairs before the United States–China Economic and Security Review Commission. He has also served as a consultant for United States and European foundations, governments and companies on their strategies and policies in Asia. Until 2009, he was a researcher at the Stockholm International Peace Research Institute, and prior to that worked with the Freeman Chair in China Studies at the Center for Strategic and International Studies in Washington, DC. His PhD and BS are respectively from the University of Southern California and Georgetown University.

Yitan Li is Chair and Associate Professor of Political Science and Director of Asian Studies at Seattle University. His research focuses on international relations, foreign policy analysis, international conflict and security, international political economy, comparative politics and Chinese and East Asian politics. He has published in *Applied Economics*, *Asian Affairs*, *Asian Perspective*, *Canadian Journal of Political Science*, *Foreign Policy Analysis*, *Fudan Journal of the Humanities and Social Sciences*, *International Studies Perspectives*, *Journal of Chinese Political Science*, *Journal of Contemporary China*, *Journal of East Asian Studies*, *Journal of Territorial and Maritime Studies*, *Nationalism and Ethnic Politics* and *Political Research Quarterly*. He is currently serving as the editor of the *Journal of Chinese Political Science*. He holds a PhD in politics and international relations from the University of Southern California.

Patrick James is the Dana and David Dornsife Dean's Professor of International Relations at the University of Southern California. James is the author or editor of over 30 books and more than 160 articles and book chapters. Among his honours and awards are the Louise Dyer Peace Fellowship from the Hoover Institution at Stanford University, Thomas Enders Professorship in Canadian Studies at the University of Calgary, Senior Scholar award from the Canadian Embassy, Washington, DC, Quincy Wright Scholar Award from the International Studies Association (ISA) (Midwest), Beijing Foreign Studies University Eminent Scholar, Eccles Professor of the British Library and Ole R. Holsti Distinguished Scholar of the ISA (West). He is a past president of the ISA (Midwest) and the Iowa Conference of Political Scientists. James was Distinguished Scholar in Foreign Policy Analysis for the ISA (2006–2007) and Distinguished Scholar in Ethnicity, Nationalism and Migration for ISA (2009–2010). He has served as president (2007–2009) of the Association for Canadian Studies in the United States, president of the International Council for Canadian Studies (2011–2013), president of the Peace Science Society (2016–2017) and president of the ISA (2018–2019). James is the editor-in-chief of Oxford Bibliographies in International Relations and also served a five-year term as editor of *International Studies Quarterly*.

Acknowledgements

Several organizations and many people have helped us along the way in this project. We are grateful to Sarah Gansen, S. Jason Giannaros, Michael Pfonner and Ian Solano for outstanding research assistance supported by the Center for International Studies and the Department of Political Science and International Relations at the University of Southern California (USC). We greatly appreciate the excellent research assistance provided by Ericka Roberts, Hao-Cheng (Tommy) Hsu, Omwattie Nerahoo, Andrea Corradi and Aleksandra (Sasha) Bausheva, supported by the Penn State School of International Affairs. Erin Baggott Carter provided an insightful commentary on Chapter 5. On multiple occasions, the Taiwan Foundation for Democracy supported this research with grants that have been invaluable in carrying out interviews. We also appreciate the contribution of Frank C.S. Liu, Institute of Political Science at the National Sun Yat-Sen University, and Emerson Niou, Duke University, who implemented the surveys reported in Chapters 6 and 7, respectively.

This volume greatly benefited from a manuscript review workshop held at Yale-NUS College on 16 May 2019. We appreciate the support from the Chinese Studies Research Program and the Dean of Faculty, Jeannette Ickovics, at Yale-NUS College. We benefited greatly from commentaries provided at that workshop from the officially designated discussants, who made extraordinary efforts to help us improve the manuscript: Andrew Thompson, Visiting Senior Research Fellow, Lee Kuan Yew School of Public Policy, NUS; Risa Toha, Assistant Professor of Political Science, Division of Social Sciences, Yale-NUS College; Steven Oliver, Assistant Professor of Political Science, Division of Social Sciences, Yale-NUS College; and Brandon Yoder, Research Fellow, Center on Asia and Globalization, Lee Kuan Yew School of Public Policy, NUS. An early version of Chapter 4 was presented at the International Studies Association Annual Convention in Baltimore and we appreciate the feedback from the discussant and panel. We also are grateful to the anonymous referees from Bristol University

Press for great insights that have made this a much better book than it would have been otherwise. Stephen Wenham, our editor at Bristol, has been very generous with his time in helping us to improve this work at every stage.

Others have helped out at various points and we apologize in advance for anyone else who should have been mentioned here. We hope that our volume will increase understanding of the interconnected and complex issues revolving around Taiwanese identity, the rise of China, cross-Strait relations and the influence exerted by the US in Northeast Asia. These matters create both danger and opportunity. The authors of this volume are united in the hope that events will play out in a peaceful and constructive way for continued security and stability in East Asia and the Pacific.

Preface

Scott and Pat visited Taiwan a few years ago for a conference. While the discussions were great and our hosts superb, what we remember most is one of Scott's interactions with a graduate student who volunteered to show him around Taipei. On the subway ride to see a temple, she berated Scott for the US position that encouraged strong bilateral economic and military relations with Taiwan but stopped short of recognizing Taiwan as sovereign. She pointed out that Taiwan had all the elements of an independent country, its own government, foreign policy, independent military and a unique currency. "Why", she asked, "does the US refuse to recognize Taiwan's independence?" She summed up her view by stating definitively: "I am Taiwanese not Chinese!"

When Scott and his Taiwanese guide arrived at the temple, however, and Scott was about to enter into the nearest entrance, the guide suddenly grabbed him: "Stop", she shouted, "we Chinese always enter temples from the right through the dragon door." (Hence the phrase, enter the dragon, exit the tiger.) Scott and Pat were struck by the rapid alternation of her stridently affirmed identities.

Many people in Taiwan identify themselves as politically Taiwanese and culturally Chinese. As Pat and Scott discussed this duality in Taipei, they wondered if the perceptions of China's ascendant economic and political power shaped these identities, making them more fluid and multidimensional, and consequently, more manipulable by leaders in both countries? To their delight Yitan and Chin, both of whom have been studying cross-Strait relations, Chinese foreign policy and US–Asia relations, also were interested in exploring these issues and our team and this book project emerged. The outcome of this joint collaboration reflects analytic eclecticism that offers bold, new insights on one of the most nettlesome security challenges in the region.

While this array of seemingly conflicting identities influenced by great power and regional politics could appear obvious to those from Taiwan and the region, it might seem hard for others to understand. But these dynamics are not unique to Taiwan. Around the world, citizen identities that culturally embrace and politically oppose a nation create the need for nuanced diplomacy and a multilayered approach for understanding identity formation (one might see seemingly similar discordant beliefs in an American Southerner's simultaneous declarations of both ribald American patriotism and defence of the Confederate flag). In Taiwan, there is no simple answer to what it means to be Taiwanese. Instead, as we will show, Taiwanese identity represents answers emerging from a series of controversial questions and as a result is fluid and relational.

1

Identity in the Shadow of a Giant: How the Rise of China Is Changing Taiwan

Overview

This volume focuses on Taiwanese identity and cross-Strait relations at a time when the ascent of China has proven to be the greatest sustained story of international relations in the new millennium. How the people who live in Taiwan view themselves is a function of great power competition. Taiwan, formally the Republic of China (ROC), exists in the shadow of one giant, the People's Republic of China (PRC), and is a key client state of another, the United States (US). Each of these features influences both the evolution of Taiwanese identity and the playing out of cross-Strait relations. Embedded in history with an eye on the future, this study will pay some attention to developments prior to the flight of the Kuomintang (KMT), the losing side in the Chinese Civil War, to the island of Formosa in 1949. However, most attention will be paid to events since that time and especially in recent years, which have witnessed dramatic changes in the capabilities of the PRC, Taiwanese identity, and cross-Strait relations. In such dynamics, the US stands out as the key third-party actor among those external to Northeast Asia, with potential to impact the direction and magnitude of further developments (Jentleson, 2016). In our approach we consider especially the pull between ideological and self-interested motivating factors on shaping identity. The overall objective of this volume is to assess the evolving nature of Taiwanese identity and cross-Strait relations in connection with a rapid rise of China. As such, it also possesses implications for the US-led world order and today's most critical great power competition.

This chapter continues with three further sections. The second section focuses on recent developments in cross-Strait relations. The third section reviews the rise of China in connection with evolving identity for Taiwan and the role of the US. The fourth and final section provides a plan of work for the chapters that follow.

The challenge of cross-Strait relations

When Ma Ying-jeou and Xi Jinping met in Singapore on 7 November 2015, it marked the potential beginning of a new era in cross-Strait relations. The heads of state for the ROC and PRC had not met in person since the end of the Chinese Civil War that produced a communist regime on the Mainland and nationalist flight to Taiwan – a gap of more than six decades. As leader of the state directly challenging the US directly for influence in Northeast Asia, the PRC's General Secretary of the Communist Party, Xi Jinping, entered the Singapore meeting in a position of strength. By contrast, Ma Ying-jeou, President of the ROC, at the time knew that his party almost certainly would lose control of both the presidency and legislature in the Taiwanese election of January 2016. Ma's KMT faced growing criticism of its policies across the board, with cross-Strait relations anchoring much of the public dissatisfaction.

For such reasons, it is not surprising that President Ma emphasized the positive legacy of policies pursued by his government, notably in relation to maintaining the status quo and peace with Beijing. At the meeting with Xi, Ma stressed the value of the 1992 Consensus – the designation of 'One China with multiple systems' – in maintaining stability (an agreement that we will see remains central to the Taiwanese identity formation process for both elites and masses). The Taiwanese president emphasized cross-Strait exchanges as something that should be expanded to mutual benefit. Ma also called for the establishment of a hotline to handle urgent matters. President Ma finished up his series of points regarding peace and prosperity by noting that both peoples are Chinese – descendants of Emperors Yan and Huang – and thus joint cooperation should be the path to follow for the Mainland and Taiwan. All of that resonated with Xi, who in representing the PRC hoped to hear affirmation of a common Sinic identity.

While widely lauded as an unprecedented *rapprochement* in cross-Strait relations, the bilateral summit had ephemeral effects. Ma's KMT lost the presidential election and its majority status in the legislature within months after the historic meeting. His successor, Tsai Ing-Wen from the Democratic Progressive Party (DPP), swept into office with a different mandate: to revisit relations with Beijing amidst growing dissatisfaction and frustration over opacity in KMT-negotiated deals with the Mainland. Tsai won the general election in a landslide. She received nearly twice as many votes as her KMT opponent, Eric Chu, and an outright victory for the DPP in the legislature. The DPP now possessed a majority in the Legislative Yuan for the first time ever. Tsai's inauguration speech in May 2016 did not re-state the previous government's acceptance of the 1992 Consensus; neither, however, has the president since taking office put forward the DPP's previously intense pro-independence rhetoric. Instead, and repeatedly, Tsai affirms that Taiwan's status is something to be resolved democratically: 'It is a decision to be made by the people here.' Unless the general public manifests a clear consensus and thereby provides a mandate, Tsai has vowed not to pursue policy action that would alter the status quo. Thus, President Tsai has situated Taiwanese identity as the driving force in the political decision making of one of the most contested and potentially violent disputes on the planet. An identity that, as we demonstrate, is fluid and ambivalent.

Further clouding our understanding of Taiwanese identity is the nature of the status quo. As will become apparent from interviews and survey data, the meaning of the status quo is subject to a wide range of interpretations. The status quo therefore provides political cover; public figures tend to endorse it but without reference to any specific content, allowing for a wide variety of understandings.

Since 2016, the focus of Tsai's government has been domestic policy – intended to spur the economy, increase wages, reform, and overhaul the pension system, and address socioeconomic challenges. On the cross-Strait front, Beijing continues to resist furthering official and semi-official communication with Taipei. The lack of resumption in cross-Strait ties, however, has not affected Tsai's popularity significantly so far (that is, in an irreversible way), even while other challenges have impacted upon the DPP's standing with the public. In fact, public confidence in her government surged when President Tsai made a phone call to US President-elect Donald Trump on 2 December 2016. This simple congratulatory call lasted ten minutes, but the symbolic politics would be hard to miss. Since US–Taiwan official relations ended in 1979, leaders from Washington and Taipei have never spoken directly to each other. While Tsai subsequently indicated that the call did not signal a policy shift, it echoed wider public sentiments about Taiwan's identity and self-confidence in maintaining pragmatic status quo positions when it comes to international standing and cross-Strait ties. Even the KMT opposition expressed approval of the diplomatic gesture from the incoming president. At the same time, Trump's willingness to speak directly with a president of the ROC raised hackles on the Mainland. This dynamic is unlikely to change as Trump's relationship with Taiwan represents one of the few policies that President Biden has largely embraced. Biden 'will most likely continue on a similar path' (Hernandez and Chien, 2020).

With a DPP government for Taipei and a historic meeting of Ma and Xi in the books, where are things headed for the ROC and PRC with relations across the Taiwan Strait? The leaders of these respective governments, Xi and Tsai, face very different situations as their time in office continues.

President Xi received from the Central Committee of the Chinese Communist Party (CCP) a second five-year mandate as party leader in October 2017. He came out of the Communist Party Congress in a more dominant position than possibly ever before. The party identified no one as waiting in the wings to be Xi's successor. Moreover, Xi showed great power through inserting his name and dogma, at the closing session, into the party's constitution. This act symbolized Xi's elevation into the highest circle of leadership in CCP history, along with Deng Xiaoping and Mao Zedong. Interestingly enough, speculation about a possible third term for Xi is already underway, along with increasingly strict controls over civil society. Moreover, in March 2018, lawmakers in China's National People's Congress (NPC) passed changes to the country's constitution abolishing presidential term limits. The constitutional change from the NPC officially allows Xi Jinping to remain in office after the end of his second term in 2023 (Doubek, 2018).

President Tsai, by comparison, has seen her approval ratings ebb and flow. This is not surprising for the leader of a democracy, of course, and cross-Strait relations are at the centre of the challenge. Embattled in her first two years in office with such divisive initiatives as labour law reform and a scale-back of an unsustainable pension system for civil servants and veterans, Tsai's popularity eventually bounced back and surged in the latter half of her term. Much of that gain can be attributed to unforeseen developments in cross-Strait relations. Tsai called, in October 2017, for movement of the ROC and PRC past historical baggage and towards a breakthrough in cross-Strait relations. The president also asserted decisively that Taiwan would not give in to pressure from the Mainland and had an inherent right to determine its destiny. Thus, Tsai attempted to occupy a middle ground on policy – assertions on behalf of Taiwan but not, at least intentionally, with a degree of intensity sufficient to provoke the Mainland.

Another development of what Beijing refers to as its proposed 'one country, two systems' model has been happening with a high profile in Hong Kong. Since March 2019, protests have been taking place in Hong Kong, with varying intensity. These protests initially opposed the government's proposed extradition bill which, if passed, would have allowed Hong Kong authorities to detain and extradite people who are wanted in Mainland China for supposed offences. Seen as a step towards further limiting freedom enjoyed by people in Hong Kong, protests against the bill started to escalate in June 2019. Tens of thousands of people have demonstrated against the extradition bill and Hong Kong has been in chaos ever since.

After the inability of Hong Kong's Special Administrative Region (HKSAR) government to get the unrest under control became obvious, Beijing took the matter into its own hands. On the eve of the 23rd anniversary of the city's handover to China from British rule, China's legislature passed a wide-ranging new security law for Hong Kong. The law reduces the city's autonomy and makes it easier to punish protesters (Buckley and Bradsher, 2020). Maintaining firm control of Hong Kong has wide-ranging implications for China's leadership, not least because the city has been upheld as a test case of the 'one country, two systems' model, under which Taiwan is to be ruled after any future unification.

Xi doubled-down on that message in his speech on New Year's Day of 2019. The president's address was timed strategically. It marked the 40th anniversary of a similar statement Beijing made to Taipei regarding unification on New Year's Day in 1979 – incidentally, also the same day that Beijing and Washington established formal diplomatic ties. Hong Kong thus stands as a barometer for the future possibility of implementing the 'one country, two systems' model in Taiwan.

Even though Beijing's unique proposal implies that Taiwan's economic and social life would continue 'as is', the latest political developments in Hong Kong occurring concurrently with the further centralization of power resulting from the outbreak and efforts to contain the COVID-19 pandemic reveal the limitations of such repeated assurances. As Bush (2019: 1) observes, under China's proposed model, 'Taiwan's institutions would be transformed into subnational bodies, and, based on Hong Kong's experience, these would be structured to prevent political forces and political leaders that China didn't like from coming to power'. Erosion of political freedoms and the right to dissent have elicited strong concerns from the electorate;

Tsai has seized on this opportunity to firmly counter and reject Xi's insistence on the 'one country, two systems' model. This move by the president has garnered increasingly favourable responses from public opinion across the political spectrum in Taiwan. At least in part, that can explain why Tsai easily won a landslide for a second term in January 2020, beating the popular KMT candidate Han Kuo-yu 57.13 per cent to 38.61 per cent.

China's rise and the identity of Taiwan

Amidst the rapidly changing security environment introduced so far, this study focuses on the rise of China in connection with cross-Strait relations, the identity of Taiwan as a democratic state and the role of the US in Northeast Asia. The purpose of this book is to obtain greater understanding of cause and effect between and among China's rise, Taiwan's identity, cross-Strait relations and US activity under conditions of fast-paced and unpredictable multidimensional change. Ever since Napoleon Bonaparte famously said 'China is a sleeping giant. Let her sleep, for when she wakes she will move the world', the wakening or 'rise' of China has been a much talked about topic of world politics. While the 'rise of China' can be viewed in both positive and negative lights, we see China's rise as a complex and multilayered process, in which China seeks the restoration of its historical glory, the momentum of modernization, economic and global ascension, and the search for its past and present identity (Kang, 2007). On the one hand, China may or may not intend to do harm through its rise to its neighbours near and afar. On the other hand, China's rise may have unintended and unexpected consequences that even those fanning the fires of its rise may not predict or even perceive. This is where Taiwan's identity, cross-Strait relations and the US role in the region enter into the complexity of China's ascent. Along the way, academic literature, accompanied by data from interviews and surveys, are consulted to obtain a comprehensive sense of causal and relational mechanisms. This process will focus on Taiwanese identity in connection with a range of critical, personal, societal, political, cross-Strait, and global factors. The character of this complex system, which provides the foundation for research on Taiwanese identity, is as follows: *We recognize that external and internal factors combine to affect identity formation. Put simply, changes outside of Taiwan and internal developments all impact upon identity and each other.*

How does this volume differ from recent scholarship examining the importance of cross-Strait relations in international politics? Broadly speaking, several axioms underlie the research carried out on

Taiwanese identity in this volume. Identities are taken to be malleable and multidimensional. A culture encompasses aspects that range from the use of one or perhaps a number of languages all the way through to historical memories that shape experiences even long after the fact. Identities are shared between elites and masses, with an interactive process of change as events within state and society impact upon each other. Identity reflects choice (Gartner and Segura, 1997); individuals respond to these dynamics differently, depending on their own personal characteristics, ideological views, and relations with the Mainland. Policy preferences and actions, in turn, are shaped by identities. National identity is thus both influenced by and influences individual identities in non-linear ways. At the same time we recognize that 'identification of individuals with social, ethnic, religious and political groups involves more flexibility and choice than many previously conceived' (Gartner and Segura, 1997: 133).

Given the complex processes that correspond to the preceding set of axioms, a multimethod approach is deemed essential for the study of identity in order to grasp its multidimensional and fluid nature. On the one hand, survey research is carried out to obtain breadth of knowledge. On the other hand, qualitative data through interviews can provide depth of understanding. The combined results are compared with what has been learned so far – an ensemble of methods suitable to an intricate and rapidly changing subject area.[1]

More specifically, this volume builds upon a number of recent books on cross-Strait relations. For instance, Syaru Shirley Lin's *Taiwan's China Dilemma: Contested Identities and Multiple Interests in Taiwan's Cross-Strait Economic Policy* offers the view that 'identity forms the basis for defining interests' (2016: 12). As identity changes, Lin finds that Taiwan's economic policies towards China evolve, and they do not necessarily correlate with the ruling party's preferences or priorities. As an example, in the early 2000s, the independent-leaning DPP ruling elites actually championed economic liberalization with the Mainland. And, even though KMT leaders advocate for closer overall ties with Beijing, at times, KMT leaders have urged Taiwanese businesses and companies to invest in China with prudence and caution. Lin's detailed case studies illustrate how Taiwan's economic policies emanate from a mix of party politics and signals from the masses on their views towards China. Notwithstanding the book's many merits, it leaves the reader eager to understand with greater precision the causes and effects of identity formation and change.

Similarly, Scott Kastner's (2009) *Political Conflict and Economic Interdependence Across the Taiwan Strait* provides a nuanced perspective on the relationship between conflict and trade between rivalries. Kastner argues that the negative impact of conflict tends to be less pronounced when leaders of the countries involved are more supportive and understanding of the mutual gains accrued from closer integration into the global economy. This argument is tested in the least likely case of China–Taiwan relations, where in spite of sustained hostilities for more than half a century, commerce endured even when there were periods of tension in cross-Strait relations. The theory and empirics validate his argument, but looking strictly at the economic dimension limits the scope and possibility of other critical factors in explaining the intricate relations between commerce and conflict in cross-Strait relations. For instance, what influence might the US or other key regional actors have had in affecting the decision-makers' outlook in Beijing and Taipei on the benefits of trade and closer economic interdependence? Furthermore, how Taiwan's democratization and emerging identity are interacting with and changing the island's cost–benefit calculus of trade, business and economic interests with China remain somewhat unanswered in the analysis.

Other volumes provide greater granularity on US role in cross-Strait political developments. Dean Chen's (2017) *US-China Rivalry and Taiwan's Mainland Policy: Security, Nationalism and the 1992 Consensus*, Gerrit Gong's (2000) edited book *Taiwan Strait Dilemmas: China-Taiwan-U.S. Policies in the New Century* and Bruce J. Jacobs and Peter Kang's (2018) edited volume *Changing Taiwanese Identities* come to mind. Chen's historical analysis primarily focuses on the 'one China' question through the lens of the '1992 Consensus' and how policy changes have occurred in recent administrations in Taipei amidst heightened US–China competition in cross-Strait relations. In Gong's edited volume, several leading scholars address issues ranging from US strategic ambiguities to Taiwan's international space and economic situation. Jacobs and Kang's volume take an eclectic approach to examine a wide range of issues related to Taiwan's identity changes ranging from linguistics, geography, political science, and culture. Drawing upon these foundational works on the US role in cross-Strait relations, the present book sharpens the analytical focus on the impact the US has had on Taiwan's evolving identity. As will be elaborated in greater detail, we find that while the US remains a Pacific power and will undoubtedly have an enduring voice in any future scenario in cross-Strait relations, it is important to contextualize Washington's role; simply put, the US is not the *only* factor shaping cross-Strait developments, let alone identity change in Taiwan.

Together, these works establish how dynamic and multifaceted identity politics can be. We seek to build on these impressive works, both by intertwining their varied strands and by generating novel approaches. Our volume pushes this issue further by delving deeper into identifying the key factors – both structural and internal/domestic – that undergird Taiwan's identity formation in the first place. How inhabitants are increasingly identifying themselves only as Taiwanese amidst increasing political and economic uncertainties in cross-Strait and US–China relations is a crucial piece of the puzzle. Thus, our approach of systemism, as will become clear in the rest of this book, provides a useful theoretical framework that complements our in-depth elite interviews and two datasets on popular reflections and surveys in Taiwan to contribute to the existing literature. Systemism is a graphic approach towards conveying cause and effect that is especially well-suited to the complexities at hand.

Moreover, understanding the complexity in cross-Strait relations and getting its theoretical and policy implications 'right' have become increasingly pressing and important. Over recent years, the rise of China has become a topic frequently commented upon, but to date, few book-length, multimethod empirical analyses have been carried out to focus on cause and effect between the PRC's rapid ascent and identity change in Taiwan. In the increasingly contentious China–US–Taiwan relationship, rising tensions between Washington and Beijing most certainly will have direct implications for Taiwan's security and cross-Strait relations. Thus, the goal is to identify a network of cause and effect among these developments in Northeast Asia, with the role of the US as an important factor considered from outside of the region.

A number of writings suggest that events involving China are heading in a dangerous direction. Especially visible in that sense are *Death by China: Confronting the Dragon – A Global Call to Action* (Navarro and Autry, 2011); *When China Rules the World: The End of the Western World and the Birth of a New Global Order* (Jacques, 2012); *The Hundred-Year Marathon: China's Secret Strategy to Replace America as the Global Superpower* (Pillsbury, 2016); *Destined for War: Can America and China Escape Thucydides' Trap?* (Allison, 2017); and *Has China Won? The Chinese Challenge to American Primacy* (Mahbubani, 2020). All of these studies predict that intense conflict between the world's leading state and the most credible, rising challenger is inevitable.[2]

Ongoing friction has been exacerbated by escalating trade wars since mid-2018 and subsequently accentuated by the finger-pointing 'blame game' with the COVID-19 pandemic from near the end of 2019 onward. If tensions persist and worsen between the US and China, then a potentially tumultuous power transition and global strategic reorientation will have consequential impact on Taiwan's identity and role in cross-Strait relations.

Beyond the structural level, Steve Chan (2019: 11) has been somewhat sceptical about the application of a concept called the Thucydides Trap to the Taiwan-China situation. He argues that using the 2,500-year-old war as an analogy could lead to a dangerous 'self-fulfilling prophecy'. There are multiple pathways to war, among which 'human agency' has been neglected in the pure structural explanation (Chan, 2019: 11). We see 'identity' as a crucial part of the 'human agency' debate; and attempt to make self-understanding the centre of cross-Strait relations and regional security.

Several pertinent, follow-up questions arise to motivate this research project further: How does the rise of China affect the degree of stability to be expected in relations with Taiwan? What implications does the extraordinary increase in the Mainland's material capabilities have for issues of political economy and security? How might Taiwan's perception of itself – even its very identity – be affected by the dramatic rise of China? If Taiwanese identity is changing, what might that mean, in turn, for cross-Strait relations? In addition, how will the policies implemented by the US administration under Donald Trump – a significant departure from the norm in foreign policy style and substance in presidential leadership – affect the relationship in the Taiwan Strait following his electoral defeat? These queries are answered in a tentative way, with the overarching objective of the book being to offer a sense of how the rise of China, political economy and security issues, Taiwanese identity, cross-Strait relations and US influence in Northeast Asia impact upon each other in today's world. All of that promises to produce insights about policies with the best chance to result in peaceful relations, stability and prosperity across the Taiwan Strait. As is often the case with critical and complex topics, our explorations lead to the emergence of new questions whose answers are beyond the scope of this volume.

Taiwanese *identity* is a topic in which interest is increasing – a natural product of its crucial role in determining how the island will react to China's rise in the short- and long-term. However, as Gries and Su (2013: 74) point out, 'knowledge about the causes and consequences of Taiwanese views on China is not extensive'. According to Wang and Liu (2004: 574–576), survey data suggest that 'political and cultural identities may not be congruent in the Taiwanese context'; in fact, some residents may feel 'politically Taiwanese and culturally Chinese'.

A few numbers about public opinion will highlight those observations. A decade ago, 43 per cent of those surveyed identified as both Chinese and Taiwanese, with four multiple identities already in place: 'Taiwanese nationalist identity, the pro-Taiwan identity, the mixed identity, and the China identity' (Wang, 2004: 302; Wang and Liu, 2004: 576). Recent polls reflect notable changes. For instance, slightly over two-thirds (67 per cent) of those surveyed identify themselves as Taiwanese. As a result, Taiwan's identity may be converging towards some degree of consensus. Figure 1.1, from the Election Study Center, National Chengchi University (2020) shows the general increase in identification as Taiwanese across time and also makes clear that this trend is not constant. More pointedly in relation to earlier concerns about identity as a catalyst for conflict, in a separate poll, 57.4 per cent of respondents indicated that they would be willing to defend the island if China launched an invasion in response to an eventual declaration of independence by Taiwan (Taiwan Foundation for Democracy, 2019).

What is causing change in Taiwanese identity, with the result being increasing complexity, over the long-term? In a word, the standard explanation for an evolving Taiwanese sense of self in recent decades is 'democratization' (Wang, 2004: 293; Li, 2014a: 132; Li, 2014b). Thus, Taiwanese identity includes both institutional and demographic elements. The more complex identity, increasingly apparent from approximately the new millennium onward, is receiving an intense outside stimulus from the Mainland's rapid ascent.

This shock of China's swift rise is impacting most obviously upon the material world – notably the economic and security spheres – in different ways. China's rise also is affecting the ideational world, where identity is a key element underlying political processes. How the two domains, material and ideational, play out together vis-à-vis overall cross-Strait relations is far from certain because the effects of rapid change must be taken into account. Complexity resulting from a combination of material and ideational forces provides the principal justification for further research as carried out in this book: *The rise of China, Taiwanese identity, cross-Strait relations and related US activity should be studied collectively to obtain maximum possible academic and policy-related insights.*

Prior research on cross-Strait relations, along with its US dimension, is vast.[3] The current project goes beyond this valuable foundation in the literature through an investigation of the rise of China in connection with cross-Strait relations *and* Taiwanese identity. A complex network of effects is anticipated to be identified and thus a multimethod research design will be implemented. Breadth and depth will be obtained from

Figure 1.1: Changes in the Taiwanese/Chinese identity of Taiwanese 臺灣民眾臺灣人/中國人認同趨勢分佈 (1992～2020.06) Changes in the Taiwanese/Chinese Identity of Taiwanese as Tracked in Surveys by the Election Study Center, NCCU(1992～2020.06)

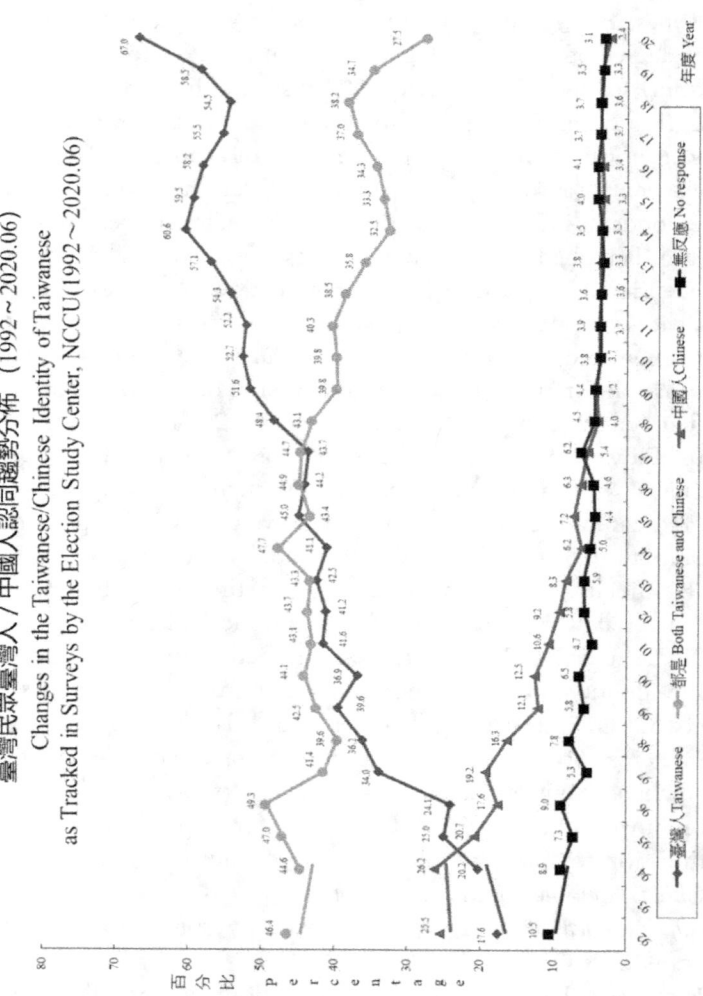

Source: Election Study Center, National Chengchi University, https://esc.nccu.edu.tw/course/news.php?Sn=166

a combination of (1) primary data gathered through interviews and surveys and (2) secondary literature.

Controversy continues over implications of the rapid rise of China for stability in cross-Strait relations, along with Taiwanese identity and the role of the US in Northeast Asia. A wide range of opinions exist. Worries about cross-Strait relations, from the perspective of American foreign policy, are long-standing. Confrontation over the Taiwan Strait, as described by an analyst from two decades ago, 'comprises the single most dangerous dispute for the US in the world today' (Tucker, 1998–1999: 150). The dangers of military conflict over Taiwan between the US and China, observes Johnston (2003: 47) just a few years later, must not be underestimated. A book from around the same time, which focused extensively on Taiwan, had a self-explanatory title: *America's Coming War with China* (Carpenter, 2006). Over a decade ago, Shirk (2007: 265) already had asserted that, with regard to cross-Strait relations, the US government 'has lost control over this dangerous situation'. Expressions of concern about Sino-Taiwanese relations continue to this day; debates about the degree of danger fill the pages of publications such as *Foreign Affairs, Foreign Policy, Issues and Studies,* and *Asian Survey*. Mounting challenges to civil liberties in Hong Kong, ongoing in 2021 and possibly beyond, raise further concerns and uncertainty about the 'one country, two systems' model, particularly with regard to its applicability for any future political arrangement and détente between Beijing and Taipei. Other studies have looked at the somewhat unique mixture of China's overly aggressive foreign policy and its comparatively high adherence to mediated outcomes (Gartner and Tannehill, 2008). All of this combines to put a priority on learning about the interconnectedness of Taiwanese identity, China's rise, cross-Strait relations and the role of the US in Northeast Asia.

Ambitious goals call for comprehensive data to triangulate substantive knowledge and thereby inform policy – hence the mixed methods approach of this book. Through multiple sources of data, much can be learned about Taiwanese identity and cross-Strait relations in the era following on from China's rapid ascent. Not surprisingly, the US is identified as playing an ongoing and influential role from outside of Northeast Asia as a supporter of Taiwan. Moving beyond these historical factors, what psychological dynamics might shape identity among those in Taiwan?

The intersection of personal and contextual factors demarcates the nature and scope of choices regarding people's identity (Gartner and Segura, 1997). We see the range of ideational choices extending to claims of national identity. This statement might represent a controversial position as legal factors, such as where one is born, or one's heritage attributes, such as one's parent's identities, are frequently seen as determining an individual's citizenship and national identity. However, there is surprisingly wide variation in the criteria for both citizenship (Money and Lockhart, 2019) and national identity (Bechhofer and McCrone, 2010). We view national identity, especially it applies to Taiwan, as a personal choice that an individual makes (Bechhofer and McCrone, 2010). Attention naturally turns to ideology versus self-interested identity motivation.

Many factors influence an individual's choice over an identity (Kou and Huang, 2015). While not excluding any extant factors, we believe that both recent literature (White et al, 2014; Narozhna and Knight, 2016: 108–116; Bortolini et al, 2018) and classical literature (Emile Durkheim and Max Weber) generally portrays two types of factors as essential for understanding ideational motivation, which we label *ideological factors* and *self-interest factors*. These are large categories of dynamics that influence identity, representing ideational bins if you like. Ideology embodies concepts such as values, ideas, emotions and factors that are largely abstract and collective (Bechhofer and McCrone, 2010). These are group interests that connect to arrays of public goods. Self-interest represents material improvements, status increases or other personal (and familial and household) advances (Huang, 2005). These gains reflect private goods: 'citizens as political subjects care about their well-being, wanting to protect and advance their material and non-material interests' (de Vries and van Kersbergen, 2007: 312).

Looking at the combination of ideological and self-interested factors driving an individual towards an identity choice (Kou and Huang, 2015), we identify in Table 1.1 four ideal-type conditions:

1. *Ideological Ideation* occurs when ideological factors motivate the ideational choice and self-interested factors play no/or a minimal role.
2. *Complementary Ideation* represents the situation when ideological and self-interested factors work together in parallel to positively support an identity.
3. *Self-Interested Ideation* occurs when self-interested factors motivate the ideational choice and ideological factors play no or a minimal role.
4. *Unmotivated Ideation* represents the situation when neither ideology nor self-interest strongly motivate an ideological choice.

Table 1.1: Ideation theoretical framework

		Self-interest	
		Yes	No
Ideology	Yes	*Complementary Ideation*	*Ideological Ideation*
	No	*Self-Interested Ideation*	*Unmotivated Ideation*

Complementary Ideation can jointly drive you towards or away from an identity, creating two sub-conditions: *Positive Complementary Ideation* occurs when ideological and self-interested factors drive you towards the identity in question; *Negative Complementary Ideation* occurs when ideological and self-interested factors drive you away the identity in question.

National identity is geographically driven (Lin et al, 2006). The question is then, which of these conditions is more likely to influence the type of ideational choice we observe by those living in Taiwan? Unlike, say, Scottish identity, where some who live in Scotland have viewed themselves as Scots for generations and others have not, Taiwanese identity is one-directional. Putting aside for a moment the aboriginal Formosans (whom we discuss later), Taiwanese identity is a recent phenomenon (Chu and Lin, 2001). In 1949, the Nationalists who came to Taiwan all identified as 100 per cent as Chinese. If anything, they identified themselves as more Chinese than the Communist Chinese who came to power in China and who had just pushed the Nationalists off the Mainland (see Chapter 2). Thus, identity in Taiwan largely follows two patterns: (1) viewing one's self as originally Chinese, or descendants of those who originally saw themselves as Chinese, and continuing to identify as Chinese; or (2) viewing one's self as originally Chinese, or descendants of those who originally saw themselves as Chinese, and seeing oneself now as Taiwanese. Note that multiple additional categories are already emerging, such as someone identifying as Chinese who is a descendent of those who view themselves as Taiwanese, and second generation Taiwanese identifiers.

Our question to examine now (as identifying as Taiwanese has only really been an option for a few decades – see Chapter 3): for those who initially viewed themselves as Chinese, or are the children of those who initially viewed themselves or currently see themselves as Chinese: what motivates someone to choose an identity as Taiwanese? Seemingly simple, this question is extraordinarily complex.

Reflect again on the example of conflicting political and cultural affinities shown by US Southerners being exceptionally patriotic (e.g. enlisting in the military at higher than average rates) while championing those who violently rebelled against their country and incorporating them and their symbols (e.g. the Confederate flag) into their identity. Imagine if another nation openly promoted the role of the Confederacy in America and encouraged its inclusion in Southern identity. This third-party promotion would add an international dynamic to the ideational tension between political and cultural identities. But this example understates the China–Taiwan dynamic because unlike supporting the Confederacy, China promotes an identity that is current, it poses an active existential threat to use force against Taiwan, and it has ascended to emerging global superpower status.

Thus, critical to these ideational formulations, and making Taiwanese identity additionally unique, is the fact that Taiwan and Taiwanese identity are challenged by a rapidly evolving and rising Mainland China.

> Taiwan's case is distinctive, for despite having some of the features of a nation-state, its quest for sovereignty has been vigorously contested by the People's Republic of China (PRC), which claims the island as a long-lost Chinese province. Although national identity is not the same thing as sovereignty, a legal term that, according to most definitions, includes recognition by the international community, Beijing has also been unhappy with Taiwan's quest for national identity. (Dittmer, 2004: 475)

What then motivates this decision to shift from seeing oneself as Chinese (or Chinese Taiwanese, all of the language here is clearly simplified to help motivate the theoretical argument)? Returning to our two essential ideational bins, ideology and self-interests, are both likely to be the driver of this identity choice or is one factor more likely to be dominant over the other in terms of influencing Taiwanese identity?

Identity represents a sense of belonging to a larger group. As a result, we expect that more collective, public good oriented factors play larger roles in motivating ideational choice than self-interested, private good based individual gains (Van Vugt and Hart, 2004; Bechhofer and McCrone, 2010). We anticipate that Ideological Ideation will be the most common and powerful process through which national identity formation processes, followed by Complementary Ideation and Self-Interested Ideation, with Unmotivated Ideation being least likely. Furthermore, identities formed through ideological processes are more likely to have political implications (Ellemers et al, 2002; Bliuc et al, 2007). Thus, if our theory of Ideological Ideation is correct, we would anticipate that Taiwanese identity is highly political and likely to converge with political characteristics and support.

Another interesting question we try to answer is whether ideational choices are static or dynamic. Looking at both ideology and self-interest, ideational formation is at least in part dependent on the socioeconomic context individuals find themselves in. When these socioeconomic factors start to change, does ideation change too? For example, as Inglehart and Welzel (2001: 19) point out, socioeconomic development often starts from 'technological innovations', 'occupational specialization', 'rising educational levels' and 'rising income levels'; these changes help diversify 'human interaction, shifting the emphasis from authority relations toward bargaining relations; in the long run this brings cultural changes', including 'changing attitudes toward authority' and 'broader political participation'. We anticipate that ideational choices are dynamic. There may be certain elements in Taiwan's cultural and identity formation that have not changed much, but as socioeconomic experiences evolve in Taiwan, ideation and identity have developed as well.

In the remainder of this book we explore these expectations through quantitative and qualitative data, examining both ideological choices of elites and masses along with history and political support. We also address how to embed this argument for identity choice into a powerful and generalizable systemist perspective as applied to the question of Taiwanese identity.

Plan for the book

Chapter 2 carries out a historical review that focuses on Taiwanese identity, the rise of China, cross-Strait relations and the role of the US within the sub-region of Northeast Asia. While the account begins in prehistoric times, the main emphasis is on the era from the establishment of the PRC in 1949 onward. This chapter creates a context within which to review the findings of academic literature, elite interviews and public opinion surveys. The historical account is also intended to make the book more accessible to readers who are not specialists in either Taiwan or Northeast Asia.

Chapter 3 assesses the secondary literature with regard to understanding the context for contemporary cross-Strait relations. A review of academic studies reveals an evolving identity for the people of Taiwan, which includes both ethnic and institutional elements. People on the island perceive a range of identities that include Sinic as well as indigenous aspects. Important also to the self-designation of identity, as it has developed, is the sense of Taiwan as a democracy. Thus, the story of identity for Taiwan is one of movement towards a more complex range of designations. The rise of China is not a simple matter, either. On the one hand, China is gaining ground and exerting greater influence in Northeast Asia and even beyond. On the other hand, the Mainland is not without identity-related challenges of its own. Insecurities fuelled by long-standing grievances make China especially sensitive about sovereignty, with nothing, not even Hong Kong, more salient in that context than the status of Taiwan. Finally, the role of the US in the nexus of Sino-Taiwanese relations is not an easy one to sum up. While Washington seeks to preserve the security of Taiwan, it must deal with a range of pressures from politics at home, occasionally worrisome actions emanating from Taipei and assertiveness out of Beijing over perceived matters of sovereignty. Taken together, the academic literature on Taiwanese identity, the rise of China, cross-Strait relations and the role of the US provides the context for theoretical work that follows.

Chapter 4 conveys theorizing. The foundation for theoretical work on identity, change in capabilities and dyadic relations is a combination of eclectic thinking and systemism. Based on the limits of what can be learned from paradigms, it makes sense to go beyond those boundaries and pursue an eclectic yet systematic theoretical approach. To avert chaos along the way – logical inconsistencies and contradictions that easily can arise from assembly of diverse ideas from across paradigms – a graphic technique is implemented to convey cause and effect coherently. The method is *systemism*, which is designed specifically to depict causal mechanisms in visual form. Taiwanese identity, the rise of China, cross-Strait relations, and the role of the US are connected to each other and depicted within a figure created under the rules put forward by systemism. The system displayed is Northeast Asia. From a systemist point of view, the US is conceptualized as an input from the environment into the system that also receives output from it. So the US role is included and visualized in that way. The causal mechanisms in Figure 4.2 from that chapter are derived from the academic literature and provide a baseline to be elaborated as data is gathered and analysis carried out in subsequent chapters. In doing so, we also capture the tension between ideological and self-interested factors that influence identity.

Chapter 5 conveys and assesses the content from elite interviews conducted in Taipei during the fall of 2015 and the summer of 2016. These meetings are introduced in summary form with regard to time, place and representativeness. The content of the interviews is assembled inductively under a set of themes – the 1992 Consensus, Sunflower Movement and other headings. Analysis and synthesis of the interview content follows and points towards an intricate set of connections for Taiwanese identity and a range of other variables.

Chapter 6 reports on the results of an online survey of public opinion conducted in Taiwan during December 2015. The survey assesses Taiwanese voters' participation and identity formation, along with their relationship to cross-Strait relations. The survey results gathered and presented in this chapter reveal further nuances of Taiwan's identity formation – in particular how the reality of China's rise is affecting popular views and sentiments among those on the island about the Mainland as well as of their own sense of self.

Chapter 7 takes a layered empirical approach from survey results obtained in 2017 to explain how people in Taiwan increasingly view their identity as separate and different from that of the Chinese people living on the Mainland. Empirical evidence reinforces the discussion and findings in Chapters 5 and 6, noting a wide variety of factors that influence elite and mass identity formation in Taiwan. In particular, the qualitative and quantitative empirical analysis discussed thus far demonstrates that, among those on the island, there has been a significant shift in identity formation; the ROC's democratization process now plays an ongoing and major role in affecting how people see themselves as Taiwanese only.

Chapters 8 turns to elaborating, in light of material from interviews and surveys, the systemist-generated figure that provided a point of culmination for theorizing in Chapter 4. In other words, given the content of the interviews and surveys, how should the causal story from the initial graphic representation be elaborated? In short, putting this range of multiple data and methods and inputs together, what did we learn? We also address both policy implications and the influence of US vs. China great power competition. The chapter concludes with ideas regarding further research and a few final thoughts about the study as a whole.

Lastly, it should be noted that throughout the book, we use the terms 'the Mainland', 'Mainland China', 'China' and/or the 'PRC' interchangeably. What constitutes 'China' and what it means may differ for different constituents, especially those in Taiwan. Our purpose here is not to make a political statement but merely to draw on the complex views and analyses that are reflected in our elite interviews and survey data results on identity formation. As will become evident in the pages and chapters to follow, what China means is multilayered and complex. China may be a political entity, but it may also be a cultural or civilizational concept (Pye, 1968; Jacques, 2012). As a result, the distinction may oftentimes be tangled. One of our key priorities, untangling this notion represents both an important contribution in this volume and a continuing work in progress.

Notes

[1] This approach takes its inspiration from Bobrow et al (1979), which implemented an ensemble of methods in the study of Chinese foreign policy during another era of very rapid change.

[2] The classic exposition on power transition theory, which focuses upon the strategic situation facing a leading state and challenger, appears in Organski (1958).

[3] A small sample of references beyond those already provided, with an emphasis on items from the new millennium, would include Bobrow et al (1979), Copper (1990), Friedberg (1994, 2005, 2010), Wu (1994), Chen and Starosta (1997), Tucker (1998–1999), O'Hanlon (2000), Hickey (2001), Tan et al (2001), Chambers (2002), Hickey and Li (2002), Clough (2003), Glaser (2004), Chan (2004, 2005, 2017), Sutter (2004), Bush (2005), Garrison (2005), Yang (2005), Bedford and Hwang (2006), Carpenter (2006), Romberg (2007), Lin (2007), Shirk (2007), Layne (2008), Kastner (2009, 2015), Beckley (2011/2012), Goldstein (2013), Huang and James (2014), Glaser (2015), Hickey (2015), Goh (2016), Hong (2016), Lin W. (2016), Liu and Li (2017), Li and Zhang (2017), Jacobs and Kang (2018) and Taliaferro (2019).

2

Taiwan in Historical Perspective

Overview

This chapter focuses on Taiwan in historical perspective. The goal is to review the most important aspects of the evolution of Taiwanese identity, cross-Strait relations, the rise of China, the role of the US, and how these matters are connected to each other. These lines of inquiry capture the essential components for an account of the likely pathway for cross-Strait relations, which in turn obviously have reverberations that further impact on cause and effect within the regional system of Northeast Asia and even beyond. Thus, emphasis is placed on a review of historical events that are believed to be important for the development of a comprehensive understanding of the situation today.

This chapter proceeds in seven additional sections. The second section moves forward from early history to the arrival of the Japanese in 1895. The third section covers the era of Japanese rule from 1895 to 1945. The initial decades of Nationalist rule are reviewed in the fourth section from 1945 to 1979. Corresponding to the 1980s, the Taiwanese economic miracle and identity-related developments appear in the fifth section. The sixth section – an era of one country with many problems – covers the 1990s. The seventh section focuses on key interactions involving the DPP in power vis-à-vis the US and PRC in the new millennium. The eighth and final section sums up the history of Taiwan as presented in this chapter.

Early history

Taiwan, also known as Formosa, is an island about 160 kilometres (100 miles) from the Asian coastline. With mountainous territory and a subtropical climate and diverse ecosystem, the approximately 36,000 square kilometre (14,000 square mile) island is well-suited to human habitation, which goes back a long way in history. Aboriginal groups with Oceanic and Chinese origins, along with others about whom less is known, can be traced back to prehistoric times (Knapp, 2007: 5–9). A short-lived Dutch colonial settlement in the 17th century brought with it intensive agriculture to complement the hunting, gathering, fishing and small-scale farming that existed already (Knapp, 2007: 11). Ming General Zheng Chenggong, also known as Koxinga, expelled the Dutch from Taiwan in 1662 (Spence, 1999: 54; Sheng, 2001: 9; Knapp, 2007: 13). Chinese dynasties then ruled the island for over two centuries.

Change came to Taiwan as challenges to its rulers in the capital then known as Peking accumulated via encroachments from more developed great powers. Confrontations escalated during the Qing Dynasty. Mosca (2013: 2) identifies a major development in the Qing state's external relations in the transition from the 18th to the 19th century: region-specific strategies for various frontiers replaced by efforts towards an integrated foreign policy. However, things did not work out well for the Qing Dynasty when China increasingly 'confronted European empires that operated simultaneously in multiple, noncontiguous areas and could not be managed, or even fully comprehended, on any single frontier' (Mosca, 2013: 2). The Qing Empire, in turn, became one of several substantial entities locked in competition with each other (Mosca, 2013: 3). Within that empire, Taiwan had the status of a territory, until it was upgraded to a province in 1885 (Sheng, 2001: 9). Japanese expansionism impacted on the island as the 19th century wore on – a story told in more detail momentarily.

From the point of Dutch arrival onward, village-based agriculture took hold and, over the course of centuries, urbanization and transportation systems developed. The process of connecting the island's residents to each other eventually included modern roads and railways in the last quarter of the 19th century (Knapp, 1999: 22–23). These developments set the stage for a major phase of modernization as a by-product of the Sino-Japanese war towards the end of the 19th century.

Japanese rule

China fought and lost, to its great amazement, a war against Japan in 1895. For the most part, China did not comprehend that it would be no match for an already modernizing Japan. When Japan invaded Taiwan in the 1870s and China had to pay in order to obtain a withdrawal, it did not shake the court in Beijing out of its false sense of security and even superiority over others (Fenby, 2008: 48–49). War ensued between China and Japan over occupation of Korea, which Beijing viewed as being under its suzerainty. China fared poorly in the war; it lost not only Korea, but also Taiwan. Japan took control over Taiwan and a 50-year period of occupation got underway.

Japanese rule over Taiwan had lasting impacts. In material terms, Taiwan experienced a quantum leap in economic development and overall modernization. Trade with Japan played an important role in that advancement. Taiwanese in cities adapted especially well to the Japanese era. Innovations such as the telephone and public post offices – even the riding of bicycles – quickly became an ongoing part of urban life (Lamley, 2007: 218). As a by-product of Japanese rule, the Taiwanese people became increasingly separated from China. After the passing of a deadline in 1897, residents of Taiwan no longer even had the status of Chinese registry or nationality (Lamley, 2007: 208). Thus, the Japanese era impacted upon Taiwan in ideational terms as well.

Parallel sets of developments – institutional and demographic – would have important implications for Taiwanese identity in later years. On the institutional side, the Japanese government experienced ongoing struggles with the question of assimilation. Taiwanese political movements, such as the New People's Society founded in 1920, rejected both restoration to China and integration with Japan. Instead, members of the Society wanted home rule for Taiwan (Lamley, 2007: 233). Japanese residents of Taiwan, however, did not like the idea of an elected legislative body within which, of course, those of Taiwanese descent would be a supermajority (Lamley, 2007: 233). Thus, the imbalance in demographics between ruled (majority) and rulers (minority) created complications throughout the period of Japanese government. Another development from the Japanese era, demographic in nature, also possessed important implications in later years for evolving Taiwanese identity. Mainlanders came to Taiwan in large numbers – even reaching a high point of more than 60,000 in 1936 (Lamley, 2007: 223). The quarrels over assimilation and democratization, along with an expanding number of people from the Mainland, would foreshadow conflict over Taiwanese identity many years later.

When the Japanese took over in the late 19th century, Taiwan had been primarily an agrarian economy. Sugar and rice production, economically speaking, continued to be the norm during the initial decades of Japanese rule. A shift towards manufacturing occurred and the most intense phase of industrialization would come to Taiwan in the wartime period from 1937 to 1945. Japan went to war against China and then the US; and that created the need for industrial production beyond what could be sustained at home. Heavy industry expanded to complement development already in place for Taiwan (Lamley, 2007: 237). Japan lost the war and Taiwan found itself back under Chinese rule just as suddenly as that had ended 50 years earlier. With defeat imminent in the Chinese Civil War, the head of the nationalist forces, Chiang Kai-shek, retreated to the island of Taiwan, took office as president of the ROC, and a period of oligarchy under the KMT (also known as the Nationalist Party) ensued. The PRC ruled the Mainland from 1949 onward and the adversaries eyed each other suspiciously across the Taiwan Strait.

Nationalist rule

One event, from 1947, provides the point of departure for assessing the ROC during its period of exile. Hundreds of local Taiwanese died in what became known as the '228 Incident', which occurred on 28 February 1947 (King, 2016: 44). A riot took place over a government officer's beating of a contraband cigarette seller. ROC troop reinforcements quickly put down the fledgling rebellion, but the incident brought out tensions between Taiwanese and Mainlanders and led to the imposition of what became known as the 'White Terror' (Tsai, 2007: 13, 14; see also Kerr, 1965). The White Terror refers to a period of 40 years with suppression of dissent. Martial law lasted from 19 May 1949 to 15 July 1987. In any number of significant ways, observes Edmondson (2002: 27), the Nationalists could not separate themselves effectively from the previous Japanese rulers of Taiwan. The people of Taiwan, unfortunately, had traded in one form of dictatorship for another.

Efforts towards assimilation simply took a different form under the ROC. The government's security apparatus – inefficient and corrupt – contributed to public dissatisfaction (Wang, 2007: 323). A process of 'Mandarinization' (Mendel cited in Rubenstein, 2007a: 390), accompanied by acts of repression, got underway in the late 1940s and alienated many Taiwanese. Inhabitants of the island did not want to live in a culture that emphasized the virtue of a Chinese identity and way of doing things above everything else. The Nationalists instituted a programme to encourage patriotic activities among youth because of concerns about student protest movements. Youth-related programming included pro-Chinese cultural indoctrination and also surveillance regarding any potentially seditious activity (Wang, 2007: 323). Beneath the surface, however, resistance to assimilation built over time.

Chiang Kai-shek's Nationalist Party controlled the National Assembly and, when needed for continuity in leadership, permitted him to serve beyond the two-term restriction. Chiang stayed in office all the way through to 1975. For decades, the KMT succeeded in preventing any effective opposition by playing factions off against each other. Through various means, the Nationalist Party also manipulated local elections (Wang, 2007: 327). In the era of KMT hegemony under Chiang, the regime had a 'Jekyll and Hyde' quality: an undemocratic political system accompanied by a high-performing economy.

Ironically, the Nationalists had failed to reform agriculture when in power on the Mainland, but succeeded after coming to Formosa (Fenby, 2008: 382). Well-educated professionals took charge of economic development and planning and had full authority to cooperate with officials from the US who had responsibility for transfer of aid (Wang, 2007: 327). In addition, the government took full advantage of the education and abilities of migrants – an important aspect of Taiwan's overall performance in terms of creating and maintaining human resources (Wang, 2007: 329).

While US aid ended in 1964, economic success continued on the island. Taiwan became one of the fastest-growing economies in the world – well-managed and with particular encouragement towards investment and export (Wang, 2007: 333). Another reason for sustained high performance comes to the fore in looking at economic data regarding wealth distribution from the 1960s. Taiwan surged ahead but, unlike so many other examples of an economic take-off, managed to maintain income equality (Wang, 2007: 333). At the same time, KMT dominance in politics continued apace. Popular culture remained under very careful scrutiny and the Nationalist government crushed most aspects of dissent in society (Wang, 2007: 335). Intellectuals made easy targets because of their liberal-sounding positions in opposition to Nationalist policies – automatically associated with communism and its Mainland-based menace to the regime. Even Lee Teng-hui, a future president of Taiwan, had a run-in with the Taiwan Garrison Command, which in 1969 arrested and questioned him for a week about possible communist affiliations.

For the ROC and PRC, major events with opposite connotations occurred in 1971. The Mainland lobbied for admission to the United Nations (UN) *and* secured its status as a permanent member of the UN Security Council. Faced with dwindling levels of international support, Chiang's UN ambassador marched out of the General Assembly meeting in protest while delegates from some of the developing states 'danced in the aisles' (Fenby, 2008: 501). As a result, the UN adopted

Resolution 2758 on 25 October 1971 and recognized the PRC as the new and legitimate government of China. These major developments took place as a by-product of the US initiative towards the PRC in the early 1970s, along with a general shift in perception among UN member states regarding legitimate representation of the Mainland. The expulsion vote and the diplomatic walkout effectively sharpened the divide across the Taiwan Strait. In one way, the switch in UN recognition might be regarded as the final shot of the Chinese Civil War, along with a wake-up call to the ROC about the unreality of any claim regarding sovereignty on the Mainland.

Even as diplomatic isolation intensified, with the vast majority of states switching recognition to the PRC, Taiwan achieved greater prosperity than ever before. Economic advancement and a degree of transformation took place in the Taiwanese economy during the 1970s. Agricultural output declined and a shift to new forms of production, such as floriculture, became significant (Rubenstein, 2007a: 368). Meanwhile, employment in the industrial sector continued to rise; productivity and wages made steady gains and an orientation towards exports worked out especially well (Rubenstein, 2007a: 371). All of this contributed to an underlying sense of dissonance with regard to the economic and political systems when juxtaposed with each other.

While the economy moved forward very well indeed, issues of identity and representation came forward in politics. Conflict during the 1970s increasingly pitted native Taiwanese against the more recent arrivals from the Mainland over control of the state apparatus (Rubenstein, 2007b: 439). During the late 1970s, the nascent opposition 'employed ethnic discrimination as the theme of national identity issues' (T. Lin, 2002: 125). During that period, tensions between state and society sometimes came out violently into the open. In the county and city mayor election in 1977, for example, voting fraud led to a riot. This confrontation became known as the Zhongli Incident when police fired into a crowd and killed two youths (Tsai, 2007: 5). The Zhongli Incident had an important legacy; it 'increased public awareness of KMT's under-handed tactics and consequently generated support for and contributed to the strength of the Dangwai movement' (Tsai, 2007: 5). Opposition to oligarchic rule, with the Dangwai movement as the incubator for what became the DPP, increasingly came out into the open.

Another prominent confrontation between state and society became known as the Formosa or Kaohsiung Incident – a pivotal event and even legendary in the history of modern Taiwan (Rubenstein, 2007b: 441). The Kaohsiung Incident refers to a 'crackdown on protesters against the shutting down of Formosa Magazine on International Human Rights Day in 1979' (Tsai, 2007: 5). Tension built as the day for a major opposition rally drew closer; telephone surveillance and other activities on the part of government authorities signalled that a major confrontation would be coming if and when the event went ahead. When the anti-government march got underway on the evening of 10 December 1979, the police attacked participants with tear gas (Rubenstein, 2007b: 441–442). Violence ensued. As Tsai (2007: 5) observes, the Formosa Incident 'exposed to the public the heavy handed tactics of the KMT government which brought charges against the accused conspirators of the protest in public trials'. The violence brought fissures within Taiwanese society out into the open more than ever before and set the stage for organized, party-based opposition to the KMT in the coming decades.

Significant changes also got underway in cross-Strait relations as the 1970s drew to a close. Since Deng Xiaoping's opening of China in 1979, connections between Taiwan and the Mainland dramatically increased (Shirk, 2007: 196). While China obviously had great sensitivity over the issue of sovereignty, the Taiwan Relations Act, signed during that same year, entrenched the status quo and in all likelihood reduced the potential for military escalation across the Taiwan Strait. Over Taiwan, Goh (2016: 62) observes,

> China and the US achieved a limited bargain during the 1979 normalization, based on the principle of 'one China.' Beijing was accorded diplomatic recognition and authority over all of China, and Washington recognized that Taiwan is a part of China and relinquished the right to encourage Taiwanese independence (though not the right to sell arms to Taiwan).

Each side might well sum up the deal by saying that half a loaf is better than none. At the very least, the bargain reduced tensions in the immediate future for all three dyads concerned.

The Taiwan economic miracle and Taiwanese identity

Development on the island took a new and further positive direction in the 1980s. The information and computer industries, with obvious strategic importance, reached a take-off point. From 1984 to 1988, Taiwan's exports of hardware products increased more than fivefold and, as the decade progressed, 'PC clones became the norm and more sophisticated hardware and software became available' (Rubenstein, 2007a: 374). The financial sector also went through a phase of liberalization that helped Taiwan adapt effectively to the changing world economy (Rubenstein, 2007a: 375–376). These developments combined to raise the level of contact with the world abroad and exposure to new ideas, which in turn had implications for politics on the island itself.

Against the backdrop of prosperity in the 1980s, long-standing identity-based grievances came more into the open and entered onto the political agenda for Taiwan. Aboriginal concerns gained special prominence. Founded in 1985, the Alliance of Taiwan Aboriginals moved into a period of activism two years later. Protests took place and the Alliance in June 1987 made the 'first published call for aboriginal self-government in Taiwan' (Stainton, 2007: 423). Moreover, aboriginal mobilization reflected a larger ongoing process within society as a whole. As the 1980s moved along, Tsai (2007: 15) observes that

> the KMT faced difficulties in maintaining the justice system, mitigating the negative effects of economic development and the increasing differentiation of the social structure, and in responding to the rise of Aboriginal movements and the establishment of the DPP, which all contributed to the development of a 'Taiwanese consciousness' that in its strength and intensity rivaled the 'Chinese consciousness' the government had intentionally promoted over the years.

Sinic versus indigenous identification increasingly shaped the main axes of conflict in Taiwan as political competition moved towards legal status.

One example of how conflict played out concerns interpretation of Taiwanese history during perhaps its most controversial era. Memories of the Japanese regime, as the 1980s progressed, 'quickly became a source of dispute between local Taiwanese (*Benshengren*) – that is, those who had been living on Taiwan prior to the KMT's arrival' and 'the two-million or so KMT "outsiders" (*Waishengren*) who had arrived in the late 1940s and 1950s' (King, 2016: 43–44). Given horrendous experiences on the Mainland during the period of occupation, those who came over to Taiwan brought with them anger and resentment towards Japan. By contrast, the era of Japanese rule in Taiwan had entailed substantial modernization, accompanied by a significantly lower level of repression than experienced on the Mainland. These differences in experiences between *Benshengren* and *Waishengren* with Japanese rule continues to shape issues that arise later on the agenda.

One prominent example would be the teaching of history in Taiwanese public schools.

Mandarinization, described earlier, encountered mounting opposition from civil society. Nationalist leaders increasingly understood that, if pushed too hard as an ongoing attempt to 'carry a torch' for a past life on the Mainland, Mandarinization could be the ultimate undoing of the KMT. President Chiang Ching-kuo and others of a pragmatic bent within the KMT also realized, by the late 1980s, that the Mainland would not come back under their control (Rubenstein, 2007a: 391). Thus one major event – a liberalizing and at the time unexpected one, with the son of Chiang Kai-shek in power – took place in 1986: 'the decision by then-president Chiang Ching-kuo *not* to crack down on those who had illegally formed an opposition party' (Brown, 2004: 239). While formation of the DPP defied martial law, the time had come for at least limited democratization as a means towards management of underlying conflicts within society. Upheaval seemed like the probable alternative to the advent of electoral competition. President Chiang Ching-kuo allowed freedom of the press and lifted martial law (Fenby, 2008: 663). Thus, Taiwan transitioned into a multiparty system, with the KMT as initially dominant. At the effective start of party competition in 1986, the KMT and DPP held 64 per cent and 24 per cent of the seats, respectively, in the Legislative Yuan (Clark, 2007: 501). The KMT remained on top for some time, but the DPP gained ground as it built infrastructure and obtained experience in electoral competition.

Taiwan, as Corcuff (2002a: 73) observes in an exposition that emphasizes the importance of symbolic change, experienced a 'deep transition' that can be traced to the critical period of 1987–1988. Prior to that turning point, the thought of Sun Yat-sen, founder of the ROC, had been hegemonic in intellectual terms. It took the form of *tridemism*: nationalism, democracy and people's welfare (Corcuff, 2002a: 75). Sun Yat-sen had put forward tridemism to cope with China's problems in the 1920s, so it is not surprising that teachers and students increasingly found it irrelevant to Taiwan in the 1990s (Corcuff, 2002a: 76). The change in mindset paved the way for further reform of the educational system to keep pace with contemporary needs associated with an expanding modern economy.

Taiwan's school system emerged as a front line of conflict for identity formation. By 1990, school history textbooks and classes (e.g. new *Renshi Taiwan* (*Know Taiwan*)) focused less on shared history with China – an emphasis associated with KMT dominance – and 'more on distinct aspects of Taiwanese history' (King, 2016: 44). School textbooks began to discuss social, educational and economic developments achieved during Japanese rule and contrasted levels of development on the Mainland with Taiwan's much greater accomplishments during this period (King, 2016: 44). The new approach towards teaching history 'embraced Taiwan's contact with Japanese and Dutch colonial forces, celebrated Taiwan's history as a trading nation that had developed extensive commercial and cultural ties with the West and Japan and appropriated Taiwan's aboriginal heritage to demonstrate that Taiwan was a pluralistic society' (King, 2016: 45). Students therefore began to process information that could impact on identity formation – notably a shift away from Sinic affiliation coupled with demonization of Japan in particular.

Politics in the new era featured great intensity because long-suppressed conflicts could come out into the open without simply being put down by security forces. Dialogue increasingly replaced detention. The DPP initially succeeded at the local level but then became more prominent and partisan as a party active across Taiwan. Lee Teng-hui took office as president in 1988 and pursued a pragmatic path in foreign policy, with an emphasis on membership in trade groups, UN-related NGOs and other items associated with maintaining prosperity and connections with the wider world (Rubenstein, 2007b: 462). Democratization also accelerated under Lee's administration. This process included ethnic, identity-related dimensions. Native Taiwanese obtained appointment, in significant numbers, to important positions in government offices and use of the Taiwanese dialect, as an alternative to Mandarin, increased in public life (Tsai, 2007: 15, 16; see also Clark, 2007: 504). The changes in the school system noted earlier stand out as a flashpoint for conflict as Taiwanization began to replace Mandarinization.

One country, many problems

From the standpoint of foreign policy ideas and infrastructure, key events took place late in 1990 and early in 1991. At the end of 1990, PRC officials proposed initial, low-level talks about reunification under a 'one country, two systems' formula (Rubenstein, 2007b: 466). The ROC took parallel actions to facilitate interactions with the PRC. The Executive Yuan created the Mainland Affairs Council (MAC) to pursue overall plans in that area. In February and March 1991, respectively, the National Unification Council and Executive Yuan adopted 'Guidelines for National Unification' (Sheng, 2001: 19–20). The relationship with the Mainland continued to expand, albeit with halting steps (Rubenstein, 2007b: 467).

These actions led up to what became known as the 1992 Consensus. This somewhat surreal agreement resulted from a meeting in British Hong Kong between two semi-official associations: from Taiwan, the Straits Exchange Foundation (SEF), and from the Mainland, the Association for Relations Across the Taiwan Strait (ARATS). From Beijing's point of view, a meeting without state-to-state connotations had the most potential to work towards some type of functional agreement with Taipei that eventually could lead to unification. In the collective mind of Taipei, the meeting in Hong Kong permitted the opportunity to obtain some kind of stabilizing arrangement outside the normal channels of diplomacy with Beijing, to which it did not have access. The net result, the 1992 Consensus, constituted an agreement on the existence of a single China but this meant very different things on either side of the Strait.

Perhaps the 1992 Consensus is most easily understood as an oxymoron – announcement of an abeyance. Each side took away a different sense of what should be understood by 'one China and two systems'. For the Mainland, it represented an agreement on eventual unification and an effective ban on independence for Taiwan. From the standpoint of Taiwan, however, it meant a commitment to self-determination accompanied by an agreement to keep talking.

With the unveiling of the 228 Monument in Taipei in February 1995, the government took an important step towards recognizing the legacy of past oppression. Family members of victims from the 228 Incident assembled in Taipei, at New Park, and received a formal apology from Lee Teng-hui, leader of the KMT and president of Taiwan (Rubenstein, 2007b: 470). From a strategic standpoint, Lee hoped to position himself between hard-liners on both sides – independence versus unification advocates – and thus be in a good position to maintain power (Rubenstein, 2007b: 471). Given the rise of identity politics, a middle ground position entailed at least some recognition of the worst excesses from the past. Moreover, greater internal stability, in all likelihood, would facilitate more cooperation between the ROC and PRC.

Just a few months later, any hoped-for calming of cross-Strait relations received quite a jolt from across the Pacific. With a reversal of its 16-year ban on visits by high ranking officials, on 22 May 1995, the US granted a visa to President Lee Teng-hui. The visa would permit a six-day visit – characterized as private rather than official – to his alma mater, Cornell University. This action 'prompted a crisis in both China-United States relations and cross-strait relations' and China responded to Lee's visit with great intensity (Sheng, 2001: 24, 26). Lee arrived in the

US and complications ensued right away; government officials greeted him with a 'formal red-carpet ceremony' (Rubenstein, 2007b: 471). This looked to Beijing in particular like an act of formal recognition. The speech by Lee at Cornell obtained significant media coverage and China reacted decisively against the visit as a whole.

Most dramatically, China launched missile tests and conducted military exercises close to Taiwan and, between July 1995 and March 1996, assembled troops in Fujian Province directly across the Strait (Sheng, 2001: 28). From 21 to 26 July 1995, observes Sheng (2001: 28), the third division of the Second Artillery Corps of the People's Liberation Army (PLA) carried out in a sea area north of Taiwan 'a surface-to-surface missile test, code-named "95 *Ziqiang*"'. Located just 170 kilometres north of Taiwan, the target zone for the missile testing sent a clear and threatening message (Rubenstein, 2007b: 472). The US responded by assembling two aircraft carrier battle groups near Taiwan – since the end of the Vietnam War in 1975, its most sizable fleet in East Asia (Sheng, 2001: 31–32). In light of obvious US military superiority, Beijing backed down and the crisis abated (Fenby, 2008: 664). This peaceful outcome did not mean, however, anything like 'forgive and forget'.

Events from 1995–1996, which reached the crisis level, strengthened Taipei's perceptions that China would be willing, for purposes of coercion, to use dangerous levels of military force (King, 2016: 45). The likely explanation for the very high intensity of the Chinese response resides in domestic politics: 'Jiang Zemin decided it was safer to appease the hawks in the army, the government, and the public by holding live-fire missile exercises toward Taiwan and risking a war with America than allow public protests – an ominous precedent for future Taiwan-related crises' (Shirk, 2007: 227). While de-escalation ensued, memories lasted as both sides realized the potential for war if and when independence for Taiwan came out openly as an issue.

Meanwhile, a new series of changes in the educational system of Taiwan had implications for the nexus of identity and cross-Strait relations. A university law, passed in 1994, permitted greater autonomy on campuses (Rubenstein, 2007a: 381). More diverse curriculum, with reduced government influence, took hold as a result. Textbook reform, in 1997, stands out in Taiwan's evolution as a 'milestone' (Corcuff, 2002a: 85). Historians worked on the new programme 'with a degree of freedom from political interference unknown until then' and, for the first time, could transcend the 'political taboo' in the education field regarding the plurality of historical experiences for Taiwan (Corcuff, 2002a: 86). The result, *Knowing Taiwan*, represented the initial stage in a new three-year high school programme and, as in the case of reform that pertained to Sun Yat-sen-inspired tridemism, change emerged from inside of the state-party apparatus (Corcuff, 2002a: 88, 90). This shift signalled KMT's awareness of the need to adapt in order to remain relevant to future political competition beyond an agenda that consisted of Sinic identity and unification.

Events involving China and the US, well beyond Taipei's control, had important implications for cross-Strait relations. Tensions increased for Beijing and Washington with US bombing of the Chinese Embassy at Belgrade in May 1999: 'China's Communist Party leaders deflected the students' nationalist outrage away from themselves onto the United States' and the Chinese public believed the bombing to be intentional (Shirk, 2007: 214, 218; see also Fenby, 2008: 666). Due to its cultivation of xenophobic nationalism – a tendency discussed at length later in this chapter – Beijing lacked flexibility in responding to an event such as the bombing of its embassy.

After the aerial assault on the embassy, a gap between pragmatic foreign policy and nationalistic public opinion became more entrenched. China then went on to blame the US for rejection of its bid to host the 2000 Olympic Games (Shirk, 2007: 220, 227). Tensions diminished, however, as economic realities for the US and PRC intervened for both sides; the relationship had become too important to allow ideological differences to interfere (Fenby, 2008: 666). Leaders in Beijing knew, however, that future confrontations with Washington, Taipei (or both) increasingly would be difficult to manage in light of highly probable domestic pressure in favour of escalation.

Leadership in Taiwan also tried to manage new difficulties arising from the three-way relationship. President Lee put forward the 'two states' theory in 1999: Before his presidential term expired, Lee hoped to lay a firmer groundwork for the future and that 'reflected his lack of confidence in the next president' (Sheng, 2001: 215). Lee had to appease his base of supporters, who wanted major policy change, notably, movement towards independence – yet he also had to deal with realities involving further confrontation with China and the US, and was reluctant to see conflict escalate (Clark, 2007: 525). The president faced an almost impossible situation in which the wrong policy profile could damage the three-way relationship while also aggravating domestic tensions – an outcome much more likely than something that would please all parties concerned.

Symbolic recognition on the island of an increasingly Taiwanese identity continued apace and promised to raise tensions with the Mainland. Reform of banknotes from the Chiang Kai-shek era, for example, took place in a gradual way (Corcuff, 2002a: 92). Over the course of decades, vegetal ornaments with traditional Chinese associations had been used for watermarks. 'The plum flower (NT$100), orchid (NT$200), bamboo (NT$500), chrysanthemum (NT$1000), and pine (NT$2000)', as Corcuff (2002a: 93) observes, all possess a strong identity as Chinese. Official status of the New Taiwan Dollar as the national currency of the Republic of China on Taiwan was confirmed in 1999 and as newspapers noted right away, represented considerable 'symbolic change' (Corcuff, 2002a: 95). Movement away from a Sinic identity – and towards a uniquely Taiwanese alternative – stood at the centre of the preceding changes.

Corcuff (2002a: 96) sums up the cumulative effects of reforms such as those involving currency:

> The disappearance of Sun Yat-sen's doctrine is near total, and though it has not officially been replaced by any other ideology, the switch is *de facto* operated amid a relatively consensual new ideology of 'soft' Taiwanese nationalism, which encompasses the defense of Taiwan's democracy, appeals to its consolidation and common defense of Taiwan's sovereignty, the necessity to put aside the question of the national title in the face of the PRC's diplomatic pressure and military buildup.

Identity evolved in a gradual way, cautiously for the most part among leaders, but in a clear direction: away from a connection with China. Change unfolded across multiple dimensions that ranged from philosophical dispositions to design of political institutions. Implicit in all of this inhered a more open embrace of Taiwanese uniqueness based on a multifaceted identity, within which a Chinese element would have a limited role to play.

Change on the island, both symbolic and material, did not escape the attention of the Mainland, which saw danger on the horizon regarding Taiwan's possible declaration of independence. When it released the *White Paper on the One-China Principle and the Taiwan Issue* on 22 February 2000, Beijing made a major policy statement. This pronouncement, as Rigger (2001: 192) observes, 'threatened force if Taiwan moved toward independence or refused to enter negotiations leading to the unification of Taiwan and mainland China. While the first condition was a familiar one, Beijing had never before offered the delay of negotiations as a rationale for military attack'. Tensions across the Strait increased as a result.

The Democratic Progressive Party, the People's Republic of China and the United States

Taiwanese reaction to the threatening stance from the Mainland worked in exactly the opposite direction hoped for among Beijing's leadership. A major changing of the guard came in Taiwan's election of 2000, when Chen Shui-bian became the first president elected from the opposition DPP. It also marked the first time that a political party other than the KMT held the seat of the ROC government in Taiwan. Chen pushed Taiwanese nationalism and appealed to his 'base', either out of necessity or preference, and this became more pronounced once he came to power (Clark, 2007: 510).

These developments took place against the backdrop of mounting Sino-American tensions over the status of Taiwan. While quite astonishing to those outside of China who hear of it for the first time, the PRC's National Humiliation Day, each September since 2001, makes sense within its historical context. Every year on 18 September National Humiliation Day commemorates horrendous experiences at the hands of Japanese occupation. The specific day of the year chosen, 18 September, recalls the Japanese bombing attack on their own railway in Mukden, which when blamed on the Chinese created the rationale for the invasion of Manchuria and further aggression. Even nine decades after the specific events in 1931, the legacy of the wartime experience should not be underestimated when processing Chinese reactions to anything that even looks remotely like a violation of sovereignty.

Tensions mounted with the US as a new president, George W. Bush, took office in 2001. Loss of US jobs to China had become an issue in the 2000 presidential election campaign and it stayed salient through the following contest in 2004. Shirk (2007: 249) summarizes a series of economic problems and associated conflict with China: 'piracy of DVDs, CDs, prescription drugs, and other intellectual property frustrated American producers'. Retaliation from the US ensued. For example, the US House of Representatives blocked the Chinese National Offshore Oil Company's (CNOOC) attempt to buy UNOCAL. The political explosion from the CNOOC bid stunned and demoralized the Chinese government, with the bid being withdrawn on 2 August 2005 (Shirk, 2007: 250, 251). Given different value systems, Washington and Beijing began to collide on economic issues as the ascent of China brought it more directly into the global system.

Conflict with a rising China included security policy as well, notably regarding nuclear missile defence. The Bush administration refused to adjust deployment plans in response to Chinese concerns.

'Forced to plan for a thick, robust missile shield around the United States (even though the technology may never succeed)', Shirk (2007: 247) observes, 'China has sought to minimize the damage to bilateral relations'. A military incident soon would aggravate Sino-American relations and draw attention to ongoing Chinese concerns about sovereignty.

Near the Hainan Island on 1 April 2001, a mid-air collision occurred between a PLA Navy interceptor fighter jet and a US Navy EP3 signals intelligence aircraft. The pilot of the Chinese military plane died, and the US aircraft had to make an emergency landing on Hainan Island. The PRC detained and questioned the crew, but released them when a sufficiently ambiguous document permitted both sides to back away without serious embarrassment. This strange episode, according to Callahan (2010: 16), reveals how identity and security issues are tied closely together even among political elites. Given concerns over Taiwan and possibly other peripheries, such as Tibet, leaders in Beijing had to avert any sense of defeat over a sovereignty-related issue such as the aircraft collision. Even a seemingly minor incident had great potential for escalation of US conflict with China, still fixated on past humiliations involving violation of its sovereignty. The EP3 incident also shows the clear cultural difference between China and the US in dealing with conflicts and China's 'apology diplomacy' (Gries and Peng, 2002).

Tensions between China and the US continued during the George W. Bush years in the White House. Independence as an issue came onto the three-way agenda in a dramatic way as the election of 2004 approached for Taiwan. Anxieties about war heightened, as noted by Shirk (2007: 204), during the presidential election campaign of 2003–2004 when Chen Shui-bian 'called for a referendum to revise the Constitution in 2006, and ratify it by 2008' – a schedule 'obviously timed to conclude with the 2008 Olympics to be held in Beijing'. The election campaign itself featured mobilization on issues of identity. The most intense moment of all, perhaps, came with the Pan-Green rally on 28 February, to commemorate the 228 Incident of 1947 but also explicitly stand up against any new threats from the Mainland (Clark, 2007: 514).

China took notice of the rising tide of nationalism in Taiwan and passed an Antisecession Law on 7 May 2004. Beijing made a clear statement against Taiwanese independence: 'The guidelines combined firmness and friendliness toward Taiwan, but the Chinese government emphasized their firm side by calling them the "Four Nevers"' (Shirk, 2007: 207). The Mainland, however, used both the 'stick' and the 'carrot' to counter the Taiwanese trend towards independence. When it allowed two Taiwanese politicians, Lien Chan (KMT Chairman) and James Soong (People First Party head) to visit and speak on live television in May 2005, the Mainland looked confident as a result. Soon after, Beijing permitted its tourists to visit across the Strait (Shirk, 2007: 208, 209). Note that with the visit from Lien and Soong, Beijing extended the olive branch to two *Pan-Blue* politicians; Pan-Green remained anathema from the Mainland government's point of view.

Over and beyond the referendum controversy, actions by Taiwan during the George W. Bush era aggravated matters in the three-way relationship with the PRC. Perhaps most notably, Chen Shui-bian abolished the National Unification Council on 28 February 2006. This action took place, in all likelihood, as a response to declining support at home (Shirk, 2007: 209). Pan-Blue leaders and the Mainland condemned the decision immediately after, with Beijing emphasizing that Taiwan had no right of secession. Mainland leaders continued to seethe over the perceived drift of Taiwan towards independence.

China's Olympics in 2008 provide a highly public instance of a performance that intertwines identity with security (Callahan, 2010: 3). Take, for instance, events connected to Grace Wang, a Chinese student from Duke University. She intervened in a confrontation involving pro-Tibet and pro-China protesters on her campus over the Olympic Torch's Journey of Harmony. The PRC called Wang a traitor because of the attempted mediation between opposing sides of the debate (Callahan, 2010: 128). It is revealing that even an effort that entailed neutrality and conciliation by an individual Mainlander would be seen as an act of betrayal vis-à-vis a sovereignty-related issue.

With the election of Ma Ying-jeou as president in 2008, an 'unprecedented détente' ensued with the Mainland (Kastner, 2015: 2). Ma shelved talk of independence and even autonomy in and of itself. The Ma administration pursued conciliation with the Mainland and impacted upon identity in doing so. The Economic Cooperation Framework Agreement (ECFA) stands out as the most important agreement from the Ma era. ECFA greatly reduced commercial barriers, notably tariffs, and had as its goal the promotion of trade between the Mainland and Taiwan. For Taiwanese, the agreement came to symbolize a *rapprochement* with the PRC. Positive views from Pan-Blue contrasted with very negative reactions from the DPP, which worried about further economic interdependence as leading, perhaps irreversibly with ECFA in place, to unification.

Ma pursued ideational as well as material reconciliation with the Mainland. The president used historical memory 'as part of a wider project to "re-Sinicize" Taiwanese history' (King, 2016: 46). Ma's policies, which pertained to the school system and beyond, constituted a reversal from curricular shifts that had characterized the 1990s. For example, the government

> re-introduced classical Chinese into the education curriculum; celebrated key aspects of Chinese cultural heritage, such as Confucius and Huangdi, or the Yellow Emperor, a Chinese deity; and returned the names of national institutions such as the Taiwan Post and the National Taiwan Democracy Memorial Hall back to their pre-DPP titles, the China Post and the Chiang Kai-shek Memorial Hall. (King, 2016: 46)

Ma's government also commemorated important events from the Second World War in ways that paralleled the approach taken on the Mainland: (a) a conference in 2013 looked back at the Cairo Conference and Declaration from 1943; and (b) a suite of material, produced by Academia Historica, the Ministry of Defence, the Ministry of National Education and the Ministry of Foreign Affairs in 2015, focused on the end of the Second World War (King, 2016: 46–47).

Ma, in sum, claimed 'China's wartime history and identity for Taiwan' (King, 2016: 47). The president and those implementing his policies reminded all who would listen that the ROC, as compared to the communists, had done most of the fighting against the Japanese. This fed into the larger objective of improving the KMT's image by linking its history to the struggle against fascism. Not surprisingly, the opposition DPP saw all of this, along with ECFA, as a poorly hidden initiative towards unification with the Mainland.

Sovereignty issues in Northeast Asia at a more general level created complications for Sino-Taiwanese relations as pursued by the Ma administration. Events involving the PRC with Japan, in light of historical memories of wartime atrocities, had especially great intensity and potential for escalation of strife. Even minor incidents created risk of major consequences. On 7 September 2010, for example, the Japanese coast guard detained a Chinese fishing boat and its crew – on the surface a trivial matter. Tokyo claimed that the boat had been fishing in Japanese territorial waters – inside of 12 miles from a disputed island chain – known as the Diaoyu Islands in China and Senkaku Islands in Japan. Japan also noted that the fishing boat had rammed a Japanese coast guard ship (Beckley, 2011/2012: 83). Nationalist anger escalated against Japan after the arrest and many on the internet 'called for a boycott of Japanese goods and for the Chinese government to adopt stronger measures' (Beckley, 2011/2012: 84, 85).

Sovereignty-related anger crept into the Sino-American dyad as a by-product of accumulated incidents at sea and mounting sensitivities in China regarding perceived imperialist encroachments. 'The combination of China's hypernationalist political environment with increasingly severe economic and social instability', observes Beckley (2011/2012: 82), 'elicited China's hard-line and unprecedented diplomatic posture against U.S. naval exercises in international waters in the Yellow Sea'. After a 21 July statement from the US that its aircraft carrier would participate in military exercises but not enter the Yellow Sea, tensions diminished (Beckley, 2011/2012: 82).

Chinese sensitivity about the status of Taiwan continues to affect even seemingly trivial matters related to sovereignty. Baron (2016: 64), in summing up a recent incident, asserts that 'deportation of 45 Taiwanese citizens from Kenya to China in early April [2016] was of nebulous legality'. Malaysia took the same kind of action at the end of April 2016 – the government deported a further 32 Taiwanese suspects to Beijing. The Chinese government insisted that the prime reason had been Taipei's leniency on acts of fraud (Baron, 2016: 64). While it is possible such a concern played some role in the decision, the more likely explanation is ongoing pressure from the Mainland.

Tensions continue at this time of writing, with the politico-economic agenda of former US President Donald Trump reverberating throughout Northeast Asia in ways that do not point in any particular direction. Trump campaigned on an 'America First' platform that, once implemented, has created mixed signals for Xi as it relates to the PRC's interests. In economic terms, tariffs were a major priority for the US president; the idea of America First focuses very directly on protection of industries that had been experiencing employment losses via relocation of plants to Asia. Tariffs in place already have caused retaliation from the PRC, with speculation underway that a trade war could ensue and greatly damage the global economy. Consider, specifically, the arrest of Meng Wanzhou, Chief Financial Officer of Huawei, a Mainland tech giant, on 1 December 2018. This occurred in Canada and followed on from US accusations that Meng had violated sanctions imposed on Iran (Horowitz, 2018). This incident put an exclamation mark on the building confrontation between Beijing and Washington.

At the same time, in the realm of security, the Trump rhetoric about America First would seem to point in a more pacific direction. The former president continues to rail against overseas security-related involvements that invariably turn out to be very costly to the US. Such statements can be interpreted, with probable justification, as signalling that the US would prefer to stay out of Sino-Taiwanese relations to the greatest degree possible. The former president's rhetoric almost certainly reflects a desire for Taiwan to take on a greater burden of its own security and national defence. Thus, a Trump administration might be seen as less likely than others beforehand, which held what might be described as a liberal internationalist worldview, to encourage independence for Taiwan. The mixed messages from the White House serve as an additional, exogenous source of concern and uncertainty affecting cross-Strait relations.

Summing up the history

This chapter began with a history of Taiwan from time immemorial onward. Essential aspects of Taiwanese identity, cross-Strait relations, the ascent of China and the ongoing role of the US have been reviewed. Contact with the Dutch, Chinese, and Japanese over the course of centuries influenced politics, economics, and identity for the inhabitants of Formosa. Arrival of the KMT after its defeat in the Chinese Civil War stands out, perhaps, as the most transforming event of the modern era. Sinic and Taiwanese elements have blended together, not always peacefully, as identity evolved on the island over the course of decades. The history of US–China–Taiwan relations demonstrates that the triangular relationship has always been based on the strategic interests of the three parties. At the structural level, the strategic relationship between the US and China has played a much more determining role. At times, US–China relations appeared to show signs of a high level of cooperation as a result of the liberal institutionalist engagements between the two countries, for example the US's assistance that enabled China to enter the World Trade Organization (WTO) in 2001 and China's rapid economic rise that followed. As China gradually became the 'factory of the world', economic interdependence between the US and China strengthened significantly. However, viewing US–China relations through a longer stretch of history and the recent escalation of tensions between the two countries, particularly during the Trump administration, suggest that liberalism may not have helped the US and China to escape 'Thucydides' Trap' (Allison, 2017). Taiwan has always been an important piece in the strategic game over Beijing's and Washington's respective interests in the region. As China continues to challenge the US in the Asian Pacific, Taiwan's role can only become more important (regardless of identity or party affiliation of the US president; Hernandez and Chien, 2020). While not intended to be complete, the preceding review of events is sufficient to provide a context for examination of academic literature, along with results from elite interviews and opinion surveys, which takes place in subsequent chapters.

3

The Problématique of Taiwanese Identity

Overview

This chapter focuses on the evolution of Taiwanese identity. The question, 'what does it mean to be Taiwanese?', has never been obvious or easy to answer. Instead, responses vary across time, geography and individuals. Since identity represents a sense of belonging to a larger group, such ideological factors as values, ideas and emotions that affect the collective contribute to identity formation. Additional important aspects of evolving Taiwanese identity include cross-Strait relations, the ascent of China and the ongoing role of the US in Northeast Asia. While it is beyond the scope of the present investigation to cover all of the relevant academic literature in the preceding interconnected subject areas, what follows is a good faith effort. The review is deemed sufficient to identify the most important patterns in what academic literature has said about Taiwanese identity, most notably in connection with the other aspects discussed in the book thus far. In peeling back the layers of Taiwan's identity choice, we also begin to uncover how and why Taiwanese identity is highly political and increasingly convergent with the changing tides of political support on the island.

This chapter unfolds in eight additional sections. The second section covers early Taiwanese identity. The third section identifies historical imperatives. The fourth section covers the politics of Taiwanese identity. The fifth section assesses the impact from the rapid ascent of China to world power status. The sixth section turns to how the PRC exerts pressure on Taiwanese identity. The seventh section explores the closely related elemental role that Taiwan plays in relation to the Mainland. The eighth section explores the nexus of the US, PRC and cross-Strait relations. The ninth and final section assesses the academic literature in an overall sense.

Early Taiwanese identity

Taiwanese identity experienced a major, Sino-centric shock with the arrival of the KMT from the Mainland after its defeat in the civil war. Over the course of subsequent decades, in tandem with democratization, state dominance declined, with identity-related elements from civil society gaining ground. Taiwanese identity today is multifaceted and includes both demographic and belief-based elements. The rise of China also impacted upon Taiwanese identity, as irredentism from Beijing exerted pressure on the nearby island. The PRC reacted quite negatively towards Taiwanese talk of autonomy and especially independence as the DPP rose to challenge the KMT. China's greatly enhanced military capabilities, in particular, worried leaders in Taiwan and the US. A review of history reveals Sino-Taiwanese relations to be interconnected with the ascent of China and evolving identity on the embattled island of Formosa. With regard to forces coming in from outside of Northeast Asia, the US as a patron of Taiwan and rival of China is by far the most important in impacting upon cross-Strait relations.

Arguments in favour of Formosa and its inhabitants as part of the Chinese nation emphasize ethnicity as a long-standing connection, with most Taiwanese being Han Chinese (Li and Zhang, 2017). Shirk (2007: 185), however, summarizes the evolution of sovereignty regarding Taiwan in a way that takes the matter of identity in a different and less Sinic direction:

> The island of Taiwan has not been an integral part of China for thousands of years. The Qing dynasty took control over it – along with Tibet, Xinjiang, Mongolia, and Manchuria – into the seventeenth century and then lost it after its defeat in the Sino-Japanese War two hundred years later. In the 1940s, Mao Zedong actually told Edgar Snow, an American journalist, that after the CCP defeated the Japanese, it would let Taiwan become independent.

Given these facts – and especially the final and quite surprising revelation from the Second World War era – it is easy to see why Chinese claims regarding Taiwan are contested. While the Mainland pursues irredentism and perceives Taiwan as integral to its existence, many on the island and beyond read history in a different way.

Taiwan experienced a shock to its demographic system and associated identity when the ROC government collapsed, lost the civil war and retreated to Taiwan. The KMT leadership and supporters rapidly fled the Mainland for the island refuge in 1949. Migration back and forth across the Taiwan Strait did not constitute anything new, but the scale of this particular unidirectional movement led to massive change on Formosa. From the standpoint of identity translated into political and state institutions, the KMT became the dominant influence on the island. The KMT party-state could dictate an official narrative because it 'controlled Taiwanese media, school textbooks, museums and memorials', with local history 'mentioned obliquely, if at all'. Instead, Taiwan became 'a site of "patriotic" Chinese resistance against Japanese colonialism' (King, 2016: 43). In fact, the KMT identified themselves as more Chinese than the CCP who seized power in Beijing. The period of KMT dominance in identity formation through the school system spanned the 1950s through the 1970s (Li and Zhang, 2017). As will become apparent from a review of academic research, movement away from the KMT-dominated, Sinic identity took place with great conflict and destabilization along the way.

The historical imperatives of Taiwanese identity

What, then, is the contemporary situation regarding Taiwanese sense of self? From a survey taken during 10 to 24 January 2014 (N = 1,072), Liu and Li (2017) derive five main points about Taiwanese identity, which, given their importance, we quote at length:

> First, unification/independence preferences and belief in Taiwan's democratic impact could explain why Taiwanese voters see Mainland China as a brother or an enemy. Second, Pan-Blue supporters tend to see Mainland China as a brother, but this does not imply that they are zealous about cross-Strait trade talks. Third, Taiwanese identifiers tend to see Mainland China as an enemy, but this does not mean that all Pan-Green supporters have this tendency. Fourth, diversity (if not a gap) exists between the older and younger generations regarding their perceptions about Mainland China. Compared to those who are 46–60 years old, Taiwanese voters who are older than 61 tend to use the brotherhood analogy in their description of the cross-Strait relation; conversely, those born after 1968 tend to use hostile expressions (such as 'enemy') to describe Mainland China

but welcome more economic connection with Mainland China. This paradox reflects the reality of the younger generations of Taiwanese. Although younger Taiwanese wish to maintain their separate and unique identity, their future may be highly dependent on Mainland China. Fifth, as the majority of Taiwanese identifiers (58.86%) tend to be conservative about trade talks with Mainland China, one-third of the respondents (30.88%) who identify themselves as both Chinese and Taiwanese are likely to be the driving and supportive force for trade talks with Mainland China. (Liu and Li, 2017: 275–276)

The preceding points, taken together, bring out the ongoing complex and dynamic nature of identity choice among the Taiwanese. Ideological and self-interested, material factors related to self-identification – not always in line with each other regarding direction of change – clearly exist. Based on the survey results, it is clear that the people of Taiwan vary in identification along issue continua such as (1) independence versus unification and (2) degree of economic integration with the Mainland via trade and other means. Cohort effects, which correlate with Mainland- versus island-based origins, also are quite apparent in shaping identity as it evolves.

Generational change in particular, for some time now, is a common theme in observations about Taiwanese identity. Lin (2002: 134–135) sums up survey results over the period from 1992 to 1997: 'except for the NP [New Party] identifiers, increasing Taiwanese identity and decreasing Chinese identity are two significant and general trends, although the growth in Taiwanese identity is relatively unstable from year to year'. As the 1990s drew to a close, a new generation identified less with the culture of the Mainland and more with an essentially Taiwanese way of life (Tucker, 1998–1999: 156). Around 1997, manifestations of a new Taiwanese identity – more ethnically inclusive – clearly had started to rise (Edmondson, 2002: 37). Discourse about identity shifted and integrated 'indigenous groups, Taiwanese of Fujian descent, Hakka, and Chinese war-era immigrants' into a community, with emphasis on 'Taiwan's strategic geohistorical Pacific Rim positionality' (Edmondson, 2002: 37). In recent years, there has been a shift in discourse in which 'the ROC is regarded as a foreign colonial regime' (Chiung, 2018: 56). All of this stimulated interest on the Mainland – and not in an approving way.

Polls, even from two decades ago, affirm the preceding trend towards a Taiwan-oriented identity, notably in connection to sovereignty. For example, a survey taken by *The United Daily* on 11 July 1999 revealed that '71 percent said Taiwan was a sovereign country, 13 percent disagreed and the rest had no opinion' (Sheng, 2001: 219). Moreover, all three candidates in the 2000 presidential election agreed that, in practice, Taiwan is sovereign (Brown, 2004: 242). While they tend to emphasize closer connection with the Mainland as a means towards economic benefits, even candidates from the Pan-Blue parties do not contradict the preceding position on the island's autonomy and distinct political culture. It therefore is not surprising that scholars increasingly recognize a shift in Taiwan's identity choice: most people on the island identify as Taiwanese rather than Chinese (Hickey, 2015; Kastner, 2015: 2).

Various efforts have been made to create taxonomies and typologies for identity among the Taiwanese. The basic story line is that identities, whether based on descent or beliefs, have become more elaborate and intertwined over time. Identity as categorized in connection to ethnicity and beliefs is reviewed in turn.

Ethnicity in Taiwan, traditionally speaking, is based on 'registration-based distinction between Taiwanese (*Benshengren*, including Holo or Minnan and Hakka) and Mainlanders (*Waishengren*)' (Marsh, 2002: 147). With regard to belief systems, all other things being equal, Mainlanders had the most direct identification with the KMT and others less so, with opposition building over time.

Tsai (2007: 10) identifies four main ethnic groups in the 21st century: 13 per cent Mainland Chinese, 70 per cent Holo, 15 per cent Hakka and 2 per cent Aborigine. Corcuff (2002b: 163) elaborates on the categories, with Aborigine and Austronesian as synonymous:

> In recent years, the validity of the traditional distinction between *Waishengren* and *Benshengren* was so challenged that it is finally becoming more and more common to divide the Taiwanese population into four main groups: the *Austronesians*, the island's original inhabitants, forced to cohabit with the *Hakka* and *Holo* peoples arriving from Fujian and Guangdong provinces of China, particularly since the seventeenth century; and fourth the *Mainlanders* coming to Taiwan during a final wave of Chinese migration from the Mainland during the watershed years 1945–1949.

Brown (2004: 10) summarizes the historical pathways that have produced the current profile of ethnic identification on Formosa. Those of Han descent bifurcate into Taiwanese and Mainlanders.

Taiwanese further subdivide into Holo or Hakka, with Mainlanders then producing many groups. Others on the island have origins that go back to the Aborigines. One descent group goes into the plains and produces the Siraya or many other groups. The other descent group, which ends up in the mountains, is responsible, in turn, for a wide range of collectivities today.

Ethnic identification beyond simply Mainland- versus island-based origins became visible in political terms during the campaign season leading up to the election of 2000. A more complex picture emerges from the presidential election of that year, and according to Rigger (2001: 197), the 'category Taiwanese must be disaggregated into Minnan, Hakka, and Aboriginal voters'. At the same time, this nuanced sense of Taiwanese identity also points towards a greater emphasis upon its context and development as something differentiated from the Mainland.

The politics of Taiwanese identity

Identity expressed in political terms begins with the long-standing division regarding the Pan-Blue versus Pan-Green coalitions. Blue partisanship means a basic commitment to eventual unification with China, with the KMT, the People First Party and the New Party as the political organizations identified with that position. A Pan-Green affiliation, which includes the DPP, New Power Party and the Taiwan Solidarity Union, refers to a preference for greater autonomy and possibly moving towards greater independence from the Mainland. A new political party, Taiwan People's Party, founded by Taipei Mayor Ko Wen-je in August 2019, straddles the middle, seeking to establish itself as a viable alternative to the traditional divide between the KMT and DPP. Adopting the slogan that 'the two sides are one family', Ko's party platform draws supporters from both camps, especially those who favour pragmatic ties with the Mainland while embracing Taiwan's distinct identity. With time, more elaborate categories of political identities will become increasingly prevalent, especially as democratization deepens on the island. So from a political perspective, two different nations have existed historically in Taiwan: Chinese and Taiwanese (Lepesant, 2018).

With a maturing electoral process in place in Taiwan, Marsh (2002: 145) identifies multiple types of national identification preferences emerging among the people of Taiwan:

- Pragmatist: agrees with Taiwan independence if no military threat from China *and* unification with China if the Mainland becomes similar to Taiwan in political, economic and social conditions.

- Taiwan nationalist: agrees with first, disagrees with second.
- China nationalist: disagrees with first, agrees with second.
- Conservative: disagrees with both.

These categories are nuanced and include both descent group and political allegiance. Notable in particular is the rise from 25 per cent in 1992 to 39 per cent in 1996 of the pragmatists (Marsh, 2002: 147). Thus, in the new millennium it is clear to see a social basis to Taiwanese identity (Brown, 2004: 2). This type of identification includes reference to political system along with ethnic origin and goes beyond a single axis of linkage to China or rejection of it.

What does a hybrid and still developing Taiwanese identity mean in relation to the familiar political spectrum – pan-Blue linked to unification and pan-Green connected to independence – in Taiwan? Tsai (2007: 9) offers the following analysis of the road travelled so far:

> Under the influence of various government policies that promoted 'Taiwanization' (*bentuhua*), the newfound openness ushered in by democratization, and the guidance of political leaders, Taiwan's national identity shifted gradually from that of belonging to the country ruled by the legitimate government of 'One China,' to a concept of 'One China' as part of 'Two regions, Two Political Entities', and then finally to today's widespread recognition of Taiwan as an independent political regime separate from China.

Note that some time onward from that assessment of national identity over a decade ago, the three major parties all eschewed support for either independence or reunification in the near future (Zagoria, 2003: 210). 'Rather than a deepening hue of Blue or Green', observe Huang and James (2014: 686–687), 'Taiwan's political spectrum is converging and shifting towards Aquamarine'. Moreover, this 'blending of the Blue and Green positions into a status quo of de facto sovereignty – seems likely, metaphorically speaking, to end up as the last colour of Taiwan' (Huang and James, 2014: 688). Thus, the overall story of identity on Taiwan is one of movement away from categories based strictly on differing ethnic origins and towards more complex formations. Such ideological factors that bind the collective group have emerged gradually and rather recently. They include a distinct set of political culture and belief systems rooted in a stronger embrace of democratization, political accountability, rule of law and respect for human rights, alongside demographic traits. This strengthens the belief that the identity of the state is subject to a variety of forces that can evolve with time (Lepesant, 2018).

The Middle Kingdom moves up

Traced back to the 1990s, the rise of China is a major topic – 'a serious issue of consideration for 21st century international relations' (Dellios, 2005: 1). China's rise, observes Glaser (2011: 80), probably will be the most important story of international relations in the 21st century, but a happy ending is far from guaranteed. Understanding the role of China in the world, Foot (2013: 1) adds, is a crucial intellectual exercise for the new millennium. The PRC's emergence as an economic powerhouse is identified by Liu and Li (2017: 266) as a key development since the 1980s, with important ongoing implications for cross-Strait relations.

China's economic take-off, which began with market-oriented reforms under Deng in 1978, includes high growth rates, greatly increased exports and attraction of significant foreign investment (Kang, 2007). Elements of the dramatic rise for China in economic terms also include a huge emerging market and low labour costs (Dellios, 2005: 1). As a result of disposable resources from rapid economic growth, China is able to increase military spending significantly. In addition, the Mainland probably possesses 'the most effective and certainly the most robust cyber-espionage system in the world' (Coker, 2015: 159). Beijing also uses its newfound wealth on the diplomatic front to establish 'hundreds of Confucius Institutes around the world, running 24-hour CCTV news channels in major languages and offering scholarships for tens of thousands of international students' (Chu and Chang, 2017: 105). Taken together, the PRC's accumulating capabilities run the gamut from hard to soft power.

Sceptics about the rise of China, notably as understood in relative terms, also exist. Beckley (2011/2012: 58), for example, observes that the 'case for the decline of the United States and the rise of China rests heavily on a single statistic: GDP. Over the last twenty years, China's GDP has risen relative to the United States' in terms of purchasing power parity (PPP), though it has declined in real terms'. Quite emphatic about limitations on the ascent of China are Brooks and Wohlforth (2015: 8), who claim to demonstrate that 'the United States will long remain the only state with the capability to be a superpower'. Obstacles exist to the further rise of China as peer state. Take, for example, lack of regulation, which in turn helps to maintain a rate of growth. Less well acknowledged, observe Brooks and Wohlforth (2015: 30), is that 'lack of environmental protection leads to an overestimation of China's economic growth rate'. Brooks and Wohlforth (2015: 34, 49) identify a 'gap between China's economic rise and its potential to attain the capabilities of a superpower', but they also acknowledge that the US's 'once unparalleled freedom of action is now declining, especially in China's near abroad'. Hence, the position of sceptics might be summed up as holding that, while change in material terms clearly is underway, its consequences in terms of China's *efficacy* in comparison to that of the US remains open to question.

Controversy is certain to continue over whether China ultimately will achieve peer status or even surpass the US. Beckley (2011/2012: 44), for example, concludes that 'China is rising, but it is not catching up' and Brooks and Wohlforth (2015: 52) add that, notwithstanding 'dramatic economic growth in the past few decades, the scope, significance, and pace of its global ascent must be kept in perspective'. The accuracy of assertions about the end-state resulting from developments underway is a subject beyond the scope of the present study, which includes a focus on whether China is gaining ground relative to the US – a point not in question.

Will the ascent of China, to the extent it is not ephemeral, be peaceful or not? Yuan (2015: 25) reveals that to be a multifaceted question:

> China's rise is transforming the global and regional geo-economic and geopolitical landscapes and has understandably generated wide-ranging discussions of and speculations on how Beijing is going to exercise its power and influence in international politics. As the country's capabilities expand, so have China's aspirations and ambitions, as well as growing expectations and concerns from the international community.

Opinions about the preceding aspects of China's rise, as will become apparent, are all over the map. The key question is whether China's goals are unlimited (Glaser, 2011: 88). An answer to that query will go a long way towards figuring out how cross-Strait relations will develop.

With an emphasis on power politics and historical examples, realists tend to be pessimistic about how the rise of China will work out for the international system. Consider, for example, the argument from Carpenter (2006) with regard to dangers accumulating from strategic ambiguity as the US posture. Similarly, Layne (2008: 13) doubts whether China can rise in a peaceful way that is consistent with ongoing claims from Beijing. Pillsbury (2016), among others, argues that China has been on a hundred-year marathon to secretly replace

America as the global superpower. Thus, the US and China cannot escape their confrontation, where the buildup of small, persistent disagreements could intensify into longer-term conflicts and even potentially war at some point (Allison, 2017). Concept formation in this context originates with the power transition theory (Organski, 1958; Organski and Kugler, 1980), which put forward the idea that the system is most in danger of war when a leading state and challenger go through a phase of approaching evenly matched capabilities. The leading state sets the global 'rules', which the challenger believes needs to be altered for it to continue its ascending trajectory. In the present case, the US is the leader and the PRC is the challenger at the system level. Thus, China, moreover, is not a status quo-oriented state. Its challenges to the US, and the global system in turn, increase the likelihood of violent confrontation as the pair's capabilities become more equal over time.

Taiwan as a flashpoint for Sino-American conflict plays a central role in all worrisome expositions. Mearsheimer (2019) urges US leadership to abandon the tradition of liberal internationalism in favour of a realist approach towards managing the challenges posed by the dynamics of power politics. Liberal internationalism, according to Mearsheimer (2019), is a long-standing but harmful approach towards grand strategy for the US and its allies. The US should not attempt to remake the rest of the world in its image and, in particular, stay out of foreign conflicts that are likely to become expensive and near-permanent commitments. A war such as Iraq would be an exemplar in this context (Mearsheimer, 2019).

With regard to Sino-Taiwanese relations, Mearsheimer (2019) supports a traditional *realpolitik*, rather than ideological, approach. Taiwan is in the near abroad for the PRC, a formidable world power, and it does not make sense for either the US or anyone else to antagonize Beijing over the issue of the island's legal status and potential independence. Instead, like the Ukraine for Russia, Mearsheimer (2019) advocates recognition of the PRC's vital interests and therefore a cautious approach on the part of the US-led coalition in reacting to whatever strife arises in the future.

Even beyond realists and their worries about shifting relative capabilities, those who focus on China's identity-related struggles also tend to be concerned about the consequences of its rapid upward trajectory. This is true especially in relation to the US as the system's current leader (Callahan, 2010: 192). Consider the following observations about the scope and scale of China's rise (Chu, 2016: 47):

China has rapidly emerged not only as the region's locomotive of economic growth, but also as the principal architect of regional integration and new rules of economic engagement, most notably with the launch of the 'One Belt, One Road' initiative and the Asia Infrastructure Investment Bank (AIIB). In a nutshell, history is no longer loading the dice in favor of Western-style liberal democracies.

For China, the ascent is a double-edged sword. China is changing the world, but the reverse also is true. For example, China's power vis-à-vis the US and Taiwan is growing, but with declining ability to control information going to the public and conceal decision-making (Shirk, 2007: 260). These properties, in turn, virtually guarantee tensions with the leading Western democracies over human rights in particular. Notable ongoing instances concern treatment of Hong Kong and the Uighur nationality in Western China. As witnessed with the Trump administration in particular, conflict also can escalate over trade policy, notably with regard to effects from protectionism and non-tariff barriers.

Rising China pressures Taiwanese identity

All of this discussion leads naturally into the matter of Chinese national identity in connection with its rapid rise and enhanced capabilities. Nationalism is a central feature of Chinese politics and dates back over a century (Ross, 2012: 78). China today is 'less totalitarian and more capitalist, less monolithic and more diverse, less drab and more colorful, less isolated and more globalized' (Shirk, 2007: 5). Interesting identity-related concept formation is put forward by Callahan (2010: 9), who describes China as a 'pessoptimist nation'. Analysis of 'structure of feeling' makes it possible to comprehend 'actions and events that emerge from different combinations of reason and emotion, and thus from various combinations of optimism and pessimism' and pessoptimism 'is deeply embedded in Chinese society in ways that continue to inform economic and military policy' (Callahan, 2010: 11). Chinese identity therefore is contested within itself – hopeful about the future but angry regarding the past and thus easily offended by anything that even remotely is perceived to resemble renewed imperialism.

China's educational system is relevant here and possesses several characteristics that seem peculiar when revealed to those who live elsewhere. Education in China stresses a history of national humiliation

(Callahan, 2010: 12). Sustained emphasis on what is known as the Century of Humiliation – the period of chaos and horrific treatment at the hands of the great powers prior to the Revolution of 1949 – accounts for 'the tremendous symbolic importance to China of the return of Hong Kong in 1997 and Macao in 1999' and why Taiwan's *de facto* independence is construed as further imperialism (Brown, 2004: 21). As Callahan (2010: 14) observes, 'the discourse of "Century of National Humiliation" (1840–1949) knits together all the negative events – invasions, massacres, military occupations, unequal treaties, and economic extractions – of prerevolutionary history that can be blamed on outsiders'. This anger about the past is manifested in various ways that potentially are harmful to China today; for example, Shirk (2007: 258) recommends that school textbooks 'stop glorifying the xenophobic violence of the Boxer Rebellion in 1900 if the Party doesn't want to see it repeated'. Furthermore, a hypersensitive and easily activated public can put leadership in an awkward and even undesirable position in the domain of foreign policy as well.[1]

Highly emotional nationalism constitutes 'a blowback from Beijing's own propaganda policy' (Callahan, 2010: 195). Path dependency is in evidence; since the state 'fanned the flames of nationalism to build support', Chinese leaders – and certainly Deng Xiaoping – had to heed popular sentiment (Vogel, 2011: 477). Johnston (2013: 12–13) adds that 'sensitivity to challenges to sovereignty is at the heart of much of China's more uncompromising foreign policy positions on territory'. Perhaps, as Callahan (2010: 192) suggests, 'to understand China's dreams, we need to understand its nightmares'. The narrative put forward by the PRC is increasingly nationalistic and steeped in intransigence and victimhood (Bitzinger, 2015: 59). None of this bodes well for cross-Strait relations.

Chinese critics frequently 'vent their anger not just at foreigners, but also at Chinese leaders (and other "traitors") for being weak in the face of foreign provocation' (Callahan, 2010: 27). The most common way to resolve humiliation, as put forward by Chinese commentators, is *xuechi* – this means 'cleanse humiliation' but also denotes 'revenge' (Callahan, 2010: 1999). It is very tempting for the government, since it finds such a warm reception from the public, to play this card. China can be understood as 'a mobilization state that both encourages and feeds off of the positive productive power of popular feelings and mass action' (Callahan, 2010: 25). It almost goes without saying that such processes, once set in motion, could become intense enough to escape government control. It is interesting to observe, in that context, how the PRC handles cyber-security and surveillance. On the one hand, it is no surprise to learn that potential collective action against the government, organized via the internet, is monitored (King et al, 2014). On the other hand, it is fascinating to learn that the Chinese government also keeps an eye on potential excesses from would-be *pro*-government collective action. The intuition on this point is that highly intense nationalist pressure over issues such as Taiwan or Hong Kong also could present a danger to the regime if it is perceived as weak in the face of such challenges (King et al, 2014).

Therefore, from China's perspective, the rise of China and the final resolution of the Taiwan issue are of extreme importance. Mahbubani (2020: 138) observes that 'China was badly trampled upon and humiliated during the century of humiliation. China's recovery today buoyed their national pride'. 'The reason why China is working hard towards reunification with Taiwan is that it wants to remove the last vestige of that century of humiliation' (Mahbubani, 2020: 223). In a word, China wants to become intact on its own terms.

Taiwan, of course, comes to the fore as a target for displacement of negative by-products from mobilization of people on the Mainland. Thus, the PRC must maintain a balance between resisting efforts towards Taiwanese autonomy while simultaneously keeping emotions among the general public on the Mainland from spinning out of control.

Chinese leadership is not without alternatives here – possibilities beyond ongoing censorship clearly exist. Consider the educational system as a possible starting point for change. Instead of casting modern China in the role of a victim, school textbooks 'should highlight the successes of its statesmen, reformers, entrepreneurs, and scientists' (Shirk, 2007: 258). This would have the salutary effect of reducing Beijing's vulnerability to finding itself in a figurative corner during interstate conflicts. The temptation to project internal conflict outward could be overwhelming at some point and especially dangerous for the three-way interaction involving Taiwan and the US.

Given the traits just described, it is clear that Chinese politics do not stop, as the old saying goes, at the water's edge. Security and identity issues are intertwined for China and linked to its rapid rise, with enhanced international status as an overriding goal (Callahan, 2010: 11, 13). Perhaps the 'heart of Chinese foreign policy thus is not a security dilemma, but an "identity dilemma": Who is China and how does it fit into the world?' (Callahan, 2010: 13). Answers to that question distinguish optimists from pessimists.

Optimists hope that, gradually, China will move away from its dual identity as an object of great power manipulation and historical victim (Shambaugh, 2004: 64; see also Hong, 2016: 67). After all, crises during the 1990s 'taught China's leaders that arousing the public's nationalist feelings is not cost free' (Shirk, 2007: 233). As such, it is realistic to hope for a Chinese foreign policy that incorporates learning and thereby moves away from an identity of victimhood. Kang (2007) reinforces that position. His vision of China rising emphasizes the fact that neighbouring states, rather than balancing against China, have pursued mutually beneficial cooperation with the new economic giant. China's ascent, from the standpoint of those nearby in particular, creates opportunities and not just threats (Kang, 2007). As the saying goes, a rising tide can lift all boats.

Coker (2015: 178), to continue expounding upon the optimistic point of view, offers a positive sense of both the context of China's rise and likely consequences from it, especially in comparison to one quite salient example from the past. Upward movement for China 'is taking place in a different context from that of imperial Germany'. China, unlike Germany at the outset of the 20th century, is 'certainly not a revisionist power' and may be in pursuit of a 'gradual modification of the international system' (Coker, 2015: 178). Other aspects also point away from a sense of China as the bumptious Germany from the early 1900s leading up to the First World War: 'it is unclear whether China is quite as resentful as Germany still less as pessimistic about its future' and it is 'doubtful whether the Chinese military will become quite as independent of political control as the German army in the period leading to 1914' (Coker, 2015: 179). Swaine (2015) adds that

> most Chinese apparently believe that China's rightful place in the international order is as a major (not singularly dominant) power whose views must be respected but who exists in general harmony with other nations. This is a far cry from the notion of China as a resurgent leviathan bent on dominating Asia and the world beyond.

Furthermore, while quite vocal, the extreme nationalists remain a minority in the PRC (Coker, 2015: 179). Thus, optimists about China tend to emphasize its differences from rising great powers that ran into trouble in the past. In sum, the PRC and US can escape the cruel logic of power transition theory if mutual interests can be identified and pursued in ways that diminish tendencies towards confrontation between the two leading states.

Parallels between the PRC and rapidly rising powers from history that stimulated conflict at a system level, in particular, may be overestimated from the outset. China and the US instead could evolve towards a high-level partnership. A precedent might be the US and UK at the outset of the 20th century – although of course it is appropriate to point out that those states shared democratic institutions and values. So the power transition between the UK and US went 'relatively smoothly as one Anglo-Saxon power was going away to another' (Mahbubani, 2020: 258). Swaine (2015) sums up the current Chinese mindset via three sets of attitudes: 'national pride alongside a strong fear of chaos; an inculcated image of a peace-loving and defensive polity alongside a strong and virtuous central government; and a unique, hierarchical yet mutually beneficial view of inter-state relations'. These views combine to create many contingencies, as opposed to an obvious pathway towards either war or peace.

Controversy exists over the degree of change in Chinese foreign policy as a by-product of its rise. How that matter is resolved possesses, in turn, implications for the degree of instability and danger to expect in the near future for cross-Strait relations and beyond. Relatively early in the rise of China, Johnston (2003: 48) observed that the scope of revisionism 'is not obvious, and that the current empirical evidence about these claims is, at best, ambiguous'. Moreover, evidence at that time of active Chinese balancing against the US to replace the unipolar order with a multipolar system can be summed up as murky (Johnston, 2003: 49). A decade later, Johnston (2013: 7) still sees continuity: 'the new assertiveness meme underestimates the degree of assertiveness in certain policies in the past, and overestimates the amount of change in China's diplomacy in 2010 and after'. Looking across events from late 2009 through 2010, Johnston (2013: 14) does not detect a new and sustained pattern of activity.

One example concerns US arms sales to Taiwan. China did not respond with any concrete sanctions against US companies and Johnston (2013: 15, 16, 32) also is unable to detect any increase in Chinese assertiveness during other events in the same time frame. Jerdén (2014: 85) argues against the presence of a 'new assertiveness' in 2009–2010 and concludes that 'China's overall foreign policy had not changed in these years'. From that point of view, the PRC might even be viewed as evolving towards a status quo-oriented state.

Other, more pessimistic, observers claim to detect significant change in Chinese foreign policy during the time frame just noted. Ross (2012: 72–73), for example, emphasizes a departure from the recent past:

> by the end of 2010 a more contentious Chinese foreign policy had elicited widespread suspicion of Chinese

intentions and of its greater capabilities in East Asia, South Asia, and Europe. China's new diplomacy elicited a countervailing U.S. policy toward China that stressed greater strategic cooperation with countries on China's periphery.

Pillsbury (2016) holds an even grimmer view about China's rise and intentions, arguing that China has taken a systematic approach to replace the US as a superpower. From a military perspective, 'through 2030, the Chinese will have more than $1 trillion available to spend on new weapons for their navy and air force', and 'the future military balance of power is slowly shifting, from a ten-to-one U.S. superiority, towards equality, and then eventually to Chinese superiority' (Pillsbury, 2016). The jury is still out regarding the degree of ambition that can be gleaned so far from Beijing's statements and actions regarding foreign policy. No matter, in that regard, is more pressing than figuring out China's intentions about Taiwan.

The elemental role of Taiwan for China

Perhaps one of the least understood and potentially dangerous aspects of China as a renewed force in world politics is the nature of its attachment to the island of Formosa. Taiwan is a key element within Mainland identity. 'For Mainlanders who personally participated in China's war with the Japanese', observes Li (2002: 109–110), 'Taiwan's independence is the last thing they want'. Independence for Taiwan would be 'a funeral knell for Mainlanders' lifetime search for Chinese pride and national identity' (Li, 2002: 109–110). From the standpoint of the Mainland, 'acquiescence to Taiwan leaving "Chinese" control would be tantamount to the CCP admitting failure to protect the territorial integrity of China, a fundamental responsibility of any Chinese government' (Roy, 2003: 241). As Johnston (2003: 38; 2013: 12–13) observed on multiple occasions, for Chinese leaders, Taiwan is the immediate and medium-term issue, rather than the US strategic presence in Northeast Asia *per se* or even 'other military contingencies such as a war on the Korea Peninsula, or power projection far beyond its periphery'. The unification of Taiwan has become part and parcel of realizing the 'Chinese dream' and achieving the 'great rejuvenation of the Chinese nation', signature priorities and initiatives of Xi's leadership (Yang, 2014). As such, the status of Taiwan is a matter of both material and ideational necessity for the Mainland.

Sovereignty is the essence of the Taiwanese issue from the standpoint of Beijing and that can lead to harmful misunderstandings with the US in particular and the international community in general. The PRC, observes Roy (2003: 246), 'misleadingly associates expression of the popular will of the ethnic Chinese inhabitants of Taiwan with the exploitation of China by the imperialist powers during the Century of Shame'. China opposes independence for Taiwan because it represents loss of a domain identified as having fallen under colonial control and might impact upon other ethnic territories currently under the PRC's control (Brown, 2004: 3). For China, the handling of Taiwan is likely to serve as a demonstration effect for other adversaries in its peripheral regions who are giving thought to secession or at least qualitatively greater autonomy. Fravel (2005) clearly demonstrates that while China has made significant compromises in many 'frontier' and 'offshore island' territorial disputes, it has never made any compromise on homeland disputes, including Hong Kong, Macao and Taiwan. And Beijing is unlikely to do so in the future.

Taiwan as independent or part of China is a political matter but also a basic question of identity (Brown, 2004: 211) and even an 'emotional blind spot' for the Mainland (Shirk, 2007: 265). Unification therefore is perceived as a *domestic* issue over which a sovereign state must exert full control (Legro, 2007: 517, 525; see also Kastner, 2015: 3). Shirk (2007: 2) adds that intense nationalist emotions are aroused in connection with the island of Formosa and 'Chinese schoolchildren have been taught the century of humiliation would finally end only when Taiwan was reunified with the Mainland'. This emotive element should not be underestimated in its implications for policy; more than specific formulations about it, the 'broad public cares more about not losing Taiwan' (Shirk, 2007: 261, 265; see also Friedberg, 2005: 22). Taiwan, moreover, 'is widely seen in China as a key "lost territory" that Beijing needs to regain before it can be a truly great power' (Callahan, 2010: 204). No leader in China, assert Li and Zhang (2017), can survive the loss of Taiwan and Xi Jinping is no exception. While the KMT left the Mainland seven decades ago after defeat in a war, identity-based struggles and policy issues linked to that migration obviously reverberate back into the PRC to this very day.

Analysts of the PRC's military buildup routinely connect it to concerns about Taiwan (Shambaugh, 2004: 86; Dellios, 2005: 5). Nationalist-oriented sources for a potential war, observe Ross and Feng (2008: 303), 'include the Taiwan issue, insofar as a weakened leadership may adopt coercive measures to achieve rapid unification'. It is unclear that China 'will wait indefinitely to gain full control of Taiwan' (Glaser, 2015: 61). Leaders in China, according to Li and Zhang (2017: 32), could be forced by rising Chinese nationalism 'to use Taiwan as a scapegoat to divert attention away from any potential domestic unrest or instability'. A domino effect is at issue here in the Chinese mindset – fear that Taiwan's independence would lead, in turn, to secessionism in Tibet, Xinjiang and maybe Inner Mongolia (Shirk, 2007: 182). This level of concern recalls near-obsession in the US with the domino theory as involvement in Vietnam expanded – quite ironic given the history of the PRC, which denounced American imperialism throughout that war.

Economic factors associated with the rise of China are important in explaining how Beijing and Taipei arrived at the respective positions occupied today. Accumulating economic interdependence across the Taiwan Strait can be traced to Deng Xiaoping's opening of China and massive economic development from 1979 onward (Shirk, 2007: 183, 196). Economic ties have gone up dramatically for the PRC with Taiwan and also the US (Kastner, 2015: 10). Taiwan, quite rapidly, has become integrated with the economy of China (Huang and Weatherall, 2017: 120).

Interdependence, however, is uncertain in its impact and controversy continues. Economic ties across the Strait appear to influence policy more in democratic Taiwan than in authoritarian China where the private businesses, coastal provinces and those who prefer economic progress over the 'one-China principle' cannot speak openly. Even at the turn of the millennium, some observers already had described cross-Strait relations as 'structurally unstable and potentially explosive' (O'Hanlon, 2000: 51). Expanding economic interdependence, as Shirk (2007: 211) sums things up, 'does not make war unthinkable'. While violent conflict would destroy accumulated wealth, identity-based concerns could overwhelm aversion to war if signals towards an independent Taiwan reach a high enough level of intensity.

The implications of China's rise are thus manifold, not least for Taiwan's identity and for our understanding and application of International Relations theory in regional security. What is clear is that closer economic integration across the Taiwan Strait has not produced the kind of spillover effect that political leaders in Beijing had expected. Taiwanese businesses and elites may benefit from riding the coat-tails of China's rapid economic ascendancy, but these material, individual gains are largely reflective of private goods and do not represent the more collective, public good oriented factors that play a more significant role in motivating ideational choice. A doubling down of China's emphasis on the material aspects of its rise could further motivate the decision for the electorate in Taiwan to shift away from seeing oneself as solely Chinese. Moreover, the political gap across the Taiwan Strait continues to widen as Taiwan's electoral politics matures and as its societal values and political cultural emphasis on democratization deepen, all of which are key ideological determinants that forge a distinct and collective sense of belonging in Taiwan's identity formation.

China, the United States and cross-Strait relations

What, then, should the US do about the rise of China and cross-Strait relations? And, what impact does US involvement (or inaction) have on Taiwan's identity? As the leading state in the global system and *de facto* manager of its flashpoints for strife, the US emerges as the natural priority for assessment. Multiple options are available to the US's competition for support in the worlds of academe and policy.

One school of thought stresses the value of strategic ambiguity. This idea originates, in its generic form, with analysis of deterrence from Schelling (1960) – namely, implementation of a threat that leaves something to chance. The threat in the present context refers to what the US is expected to do in response to any Chinese escalation of conflict across the Taiwan Strait. Ambiguity in this form is regarded as 'the only prudent policy' and 'safer and wiser, as well as more realistic, than attempts at clarity' (Tucker, 1998–1999: 162, 163; see also O'Hanlon, 2000). The US finds itself 'under pressure to protect Taiwan against any sort of attack, no matter how it originated' (Glaser, 2011: 87). Public opinion can be cited to reinforce a line of reasoning in favour of ambiguity as opposed to a clear public commitment to military action: 'the overwhelming majority of the American public (71 percent) opposes sending troops to defend Taiwan if it is attacked by China' (Hickey, 2015). Elite and mass opinion in the US are not in sync regarding Taiwan. Maintaining strategic ambiguity is ideal from a US standpoint because it does not draw too much attention to a foreign policy issue on which the leadership in Washington lacks support from the general public. Forcing the issue could weaken Washington's ability, as a result of a public backlash, to achieve existential deterrence.

Others favour engagement for the US and China as a pathway to peace. Beijing and Washington, according to Coker (2015: 181), 'should seek to enter into a constructive cultural dialogue about their respective values while holding each other accountable for how they interpret them'. Such engagement is likely to be well-received; 'an increasing number of China's neighbors welcomed a reinvigorated American presence and made efforts to seek close diplomatic and military ties to the US' (Zhao and Qi, 2016: 492). In other words, an isolationist US would be about as welcome in Northeast Asia as an aggressive China.

Others, usually from a particular kind of realist-inspired viewpoint, have argued for years in favour of retrenchment. The PRC, according to Layne (2008: 14), 'is pursuing a peaceful policy today in order to strengthen itself to confront the United States tomorrow'. So war with China is not inevitable and, interestingly, escalation will depend more on strategic choices in Washington than those of Beijing (Layne, 2008: 13). Containment is inadvisable because it would 'require the United States to pledge explicitly to defend Taiwan while bolstering Taiwanese military capabilities' (Layne, 2008: 15). The tail could end up wagging the dog. Taliaferro (2019), in a review of US foreign policy towards 'frenemies' – nettlesome allies who at times act in ways not helpful to their patron state – includes Taiwan on the list. Analysis of the Taiwanese nuclear programme produces a warning for the US in terms of ongoing matters of policy related to the island ally, that is, support is appropriate but not in the form of a blank check at any time (Taliaferro, 2019).

Instead, the US should let events play out and intervene only if and when core national interests are threatened. Furthermore, the US should give up efforts to promote political liberalization on the Mainland, a policy that comes across as 'a form of gratuitous eye-poking' (Layne, 2008: 17; see also Mearsheimer, 2019). All of this fits in with a pessimistic point of view based on whether it is possible to use engagement to socialize China into the norms of the Western-led international system (Yang, 2017).

Controversy persists over the US role in Northeast Asia, notably in regard to involvement with Taiwan. Realists and liberals advocate a range of policies that run the gamut from low to high activity in response to Chinese initiatives. Given long-standing sensitivity on the Mainland about any issue that seems connected to sovereignty, the appropriate degree of support from the US for Taiwan, especially when it tilts more in the direction of independence, is far from obvious.

What is striking to observe from the extant literature is how Taiwan's identity has evolved in the context of decades of strategic ambiguity in US policy towards Taiwan and on cross-Strait relations. There is a certain degree of agency in the formation of Taiwan's identity choice. US reassurances to Taiwan may form a key part of the island's bargaining tactics with the Mainland, but US support has its limitations and is strategically bound. Political leaders in Taipei may try to capitalize on Washington's support to push the envelope vis-à-vis Beijing, but the Taiwanese electorate has shown to be wary whenever its leadership moves the island's foreign policy orientation too rapidly towards the US. Similarly, a move in the opposite direction towards closer partnership with Beijing has backfired. The ideological values, beliefs and political culture shaping Taiwan's identity choice may be closer to liberal democracies like the US, but thus far we have not seen major changes or departures from the status quo with regard to Taiwan's political status or US policy of strategic ambiguity towards Taiwan.

Summing up the state of the art on Taiwanese identity

Identity in Taiwan experienced a huge shock with the ethnically Chinese influx after the ROC's defeat in the Chinese Civil War. The KMT enforced an identification with China in association with its hope to reclaim the Mainland. Taiwanese identity then evolved in a more multifaceted and less Sino-centric direction, most notably as democratization gave voice to those with roots on the island itself. The dramatic rise of China impacted significantly on Taiwan as well. The threat of imposed unification with the Mainland, and destruction of Taiwan's democratic institutions and multifaceted identity, loomed large. Chinese sensitivity over sovereignty-related issues, and fixation on humiliation from the past, worried the Taiwanese in particular. Would the PRC simply invade if it had one too many confrontations with the ROC or, for that matter, the US? The role of the US in cross-Strait relations, in light of China's rapid rise, tilts towards uncertainty and continued ambiguity today.

What does it mean to identify as Taiwanese and who and why do people do so? Theorizing will move forward in the following chapter. Causal mechanisms located within the studies reviewed by the current chapter – which focus on Taiwanese identity, the rise of China and cross-Strait relations in connection to each other and US activity from outside of Northeast Asia – will be identified and assembled into a coherent whole. The resulting systemist visualization of cause and effect will provide a baseline model that can be elaborated in light of evidence from interviews and surveys reported in subsequent chapters.

Note

[1] The concept of '*Minzu*', which corresponds to 'nation', refers in China to concepts that are diametrically opposed to each other: 'patriotic nationalism that is encouraged by the state, and ethnic nationalism that is seen as a threat' (Callahan, 2010: 127).

4

Theorizing about Identity, Change in Capabilities and Dyadic Relations: An Approach Based on Analytic Eclecticism and Systemism

Overview

This chapter theorizes about identity, change in capabilities and dyadic relations. The frame of reference for this work combines analytic eclecticism and systemism. Analytic eclecticism guides assembly of causal mechanisms into an integrated whole, while systemism – a means towards visual representation of hypotheses – provides the method. The intended empirical domain of application concerns Taiwanese (and to some extent Mainland Chinese) identity, the dramatic rise of the PRC, dyadic cross-Strait relations, and the role of the US as the key ingredient from outside of Northeast Asia.

Why bother with analytic eclecticism and systemism in the turn towards theorizing? Consider, as the obvious alternative, implementation of a particular school of thought as the foundation for theory. Carried out in Chapter 3, a review of paradigmatic research reveals that realist and liberal perspectives, while offering a range of insights, are not sufficient to explain the dynamics of the rise of China, cross-Strait relations, Taiwanese identity and US influence. Thus, attention turns to analytic eclecticism as a guide for assembly of causal mechanisms from diverse points of origin (Sil and Katzenstein, 2010a, 2010b). Our approach emphasizes theorizing that is inclusive, notably going beyond paradigmatic boundaries. Analytic eclecticism also stresses the importance of relevance to policy.

Analytic eclecticism is not without its limitations. An important shortcoming of analytic eclecticism in its original form is the potential for research findings to lack coherence because there no longer is a paradigm to guide investigation. To head off the problem of contradictory theorizing and evidence, systemism is incorporated into the process. Systemism is a graphic technique for representing causal mechanisms in a logically consistent and comprehensive way (Bunge, 1996; see also James, 2012, 2019a, 2019b; Pfonner and James, 2020). The principal result of this chapter is a diagrammatic exposition of cause and effect, based on research reviewed in Chapter 3, which connects Taiwanese identity, the rise of China, cross-Strait relations, and the role of the US. This graphic version of what is known so far provides a baseline of expectations, upon which research in this volume will build. The combination of analytic eclecticism and systemism is also an attempt to extend the effort made by Yu (2017) to broaden and deepen the methodological approach to study China.

Work proceeds in four additional sections. The second section reviews paradigmatic thinking and concludes that it is insufficient to provide a basis for theorizing in the complex and fast-paced context of the rise of China, shifting Taiwanese identity, cross-Strait relations and US influence. The third section focuses on the means towards building and depicting theory: analytic eclecticism and systemism. The fourth section assembles causal mechanisms gleaned from the diverse academic literature into a visual representation. Fifth and last is a summing up of this chapter's contributions, along with an entrée into analysis of multiple data sources that will follow.

Paradigmatic views: realism and liberalism

Prominent paradigms from International Relations conceptualize China's rise as either a threat or an opportunity for Taiwan's identity and future prospects. These views correspond, respectively, to realism and liberalism. Each point of view will be covered in turn, followed by a critique that comes from outside of the boundaries of either paradigm.

For realists, the preponderance of power will continue to favour China in Northeast Asia over the decades to come. China's newly acquired material capabilities will allow it to push the US out of the vicinity, assert itself as the regional hegemon, and dominate Taiwan without much resistance. Mearsheimer (2014a; see also Brzezinski and Mearsheimer, 2005) asserts that only a realist theory of great power politics can anticipate the foreign policy of a rising China towards its neighbours and the US. China's nationalism and the country's security imperatives, according to Mearsheimer (2014a), are the two key logics that undergird the turbulent nature of great power politics, all of which would produce the same result: unification of China and Taiwan leaders. Leaders in Beijing repeatedly have vowed that both sides of the Taiwan Strait are bound to be unified in the course of a great renewal for the Chinese people. China also has made it clear that war would ensue against Taiwan if it declares independence. The 'Anti-Secession Law', which China passed in 2005, states explicitly that, if and when Taiwan moves towards formal independence, 'the state shall employ non-peaceful means and other necessary measures'. Thus, cross-Strait relations inherently are fraught with danger, from a realist point of view, with China rising and Taiwan equivocating about its identity and role in the international system. Under such conditions, China easily could be provoked into military action in a situation increasingly unlikely to produce an effective US response.

From a realist standpoint, the structure of the international system forces China to pursue power in a zero-sum manner and establish dominance and hegemony in its region of the world. As Brzezinski and Mearsheimer (2005) contend,

> Why should we expect China to act any differently than the United States did? Are Chinese leaders more principled than American leaders? More ethical? Are they less nationalistic? Less concerned about their survival? They are none of these things, of course, which is why China is likely to imitate the United States and try to become a regional hegemon (in East Asia).[1]

The preceding line of reasoning paints a tumultuous picture ahead for Taiwan and cross-Strait relations.

Changes in US foreign policy from the Obama era include an increasing presence in the South China Sea and a significant rise in the US military budget for the coming years (Thrush et al, 2017). Things became more volatile when Donald Trump took office as president of the US in January 2017. The Trump administration revealed a more confrontational approach in dealing with its trade imbalance and in protecting US business interests in China. Even with a bilateral trade deal in place, there remains much uncertainty over its enforcement and the lingering question of 'when and how much?' tariffs might be reinstated if and when key terms of the bargain are not met.

Washington, from a standard realist, balance of power point of view, is anticipated to work at preventing Beijing from dominating its periphery and building towards a potential global threat. Thus, the US can be expected, at first, to attempt incorporation of Taiwan into an anti-China coalition. Interestingly, the then President-Elect Donald Trump's remarks on 11 December 2016 on Fox News questioning why the US should accept the 'One China' policy in the absence of a deal with Beijing that includes other items could seem very alarming in some quarters.[2] Trump's assertions, which continued to wander around on the most intense issues, call into question whether his administration would defend Taiwan or only use it as a bargaining chip to defend US interests in the region on a greater scale. However, as the preponderance of power shifts in Beijing's favour in the decades to come, Washington is likely to be compelled to accommodate the ambitions of the Mainland and strike a 'grand bargain' with Beijing and even abandon Taiwan.

With a contrast to realist thinking, a liberal approach would argue that institutions and the benefits of increasing economic interdependence can lead to greater gains for all concerned. The last three-and-a-half decades of reform and opening on China's part have seen burgeoning trade and economic interactions. These developments provide the foundation for long-term stability, raise the costs of war and conflict and incentivize China to become a 'responsible stakeholder' in the international community. The liberal view sees increasing trade with China and its transformation into an economic powerhouse as a positive-sum development, not least because China is rising up inside rather than working outside (and skirting) the existing international order, rules and institutions.

For cross-Strait ties, such developments mean that cooperation becomes more likely through these institutionalized mechanisms. Spillover effects from closer trade, business and economic ties can help to forge further dialogue, *rapprochement*, and even lead to greater political convergence. As the weaker party in military and increasingly economic terms, all incentives for Taiwan point towards cooperation with the Mainland. Moreover, from one point of view, a highly capable China is likely to make the neighbourhood as a whole more rather than less stable (Kang, 2007). China's rise is not a phenomenon that occurred overnight; instead, many in the region, including Taiwan, have been investing in various forms of political, diplomatic, sociocultural and economic engagement with Beijing, cultivating the necessary ties that would bind the region more closely while minimizing conflict.

Realism and liberalism, the two most long-standing and still largely prevailing schools of thought in International Relations, provide clear and opposing perspectives. Liberal optimism contrasts with realist pessimism. Each paradigm, however, risks being ultimately deterministic in its analysis and policy recommendations. While various accounts focus on the recent largely economic agreements between Beijing and Taipei, these treatments continue to leave out an important part of the story. Missing from the ongoing debate, most importantly, is a more nuanced consideration of how Taiwan and its policy elites view themselves and their position in cross-Strait relations. In other words, the future of Taiwan's cross-Strait policies and its identity may not derive strictly from either a military balance-of-power consideration or how increasing economic interactions develop.

Current cross-Strait relations raise an interesting puzzle: why have Taiwan and the Mainland drifted further apart in their political integration despite decades of deepening economic ties? Contrary to the liberal point of view – that closer economic ties would lead to increased desire for closer political integration – people on the island of Formosa increasingly think of themselves as Taiwanese instead of Chinese. In short, opinion growingly rejects institutional integration for Taiwan with the Mainland. At the same time, realist concentration on shifting material capabilities, with generally dire consequences inferred from the changes taking place, seems deterministic and ultimately unconvincing as a proffered overarching explanation. For one, Taiwan has refused to capitulate in spite of the Mainland's increasing levels of material power capabilities. What, then, is a better way to theorize when paradigmatic alternatives just seem too black and white?

Reference to even one alternative theoretical outlook – constructivism, or the study of ideas, institutions and norms – is enough to explain why the prevailing paradigms of realism and liberalism are insufficient to account for the dynamics of China rising, evolving Taiwanese identity, cross-Strait relations and the US factor.[3] In general, constructivism accepts the anarchical nature of the international system. However, constructivists argue that anarchy itself does not necessarily cause either state to balance against, or cooperate with, each other. Put differently, anarchy does not indicate anything in particular until it is assigned certain meaning through social interactions of agencies under those conditions (Wendt, 1992; Bertucci et al, 2018). What results from anarchy, according to a constructivist point of view, depends on the meaning or identity that is acquired during the socialization process involving respective actors. Thus, anarchy can be good or bad in terms of the social norms it ultimately reproduces.

For cross-Strait relations, identity becomes an important explanatory variable with regard to the relationship between Taipei and Beijing. Since their separation after the Chinese Civil War, Taiwan gradually has become a multiparty democracy. China, despite its unprecedented economic transformation and growth, largely remains a single-party authoritarian system. Taipei and Beijing therefore have taken two completely different political-socialization paths, democracy versus autocracy, and identities have diverged. The majority of those living on the island of Formosa today consider themselves as Taiwanese, a separate identity that derives significantly from their collective democratization process that started in the 1970s. People on the Mainland, however, live with the long-standing and ethnic-based Chinese identity. From that point of view, the Chinese identity automatically includes the 23 million people on the island of Taiwan. The Taiwanese see these two identities as different, while those on the Mainland view the self-designations as essentially the same. The situation becomes even more complex and challenging when nuances in Taiwanese identity are recognized as well. Conflict over sovereignty naturally ensues and intensifies for Taipei and Beijing.

For Taiwan to maintain the status quo, identity has been used to reconstruct cross-Strait relations in a way that one can either be Taiwanese or Chinese, but not both. This is because each identity is associated with a different political socialization process. On the part of Taiwan, any potential unification would mean reversal of the democratization process that many of its people have fought so hard to achieve since the 1970s. On the part of Mainland China, allowing people in Taiwan to call themselves 'Taiwanese' would mean the denial of the historical lineage to the Mainland. As a result, competing identities have prevented the two sides from getting closer in political terms.

For those sounding alarm bells – that the regional security dilemma is intensifying, balancing against China is in the offing, and cross-Strait relations are all but ripe for renewal of militarized rivalry – some aspects prove difficult to explain. It is puzzling, but not impossible, to account for why China already has risen to regional dominance without provoking war with Taiwan or other regional competitors (Kang, 2007). China's share of regional GDP grew from 7 per cent in 1988 to 46 per cent in 2014, while Japan's fell from 72 per cent of regional GDP in 1988 to 24 per cent today. China clearly already is well above Japan as an economic power in Northeast Asia and even competes with the US along some dimensions. Indeed, the debate over whether China's rise will provoke fear in its Northeast Asian neighbours and concomitant balancing behaviour has been raging for at least two decades. Those who expect a counterbalancing coalition to form against China in the future need to explain why this has not yet occurred, despite three decades of rapid Chinese economic and military growth.

Whether Taiwan's policy preferences move towards closer cooperation or conflict with China depends largely on its policy elites' perception of the evolving security situation in the region. As will become apparent, it is essential to recognize that views among decision-makers in Taipei are affected deeply by, and interact with, factors and institutions on and beyond the island. This study will look more closely at the importance of agency within the broader structural arguments that realist and liberal approaches follow, examining in particular such ideational variables as social interactions, public opinion, and culture in shaping Taiwan's identity and outlook on cross-Strait relations. This is done without endorsing constructivism as a method but instead simply allowing for ideational variables within an eclectic collection assembled to explain the dynamics between and among Taiwanese identity, China rising, cross-Strait relations and the role of the US in Northeast Asia.

After pondering the opposing points of view offered by realism and liberalism, along with pursuing a constructivist critique, some priorities seem clear. Given the complexity of China rising, Taiwanese identity, cross-Strait relations and US influence, paradigmatic restrictions make it unlikely that a comprehensive and satisfying account can be obtained within such boundaries. A more inclusive approach is called for, which leads into an exegesis of analytic eclecticism and a method, systemism, which is tailor-made to go with it.

Analytic eclecticism and systemism

What is analytic eclecticism and why is it a priority for implementation in this study? Analytic eclecticism focuses on problems that transcend paradigmatic boundaries (Sil and Katzenstein, 2010b). The approach is pragmatic and encourages research on matters significant to the real world. To obtain solutions with practical application, analytic eclecticism stresses the value of combining ideas from across paradigms in original ways. While analytic eclecticism searches for improved explanations, it does not seek a grand theory. The goal instead is to build theories of the middle range.

Given the subject matter at hand – the rise of China, Taiwanese identity, cross-Strait relations and US influence – analytic eclecticism seems to make more sense than a paradigm-driven approach. Evidence so far would support neither the generally positive and negative stories told, respectively, by the liberal and realist schools of thought. Given the complexity inherent in the interactions between and among the rise of China, identity in Taiwan, cross-Strait relations and the US from outside of the region, it would seem appropriate to put together an explanation that is highly inclusive. Analytic eclecticism, which transcends paradigmatic research, thus comes to the fore.

Three traits distinguish analytic eclecticism in practice (Sil and Katzenstein, 2010a: 412). Analytic eclecticism: (1) includes 'a pragmatic ethos, manifested concretely in the search for middle-range theoretical arguments that potentially speak to concrete issues of policy and practice'; (2) 'addresses problems of wide scope' that 'incorporate more of the complexity and messiness of particular real-world situations'; and (c) 'generates complex causal stories that forgo parsimony in order to capture the interactions among different types of causal mechanisms normally analyzed in isolation from each other within separate research traditions'. These characteristics combine to create an alternative to paradigm-driven research that is gaining support for good reasons. In comparison, paradigmatic warfare, with litmus tests for allegiance, seems quite self-limiting.[4] Analytic eclecticism encourages creativity and openness to new ideas and ways of putting together old ones, all of which bodes well for improving both theory and research. Implicit is the belief that these hybrid combinations may create new programmes of research that are not disposed towards paradigmatic parochialism. Sil and Katzenstein (2010b) provide numerous examples of analytic eclecticism in action, with subject matter spanning security studies, political economy, and order and governance.

Within the present context, the material to be assembled into a story of cause and effect for the rise of China, Taiwanese identity, cross-Strait relations and US influence appeared in Chapter 3. The state of the art in academic research reviewed in that chapter contained numerous linkages that can be put together into an overall picture of cause and effect. One method for creating such a picture of causal mechanisms is systemism.

Systemism's essence is conveyed by its most long-standing exponent, Bunge (1996): a commitment to building comprehensive explanations. Systemism transcends individualism and holism as the other available 'coherent views' with respect to operation of a social system (Bunge, 1996: 241). Rather than theorizing at the level of the system (holism) or its components (reductionism), systemism allows for linkages operating at macro- and micro-levels, along with back and forth between them. Systemism facilitates comparison of alternative visions regarding cause and effect. Thus, systemism is an *approach* rather than a substantive theory (Bunge, 1996: 265). Systemism as a method emphasizes diagrammatic exposition of causal mechanisms. While the idea of 'more box and arrow diagrams' might sound banal, in this context it is not. Systemism imposes rules for visual conveyance of cause and effect that promote comprehension and rigour. Thus, the overall value of systemism is that its visual representations clarify relationships expressed in a theory.

Systemism goes beyond holism and reductionism through a focus on *all* types of causal linkages required to fully specify a theory.[5] Figure 4.1 depicts functional relations in a social system from a systemist point of view. (The varying shapes that appear will be explained momentarily.) An alphabetized series of figures is used to convey in stages what ultimately appears in the full version for this diagram.[6]

Figure 4.1a depicts the system and its environment. Variables that operate at macro (VARIABLE X, VARIABLE Y) and micro (variable x, variable y) levels of the system are added in Figure 4.1b. In this diagram and others based on systemism, *UPPER- and lower-case characters correspond to MACRO- and micro-level variables*, respectively. Four basic types of linkages are possible: macro–macro (VARIABLE X → VARIABLE Y), macro–micro (VARIABLE X → variable

Figure 4.1: Functional relations in a social system

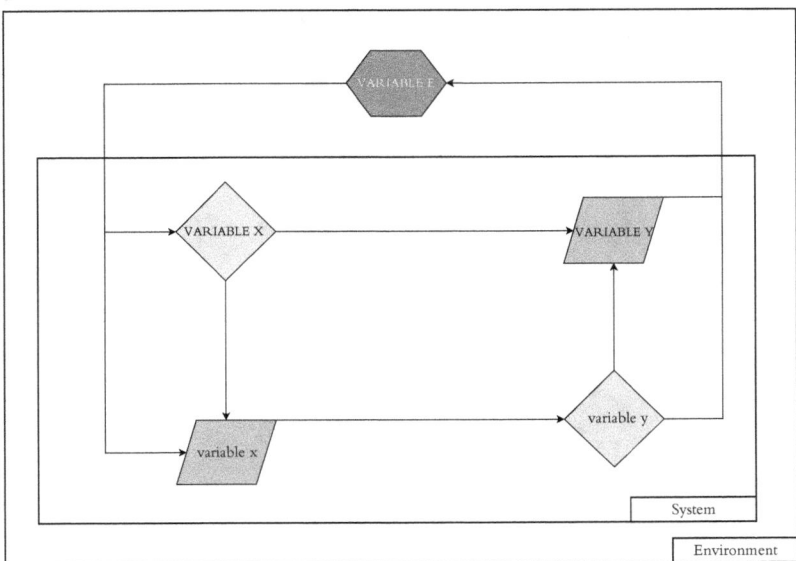

Source: Adapted from Bunge (1996: 149)

Figure 4.1a: Functional relations in a social system

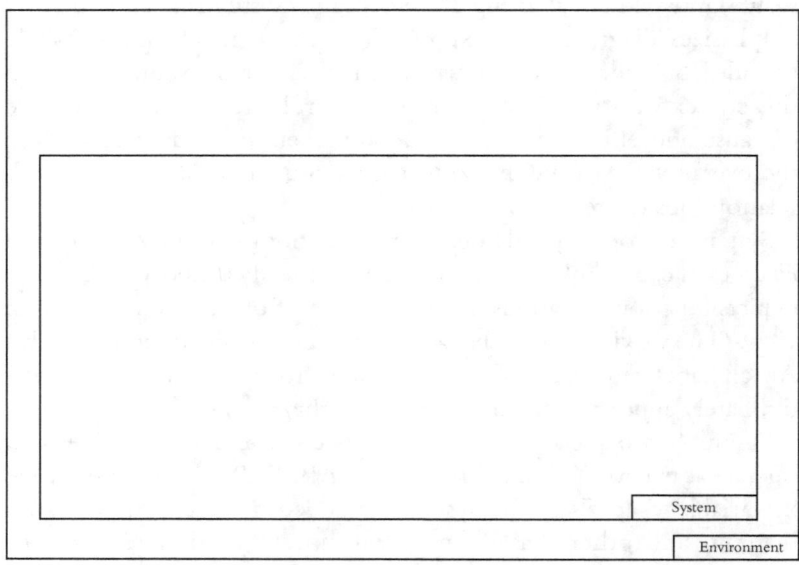

Figure 4.1b: Functional relations in a social system

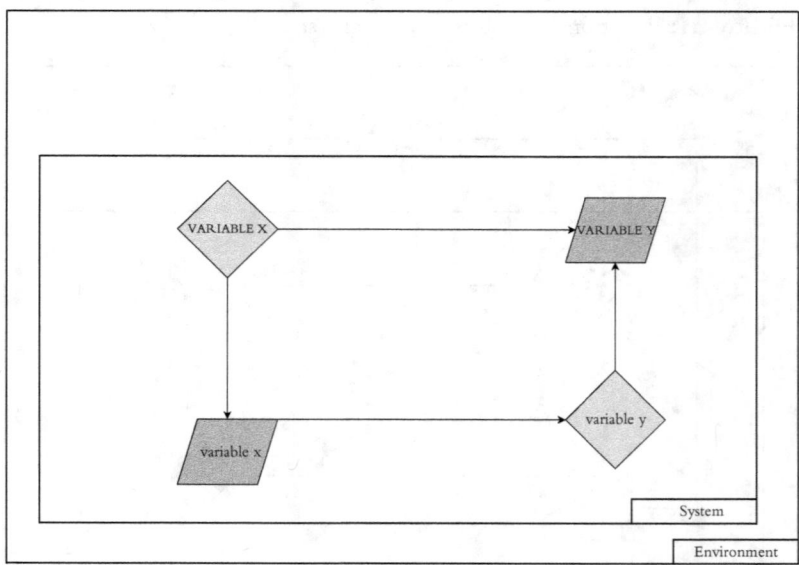

Figure 4.1c: Functional relations in a social system

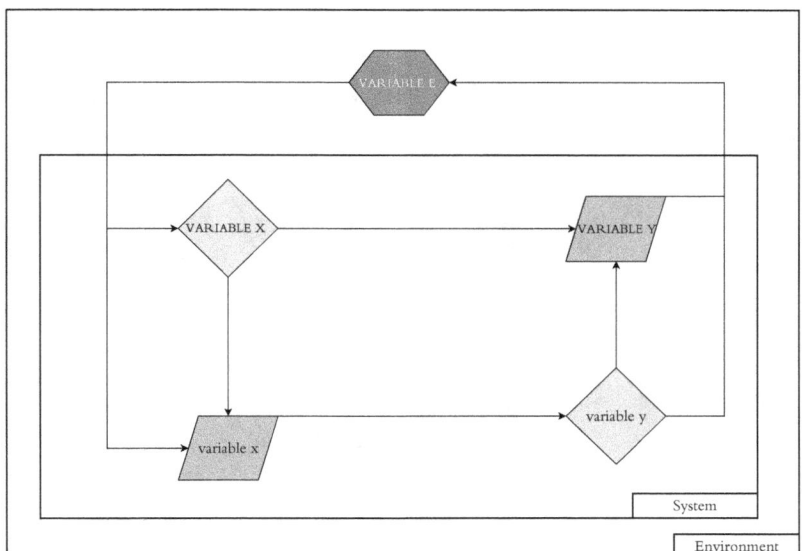

x), micro–macro (variable y → VARIABLE Y) and micro–micro (variable x → variable y). Figure 4.1c adds a variable to represent the environment (VARIABLE E). The environment can be expected to stimulate the system and vice versa: (1) 'VARIABLE E → VARIABLE X' and 'VARIABLE E → variable x' and (2) 'variable y → VARIABLE E' and 'VARIABLE Y → VARIABLE E'. All potential types of connection for a theory to incorporate now are in place.[7]

Table 4.1 provides the notation for systemism figures. Shapes are used to designate roles for variables. An initial variable takes the form of an oval, while a terminal variable is depicted as an octagon. With exactly one connection coming in and out, a generic variable appears as a plain rectangle. A parallelogram (diamond) designates a point of convergence (divergence) for pathways. A hexagon denotes both convergence and divergence – a nodal variable. A co-constitutive variable – one with mutually contingent variables – appears in bifurcated form. Line segments are depicted in different ways, depending on what they are supposed to represent, and will be explained as relevant within respective figures. For example, a small u-shape in a line means that it is crossing over another line and thus there is no connection between them.

Table 4.1: Systemist notation

Initial variable	⬭	The starting point of a series of relationships.
Generic variable	▭	A step in the process being depicted.
Divergent variable	◇	Multiple pathways are created from a single linkage.
Convergent variable	▱	A single pathway is created from multiple linkages.
Nodal variable	⬡	Multiple pathways are created from multiple linkages.
Co-constitutive variable	▭	Two variables that are mutually contingent upon each other.
Terminal variable	⯃	The end point of a series of relationships.
Connection stated in study	→	A linkage explicitly made by the author.
Connection crossing over	—⥛—	Two separate linkages that do not interact.
Connection inferred from study	┈┈▸	A linkage inferred by the reader but is not made explicit by the author.
Interaction effect	⟷	Two variables that depend upon the effect of each other.

Source: James (2019b)

Visualizing causal mechanisms

Work begins with specification of the system and environment. The system is Northeast Asia, with its conventional boundaries, and the environment is all that resides outside of it. The system is made up of states and other actors at the international level. Their interactions, back and forth, constitute the macro–macro component of the system. One example of a macro–macro linkage would be system stability as a function of its polarity; more specifically, Waltz (1979) claimed that a bipolar structure would be least prone to war. The unit or micro–micro component corresponds to what goes on within states. Gurr (1970) and many others, for instance, evaluated the potential of relative deprivation to produce civil strife. The approach to units implemented here, it should be noted, is not an endorsement for state-centrism but instead a convenient shorthand. Non-state actors of various kinds, such as NGOs, can and do appear in a given figure meant to represent cause and effect within the international system or one of its subsystems.

Hybrid linkages – macro–micro and micro–macro – tend to be overlooked. However, holding such connections constant is not a good practice in theorizing. Incompleteness is the result and leads to a vain attempt to explain everything with the pure connections – macro–macro and micro–micro – but with no *a priori* justification for doing so. Consider, for example, the insights from Gourevitch (1978) about the second image reversed. The basic idea is that events within a state can be influenced by those from outside – a macro–micro connection. For example, a state might experience a downturn in economic growth and employment as a result of sanctions or tariffs, with contemporary Iran as a salient example. Important micro–macro processes also can be identified. Levy (1989), for instance, offers a valuable review of academic research on diversionary conflict. The intuition is that, when faced with problems at home, embattled leaders may initiate strife with a foreign target in order to divert public attention away from a weak economy or other ongoing difficulties.

Many expositions about Northeast Asia are put forward in ways that rely, implicitly, on the language of systemism. Two examples are provided here.

First, Marsh (2002: 144) asserts that 'to analyze the future national identity of the people of Taiwan, two considerations are central: the will of the people and geopolitical constraints on Taiwan's independence'. From a systemist point of view, impact from the will of the people on national identity constitutes a micro–micro connection – contained entirely within the state itself. Geopolitical constraints on independent status clearly involve a force exerted from outside of the state onto an internal characteristic. This linkage therefore is identified as macro–micro within systemism.

Second, Shirk (2007: 187) claims that a Chinese leader's approach to Taiwan 'depends on three factors: domestic politics, the current situation on Taiwan, and the current U.S. stance on cross-Strait issues'. When the focus is on how politics inside of a state impact on foreign policy, either for its government or elsewhere, a micro–macro connection is observed. The designation is the same for how the situation in Taiwan affects Chinese foreign policy – another micro–macro linkage. Finally, the US stance on Sino-Taiwanese relations comes from outside into the system – a link from the environment to the macro level.

All four basic types of causal mechanisms – macro–macro, macro–micro, micro–macro and micro–micro – and effects back and forth with the environment have been identified within the academic literature on the rise of China, Taiwanese identity, cross-Strait relations and

US influence. Figure 4.2 draws on that research to provide an initial systemist representation of cause and effect. Sub-figures 4.2a–r combine to tell the story from the academic literature of cause and effect for the rise of China, Taiwanese identity, cross-Strait relations and the role of the US.[8] The sub-figures are provided to enhance understanding and retention and thus appreciate in value for especially complex models that contain many variables and multiple types of connections along the way. The argument in favour of this approach, grounded in educational psychology, is available in James (2019a, 2019b) and Pfonner and James (2020).

Figure 4.2a introduces the system and its environment: Northeast Asia and the international system, respectively. The micro and macro levels in Northeast Asia, in turn, correspond to (1) events within states and other individual actors, notably the PRC and ROC; and (2) processes at the level of the region, that is, beyond the boundaries of individual states or other actors. Figure 4.2b starts a pathway downward from the macro to the micro level of Northeast Asia: 'KMT MIGRATION FROM MAINLAND' → 'promotion of Sinic identity for Taiwan'. As an initial variable 'KMT MIGRATION FROM MAINLAND' is depicted as an oval. The linkage conveys the ROC's initial overwhelming identification with the Mainland, which it began to transmit throughout society upon arrival in major waves from the 1930s through to 1949. Figure 4.2c continues this route with a micro–micro connection: 'promotion of Sinic identity' → 'democratization and DPP pressure'. As a convergent variable, the latter appears as a parallelogram. While ROC stalwarts readily endorsed an orientation towards Chinese culture, along with an authoritarian and militarized regime, dissent emerged and eventually took the form of a rival political party once such an entity became legal.

Figure 4.2d conveys a converging macro–micro connection: 'MAINLAND THREAT' → 'democratization and DPP pressure'. As an initial variable, 'MAINLAND THREAT' appears as an oval. This is a mixed force in operation. All other things being equal, a threat from Beijing puts the brakes on the process of democratization and reduces the ability of the DPP to engage in active dissent against ROC rule. At the same time, the menace from the Mainland also creates resentment in Taiwan. Figure 4.2e completes this pathway with 'democratization and DPP pressure' → 'Taiwanization'. As a terminal variable, 'Taiwanization' is depicted as an octagon. This connection shows the impact over time as a product of institutional change; identity on Formosa gradually becomes less Sinic, more democratic, and ultimately distinct from that of the Mainland. Another terminal

THEORIZING ABOUT IDENTITY

Figure 4.2: Cause and effect for Taiwanese identity, the rise of China, cross-state relations and US influence in Northeast Asia

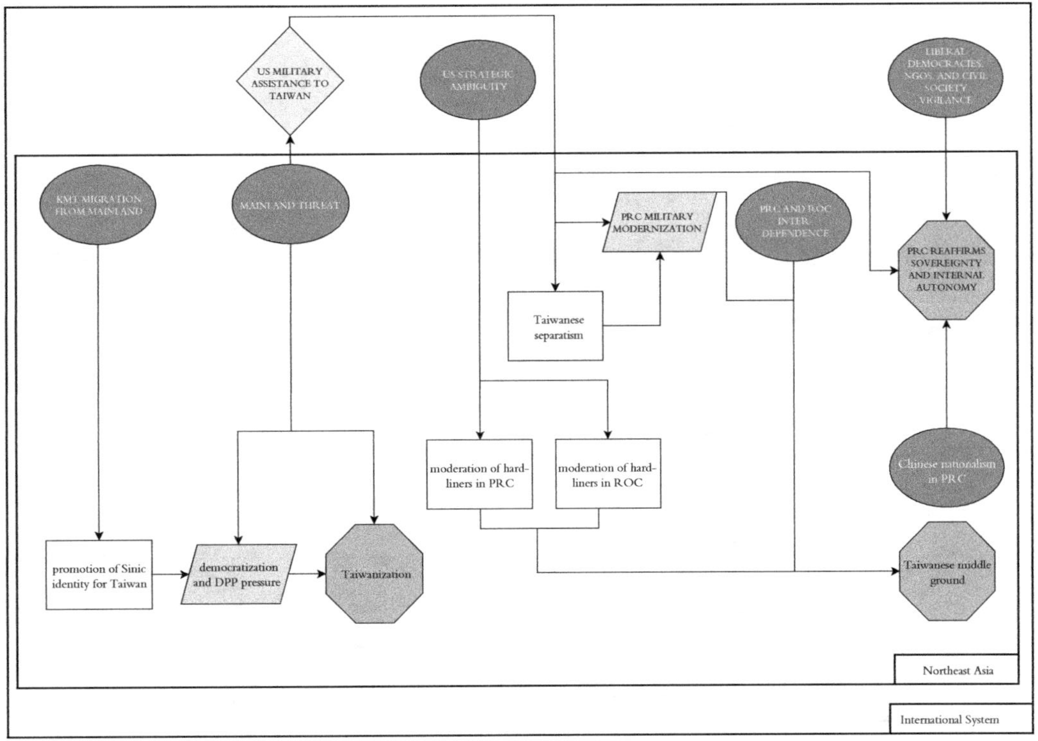

IDENTITY IN THE SHADOW OF A GIANT

Figure 4.2a: Cause and effect for Taiwanese identity, the rise of China, cross-state relations and US influence in Northeast Asia

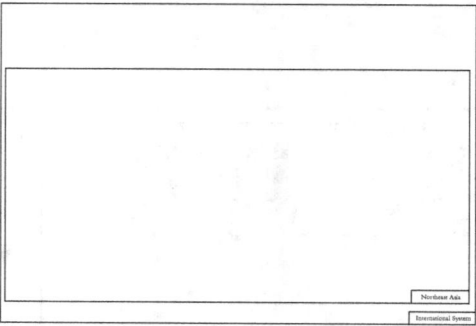

Figure 4.2b: Cause and effect for Taiwanese identity, the rise of China, cross-state relations and US influence in Northeast Asia

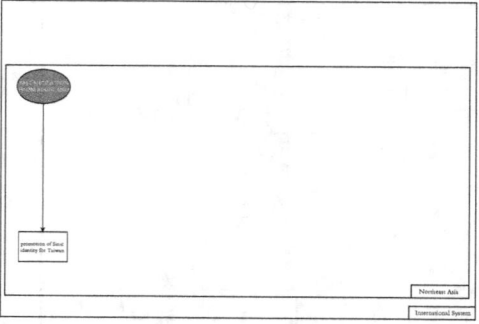

Figure 4.2c: Cause and effect for Taiwanese identity, the rise of China, cross-state relations and US influence in Northeast Asia

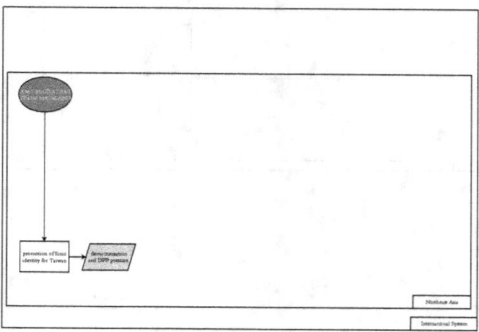

Figure 4.2d: Cause and effect for Taiwanese identity, the rise of China, cross-state relations and US influence in Northeast Asia

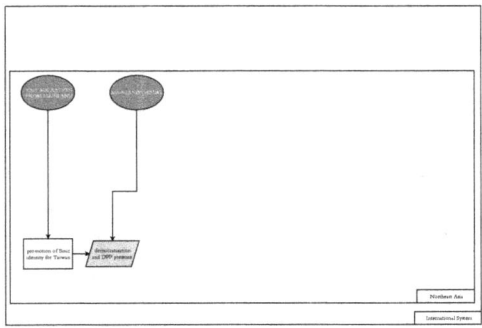

Figure 4.2e: Cause and effect for Taiwanese identity, the rise of China, cross-state relations and US influence in Northeast Asia

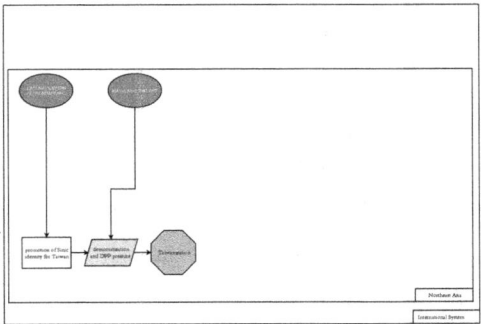

Figure 4.2f: Cause and effect for Taiwanese identity, the rise of China, cross-state relations and US influence in Northeast Asia

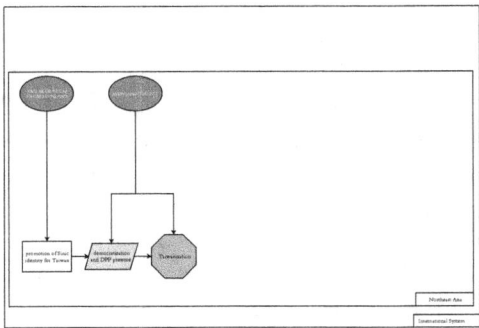

connection appears in Figure 4.2f: 'MAINLAND THREAT' → 'Taiwanization'. The force exerted here is the opposite – slowing down development of a distinct identity as leadership moves in the direction of what Lasswell (1941) famously designated as a 'garrison state' in response to a major external threat.

Figure 4.2g depicts the beginning of a new pathway, from the macro level of Northeast Asia out into the international system: 'MAINLAND THREAT' → 'US MILITARY ASSISTANCE TO TAIWAN'. This connection is straightforward. As the principal patron of Taiwan, the US is anticipated to increase its support when threats from the PRC are on the rise. Note that 'US MILITARY ASSISTANCE TO TAIWAN', a divergent variable, appears as a diamond.

Figure 4.2h shows a one-stage pathway from the international system into Northeast Asia: 'US MILITARY ASSISTANCE TO TAIWAN' → 'PRC REAFFIRMS SOVEREIGNTY AND INTERNAL AUTONOMY'. Note that the latter variable, a point of termination, is depicted with an octagon. The net result of any Taiwanese military buildup assisted by the US is expected to be greater resolve on the part of the PRC to maintain its position about Taiwan as a hybrid entity. On the one hand, the PRC must rein in ambitions about taking away internal autonomy from the ROC. On the other hand, to avert any sense of weakness, Beijing also reaffirms its sovereignty over Formosa.

Figure 4.2i follows up with a single-step pathway leading into the same variable: 'LIBERAL DEMOCRACIES, NGOS, AND CIVIL SOCIETY VIGILANCE' → 'PRC REAFFIRMS SOVEREIGNTY AND INTERNAL AUTONOMY'. As an initial variable, the former of these two appears as an oval. While Beijing might regard outside pressure as annoying and even offensive, it cannot be ignored altogether. Thus, the effect of the international community as an outside observer is to reinforce tendencies towards a hybrid approach on the part of the PRC in relation to Taiwan. In other words, for Taiwan, *de facto* rather than *de jure* independence remains the status quo.

Figure 4.2j conveys a one-step connection: 'Chinese nationalism in PRC' → 'PRC REAFFIRMS SOVEREIGNTY AND INTERNAL AUTONOMY'. As an initial variable, 'Chinese nationalism in PRC' appears as an oval. While many on the Mainland would prefer to go even further, assertion of sovereignty over Taiwan and grudgingly putting up with some degree of autonomy ends up as the outcome. At the same time, leadership in Beijing is aware of danger from the excesses of nationalist sentiment, which could lead to extreme violence and even 'shaming' of the government into more drastic and dangerous aggression against Taiwan. Thus, the effects of nationalism in the PRC

Figure 4.2g: Cause and effect for Taiwanese identity, the rise of China, cross-state relations and US influence in Northeast Asia

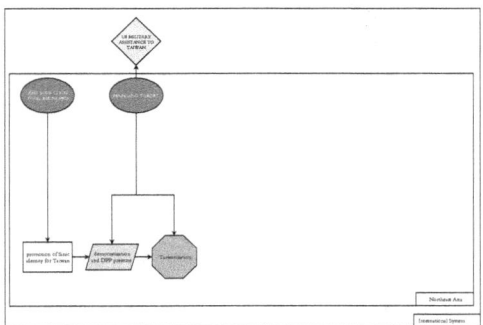

Figure 4.2h: Cause and effect for Taiwanese identity, the rise of China, cross-state relations and US influence in Northeast Asia

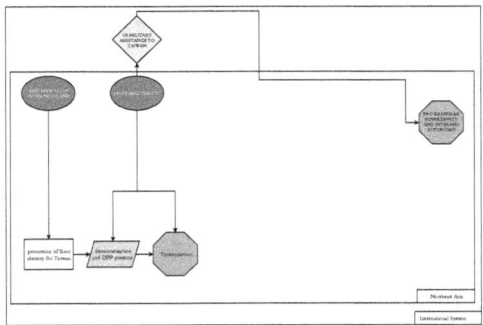

Figure 4.2i: Cause and effect for Taiwanese identity, the rise of China, cross-state relations and US influence in Northeast Asia

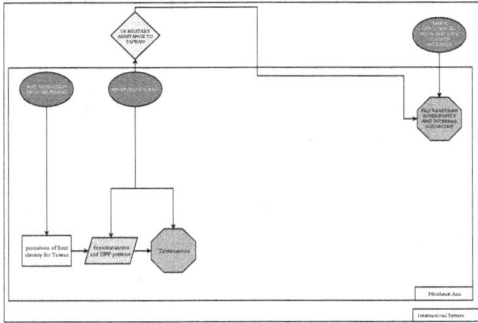

Figure 4.2j: Cause and effect for Taiwanese identity, the rise of China, cross-state relations and US influence in Northeast Asia

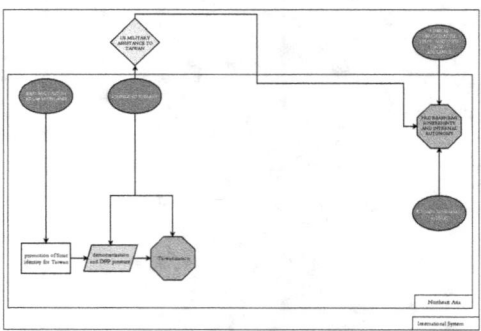

Figure 4.2k: Cause and effect for Taiwanese identity, the rise of China, cross-state relations and US influence in Northeast Asia

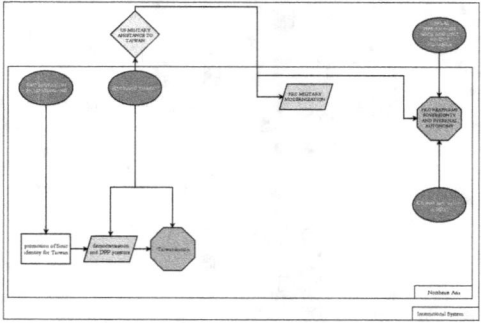

are real but also limited by other forces at work, such as the role of the US, which limits the capacity of Beijing to act decisively against Taiwan.

Depicted in Figure 4.2k, another pathway moves forward with 'US MILITARY ASSISTANCE TO TAIWAN' → 'PRC MILITARY MODERNIZATION'. As a convergent variable, 'PRC MILITARY MODERNIZATION' is depicted as a parallelogram. The PRC is deemed likely to modernize its military in response to US support for Taiwan, which is regarded as inherently threatening because it might encourage movement towards independence (Johnston, 2003: 45). According to Johnston (2003: 52; see also Callahan, 2010: 204; Hong, 2016: 67), the PRC therefore has turned to Russia and elsewhere for acquisition of military technology to keep up, to the extent possible, with US transfers to Taiwan that always raise suspicions about what will happen next.

Figure 4.2l extends an existing pathway from the international system back into the micro level of Northeast Asia: 'US MILITARY ASSISTANCE TO TAIWAN' → 'Taiwanese separatism'. As Taipei obtains greater military capabilities from the US, it can be expected to follow a more independent way of thinking. The next step, 'Taiwanese separatism' → 'PRC MILITARY MODERNIZATION', is micro to macro and appears in Figure 4.2m. The intuition is obvious; as Taiwan pursues separatism, this provokes the PRC, which turns to military modernization as a way of warning Taipei not to go too far.

Figure 4.2n displays a connection from the macro level to a new terminal variable at the micro level: 'PRC MILITARY MODERNIZATION' → 'Taiwanese middle ground'. The terminal variable, 'Taiwanese middle ground', appears as an octagon. The intuition behind this linkage is that the long-term trend towards autonomy is reined in, to some degree, as the much larger PRC also becomes a more formidable military power. At the same time, Mainland militarization adversely affects beliefs about the likelihood of evolution towards democracy in the PRC and thus stiffens resistance. The result for Taiwan is opinion that converges towards a position in the middle – increasingly distant from either unification or independence.

Figure 4.2o depicts a one-step pathway: 'PRC AND ROC INTERDEPENDENCE' → 'Taiwanese middle ground'. As an initial variable, 'PRCE AND ROC INTERDEPENDENCE' appears as an oval. This effect is a standard from the neo-Kantian outlook, within which economic interdependence helps to build peaceful cooperation. One aspect of this would be movement of public opinion in Taiwan towards a middle ground – away from both unification and independence. The same type of process would be expected on the Mainland, which would reap rewards from economic exchange and become increasingly reluctant to absorb the costs of war to alter significantly the political situation on Formosa.

Figure 4.2p starts another pathway, this time from the international system into the micro level of Northeast Asia: 'US STRATEGIC AMBIGUITY' → 'moderation of hard-liners in PRC'. As an initial variable, 'US STRATEGIC AMBIGUITY', appears as an oval. Figure 4.2q shows another connection with the same origin: 'US STRATEGIC AMBIGUITY' → 'moderation of hard-liners in ROC'. In each instance the logic is the same; the greater the degree to which the US plays its cards close to the vest, the more difficult it becomes for hard-liners in Beijing and Taipei to make the case for confrontation politics.

Figure 4.2l: Cause and effect for Taiwanese identity, the rise of China, cross-state relations and US influence in Northeast Asia

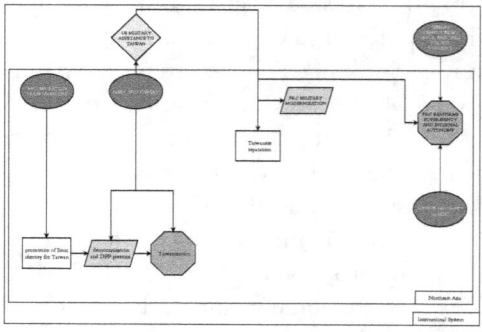

Figure 4.2m: Cause and effect for Taiwanese identity, the rise of China, cross-state relations and US influence in Northeast Asia

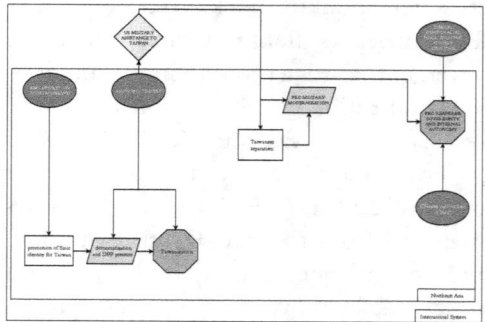

Figure 4.2n: Cause and effect for Taiwanese identity, the rise of China, cross-state relations and US influence in Northeast Asia

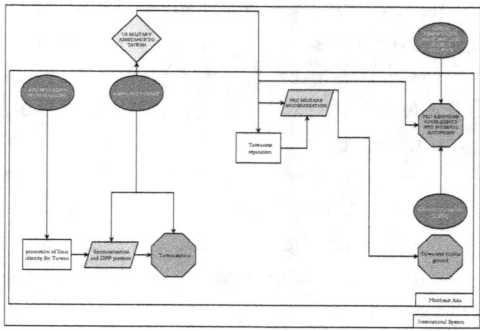

Figure 4.2o: Cause and effect for Taiwanese identity, the rise of China, cross-state relations and US influence in Northeast Asia

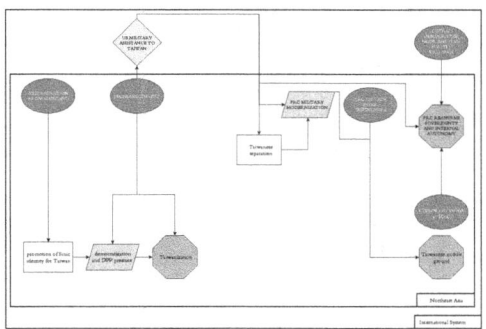

Figure 4.2p: Cause and effect for Taiwanese identity, the rise of China, cross-state relations and US influence in Northeast Asia

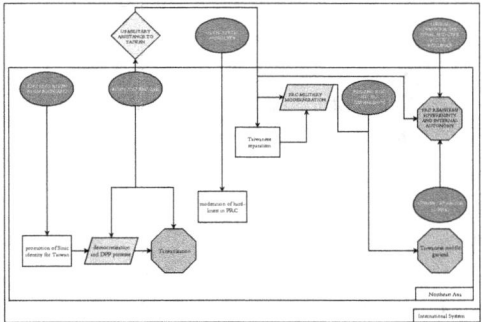

Figure 4.2q: Cause and effect for Taiwanese identity, the rise of China, cross-state relations and US influence in Northeast Asia

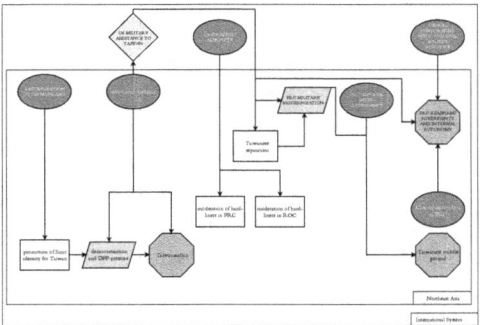

Figure 4.2r: Cause and effect for Taiwanese identity, the rise of China, cross-state relations and US influence in Northeast Asia

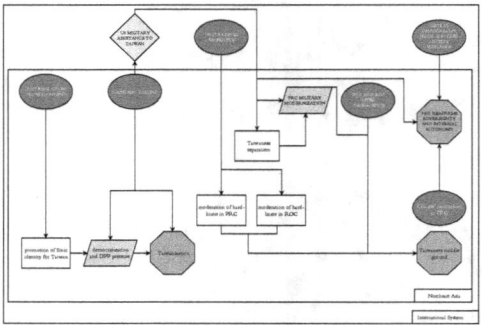

Figure 4.2r completes the final pathway with 'moderation of hard-liners in PRC' → 'Taiwanese middle ground' and 'moderation of hard-liners in ROC' → 'Taiwanese middle ground'. The extremes of opinion on the Mainland and Formosa, respectively, tilt towards a military takeover and declaration of independence. As each group occupies a smaller share of public opinion, the distribution of views in Taiwan concentrates into the middle of the political spectrum.

With Figure 4.2 in place, a graphic summary of academic literature becomes available to set a baseline for further research. The goal is not to stand still, but instead elaborate upon this diagram as more is learned. This could include both addition of new links and adjustment or even subtraction of those already in place.

Rising China, Taiwanese identity, cross-Strait relations and United States influence

When the rise of China, identity in Taiwan, cross-Strait relations and the role of the US are put together as subject matter, this chapter confirms that something beyond paradigmatic research is needed to obtain a satisfactory account of cause and effect. A convincing answer to the problems associated with paradigmatic narrowness is analytic eclecticism, which emphasizes development of middle range theory and relevance to policy. At the same time, chaos from ever-expanding sets of explanatory variables also is not welcome. What should be done to head off incoherence resulting from a highly inclusive intellectual approach such as analytic eclecticism? Implementation of systemism, a graphic technique for conveying cause and effect, solves that problem. Systemism permits combination of variables from across paradigmatic boundaries into a coherent whole and protects logical consistency through its explicit visual representation of causal mechanisms. The systemist perspective also emphasizes the need to avoid *ceteris paribus* clauses through a complete specification of causal linkages across all of the possible types. This is essential to obtain an overall sense of where identity stands vis-à-vis the possibilities enumerated in Table 1.1: Complementary (ideological and interest-based), Self-Interested (interest-based, ideology minimal at most), Ideological (ideology-based, interest minimal at most) and Unmotivated (neither ideology- nor interest-based).

With an initial graphic representation in place via Figure 4.2, based on previous academic treatments, work moves forward with new research that implements multiple methods. Chapter 5, which conveys results from interviews, is the first of three empirical chapters. The overarching goal is to build on the state of the art as conveyed here and construct an elaborated systemist figure in Chapter 8. Thus, we next examine the ability of a wide variety of observations of elite and mass attitudes to match up with some (but not all) of the relationships captured from our systemist approach.

Notes

[1] This corresponds to the logic behind the theoretical framework known as offensive realism (Mearsheimer, 2014b).

[2] The then President-Elect Donald Trump made the following comment: 'I fully understand the "one China" policy, but I don't know why we have to be bound by a "one China" policy unless we make a deal with China having to do with other things, including trade' (*Newsweek*, 2016).

[3] Constructivism may be thought of more as a method than a paradigm in and of itself. For a treatment of concept formation in this area, see Bertucci et al (2018).

[4] This is a critique of how paradigmatic research is working out in practice for International Relations as a social science. In principle, things could have evolved differently.

[5] The diagrammatic exposition that follows is based primarily upon James (2019b; see also Bunge, 1996; James, 2019a; Pfonner and James, 2020).

[6] Bunge (1996) does not provide instructions on how linkages might be 'unpacked' in the course of explaining each in turn. The specific orderings and combinations of linkages that appear in each set of figures reflects a pragmatic effort towards ease of explanation.

[7] Beyond the scope of the present exposition is specification of functional form for proposed connections; this is required by systemism for complete articulation of a theory (Bunge, 1996). While incremental change is assumed as the default position, it is important to recognize that functional relationships can be non-linear as well.

[8] The source(s) for each connection in Figure 4.2 are as follows: US STRATEGIC AMBIGUITY → restrains hard-liners in PRC and ROC (O'Hanlon, 2000: 83–84); democratization and DPP pressure → Taiwanization (Rigger, 2001: 206;

Brown, 2004: 239); MAINLAND THREAT → democratization and DPP pressure; Taiwanization (T. Lin, 2002: 231, 232; Brown, 2004: 241); LIBERAL DEMOCRACIES, NGOS AND INTERNATIONAL CIVIL SOCIETY VIGILANCE → PRC REAFFIRMS SOVEREIGNTY AND INTERNAL AUTONOMY (Johnston, 2003: 15); TAIWANESE SEPARATISM → PRC MILITARY MODERNIZATION (Johnston, 2003: 27); PRC MILITARY MODERNIZATION → Taiwanese middle ground (Roy, 2003: 243); KMT MIGRATION FROM MAINLAND → promotion of Sinic identity for Taiwan (Brown, 2004: 232); democratization and DPP pressure; Taiwanization → MAINLAND THREAT (Shirk, 2007: 182); MAINLAND THREAT → US MILITARY ASSISTANCE TO TAIWAN (Friedberg, 2005: 22); US MILITARY ASSISTANCE TO TAIWAN → PRC MILITARY MODERNIZATION (Friedberg, 2005: 22); PRC AND ROC INTERDEPENDENCE → Taiwanese middle ground (Kastner, 2015: 14); PRC REAFFIRMS SOVEREIGNTY AND INTERNAL AUTONOMY → Chinese nationalism in PRC (Hong, 2016: 67); Chinese nationalism in PRC → PRC REAFFIRMS SOVEREIGNTY AND INTERNAL AUTONOMY (Hong, 2016: 67); promotion of Sinic identity for Taiwan → democratization and DPP pressure (Rubenstein, 2007a: 391). The linkages not referenced, but inferred to complete the network of cause and effect in Figure 4.2, are as follows: US MILITARY ASSISTANCE TO TAIWAN → Taiwanese separatism; moderation of hard-liners in PRC; moderation of hard-liners in ROC → Taiwanese middle ground.

5

Elite Reflections

Overview

This chapter conveys and assesses elite reflections obtained from multiple waves of research interviews conducted in Taiwan. Material from those dialogues will facilitate our reassessment of the conventional wisdom identified in Chapter 4 and reflect support for the construction of our diagrammatic approach. Recall the systemist Figure 4.2, which conveyed cause and effect for the rise of China, Taiwanese identity, cross-Strait relations and the role of the US as gleaned from the academic literature. The depth from descriptive analysis of interviews in this chapter is intended to complement the breadth obtained from survey research assessed in Chapters 6–7. All of this will be compared in Chapter 8 with the graphic story of cause and effect told by the academic literature and encapsulated in Figure 4.2 from Chapter 4. Analysis will culminate in an elaborated systemist visualization that builds upon Figure 4.2 through incorporation of what has been learned in Chapters 5–7.

Content from the interviews is assembled into the following categories: meaning of identity; the 1992 Consensus and identity; deepening business, trade and economic ties; Sunflower Movement of 2014; textbook controversy and colonial legacy; China's rise, identity and the US role; and Tsai's presidency and cross-Strait relations. This is an intentionally inductive approach that covers sets of issues as these combine together naturally through the interviews. Moreover, this comprehensive approach is in line with principles from analytic eclecticism and systemism that underlie the project as a whole.

Work continues in four additional sections. The second section introduces the interviews in terms of time, place and representativeness. The third section contains the content of the interviews organized into the categories enumerated in the previous paragraph. Analysis and synthesis of that material, notably in terms of (dis)agreement among interviewees, takes place in the fourth section. The fifth and final section sums up the chapter's contributions.

Characteristics of the interviews

Chin-Hao Huang and Patrick James carried out the bulk of the research interviews in Taipei during September and October of 2015, respectively. Given the proximity of those visits to the presidential election of 16 January 2016, political issues held an even greater importance than under normal conditions for both elite and public. On the one hand, this closeness to the election might have the disadvantage of evoking more emotional responses than otherwise would be expected. On the other hand, the overall impact of the timing would seem to be favourable because all of those interviewed revealed a strong interest in sharing their views. To address some of these methodological issues, Huang carried out an additional set of semi-structured research interviews in July 2016 (post-election and post-inauguration of the new government in Taipei) with some of the same policy elites and interview questions.

Appendix A lists the set of questions passed along to interviewees ahead of the time spent together in person. While the questionnaire would not have surprised anyone familiar with Taiwan and its policy issues, provision of the document helped to create structure for subsequent discussions. Most questions, such as potential connection of Taiwanese identity to the Chinese military buildup, are phrased in an encompassing way. A few others, such as the query regarding ECFA, focus on more specific matters.

During the September 2015 research visit, seven meetings took place with a total of eight interviewees. Discussions with 25 interviewees took place at 15 meetings during the October 2015 trip. One large gathering occurred during the latter visit, with other sessions including either one or two interviewees. The July 2016 research visit included five meetings with a dozen interviews. All of those interviewed certainly can be described as elite and politically aware. Their employment includes government, academe, foundations, media and research institutes. Some interviewees previously have occupied roles that span categories, such as academics who once served in government. Based on advice from those with greater knowledge of Taiwan, along with previous personal experience in interviewing, the interviewers did not raise the possibility of taping sessions. Instead, material in the next section reflects integration of detailed notes taken during conversations that lasted on average between one and two hours.

Sampling is a natural question regarding interview material. What about the problem of representativeness? The collection of elite interviews here is conventional in that it came about through what is known as the 'snowball/chain referral' approach (Tansey, 2007: 770; see also Goldstein, 2002 on obtaining access to interviewees). The main axis of partisanship in Taiwan continues to be Pan-Green versus Pan-Blue; interviews are distributed evenly that way, so concerns about ideological bias should be at a minimum. In terms of format, the present study relies on semi-structured interviews, which are recommended for highly knowledgeable subjects (Aberbach and Rockman, 2002; Leech, 2002).

Responses are blended together to highlight themes and patterns. Material is paraphrased for ease of exposition, but always bearing in mind the need to convey the original meaning to the greatest extent possible. Thus, quotation marks do not appear in the text of the section that follows. Instead, the exposition combines interview material to communicate points of consensus and disagreement coherently, which in turn facilitates analysis and synthesis. It also should be noted that, to convey sentiments most accurately, the wording reflects the timing of the interviews from the fall of 2015, with the exception that the Tsai government is referred to in the present tense.

One further qualification, regarding possibly biased responses, seems in order. The interviewers did not prompt or 'coach' respondents by introducing terminology from strategic studies, political science or other academic fields. In a few instances, interviewees spontaneously utilized such language because of their prior academic training. For these cases, the interviewers obviously then felt free to engage the interviewee directly in a discussion that included open references to academic concepts.[1]

Content of the interviews

Content is presented in a way intended to convey how interviewees tended to organize their thoughts into respective topical areas. The sub-sections that follow include both panoramic and specific subject matter – a reflection of wide-ranging discussions that took place. The viewpoints and, where possible, words are from our interviewees. A few citations appear and it should be noted that, in each instance, the *interviewee* rather than the interviewer introduced the material cited. Occasional clarifying footnotes are included to help those less familiar with Taiwan follow the discussion. Here are the voices and views of our interviewees.

What does identity mean in Taiwan?

Valuable as a starting point for discussion is the set of three forces identified by one interviewee as essential to understanding identity. The first is demographic evolution – as years go on, older people pass away and are replaced by those younger. The second force is policy-related – whoever is in power in Taiwan can shape popular perceptions. The third influence is connected to what the PRC is saying and doing. As will become apparent, this summary works reasonably well as a lead-in to what interviewees offer about Taiwanese identity across the board. It also becomes obvious that cause and effect are operating in both directions with regard to policies of the ROC and PRC.

Over and beyond the three factors and their dual roles as cause and effect, a range of other subjects emerge in connection with Taiwanese identity: the role of the US; likely profile and legacy of a Tsai presidency and DPP-controlled Legislative Yuan as events move forward; potential political realignment; direct expressions about identity; and the future.

Reflections from a self-described second-generation Mainlander convey the demographic factor already noted in a revealing way. He is not sure how to identify himself and still hesitates to reply when asked "Where are you from?". The answer could be Chinese, Taiwanese or something else – and the question seems increasingly difficult to answer. Prior to the age of 40, he had been considered by the ROC government to be from a province in China, where his family lived previously. However, in 2000, President Chen changed this policy; the government removed 'belonging' to a location on the Mainland from birth certificates. Thus, legal identification for this second-generation Mainlander shifted to a place in the northern part of Taiwan. He added that his son already sees himself as Taiwanese, with reasons for this self-identification being traced to peers and school textbooks.

Movement towards a Taiwan-centred identity is true especially of younger age cohorts. While cultural identity is a hybrid of Taiwanese and Chinese elements, political identity is exclusively Taiwanese. A supermajority of younger people – 80 to 90 per cent in survey results – identify as Taiwanese and only about 10 per cent respond as Chinese. (With a *flexible* definition of 'Chinese' that number can go up to 40 per cent.) Pro-independence sentiment among youth is significant, along with fear of the future regarding (1) economic opportunity and (2) momentum inherent in Ma's policy towards linkages with the PRC. Furthermore, some complain that Chinese identity is too present in the public sector, thanks to the KMT, at the expense of representing a Taiwanese identity.

Older people, by contrast, are more cautious about anything that seems to approach *de jure* independence in particular, a sentiment confirmed by a number of respondents during the interviews. It is natural for a more advanced generation to have closer sentiments about unification or to support maintaining cordial relations with the Mainland. This demographic in Taiwan's population, however, is dwindling. The key divide is between those born (approximately) before and after 1990. Those born beyond that date have been educated *after* the period of martial law and tend to see independence as something close to a birthright. Taiwan, to the younger generation, means emotional attachment to the island. Belief that Taiwan is a separate country is one reason behind the Sunflower Movement, which will be discussed a bit later.

The 1992 Consensus and Taiwan's evolving identity

With regard to government policy as it relates to identity, the 1992 Consensus is cited by our interviewees as the foundation for future developments. In particular, they addressed the questions: how does the evolving Taiwanese identity affect the ongoing relevance of the 1992 Consensus and vice versa? As a point of departure, it is appropriate to consider the context of Sino-Taiwanese relations at the time of the 1992 Consensus. Throughout the 1980s and 1990s, the ROC and PRC lacked a formal mechanism to contact one another. This affected adversely even basic, functional matters. Examples include radio contacts for humanitarian operations, search and rescue, and providing disaster relief for fishermen and boat passengers in distress in the Taiwan Strait. The 1992 Consensus set up some fundamental operating procedures for initiating and maintaining contact for Beijing and Taipei. Underlying the agreement is the premise that both sides could work together on *functional* issues first. The 1992 Consensus implicitly recognized that Taiwan enjoys *de facto* separation and independence from the Mainland. From the standpoint of those on the island, the 1992 Consensus means that (1) culturally, we are all Chinese; and (2) we are 'One China'. From an identity standpoint, the two preceding components are so encompassing as to lack any specific meaning – almost certainly the intention at the time.

Larger and more complex questions, most obviously about sovereignty in the *de jure* sense, had no place in the initial discussion for Beijing and Taipei that resulted in the 1992 Consensus. Both sides purposefully avoided that volatile subject due to its likely derailment of the limited and pragmatic agenda at hand. At the time, Beijing and Taipei agreed on the existence of a common notion of One China but different incarnations, respectively, for the PRC and ROC.

For some time, in spite of agreeing to it, Beijing remained sceptical about the 1992 Consensus. However, in 2000, Chen Shui-bian became the first candidate from an opposition party to win a presidential election. At that point the Beijing leadership realized that value existed in preserving the 1992 Consensus and in using it as the basis for eventual resumption of cross-Strait negotiations. In fact, Chen Shui-bian on a number of occasions referenced and reaffirmed the 1992 Consensus throughout his tenure as president. In these ways and others, the 1992 Consensus became identified with the idea of a status quo in cross-Strait relations.

While about three decades have passed since the advent of the 1992 Consensus, a majority of the interviewees point out that it remains relevant today. The agreement represents the largest common denominator in cross-Strait relations and a starting point for any discussion of potential change. The Consensus is neither a legal nor binding pact. It functions as long as each party agrees to honour the principal points of the agreement: both sides of the Taiwan Strait understand that there is One China and each side of the Taiwan Strait would interpret that differently. This basic understanding (and unique arrangement) is something the general public and the government in Taipei have accepted and lived with for a significant period. At a minimum, the 1992 Consensus does not contradict the ROC's constitution and sustains a status quo with effective independence if not legal recognition. The 1992 Consensus, for example, provided the functional framework for Ma's efforts towards cross-Strait economic integration over his term in office.

Given Taiwan's democratic system of governance and accountability, the general public possesses the ultimate veto in determining the scope and scale of any future cross-Strait engagement. It is fair to say that the 1992 Consensus increasingly is questioned by the public in Taiwan, albeit for very different reasons than those that motivate the PRC's interest in change (a topic we explore at the mass level in Chapters 6 and 7). The 1992 Consensus thus may be tweaked, revised or even replaced with something new and different, if that is what the Taiwanese people seek. Given trends on the island, any such proposal would bear close resemblance to what President Tsai is advocating – the idea of a Taiwan consensus first. At the same time, the electorate of Taiwan is expected to be pragmatic and practical. Any replacement of the 1992 Consensus will not yield a radical change from the status quo that could stimulate a military response from the Mainland.

Consider Tsai's careful rhetoric on the 1992 Consensus in the lead up to the January 2016 presidential election and her inauguration speech in May 2016. In our interviews, scholars familiar with the DPP and Tsai's National Security Council officials point to the fact that, while the president has not publicly endorsed the 1992 Consensus, she does not deny the fact of the historic dialogue that took place at that time. Tsai also does not dispute the context under which the consensus was forged – a desire of the two sides at the time to advance cross-Strait relations to work on pragmatic areas of cooperation and by fostering mutual understanding and respect. President Tsai does not object, at least openly, to a priority on the return to the *spirit* behind the 1992 Consensus, which is to set aside differences and seek common ground.

With both sides governing separately for 70 years, divergence along at least some dimensions becomes only natural for the Mainland and Taiwan. In some respects, Taiwan has moved on from its wartime origins and matured into a more developed state, ushering in key ideological factors that have influenced the island's shifting identity. In particular, democratization is driven by internal political developments, not the PRC. Taiwan is the only ethnically Chinese democracy with a competitive electoral process that has seen at least three transitions of political power for the presidency. The values, ideas and political culture associated with a more free and open society, such as religious freedom, freedom of speech and the press have all occurred in tandem with increasing levels of political accountability and transparency. The political system stands as one of Huntington's Third Wave success stories, with very little political violence in the process of democratization. A natural progression occurred towards peaceful outcomes for contested elections.

Given such developments and characteristics, it is realistic to expect a greater demand from the Taiwanese people for the Mainland to affirm the existence of the ROC's democratic values and system of governance. The rationale for doing so is to clarify and reinforce the fact that Taiwan is not Hong Kong or Macau. Unification under the 'one country, two systems' model – Beijing's interpretation of where negotiations ultimately would lead – is a non-starter for the electorate in Taiwan, a consolidating view among the younger electorate that our interview respondents underscored. Notwithstanding the level of economic integration or interdependence, the more Beijing insists on sidestepping, undermining or ignoring Taiwan's *de facto* independent system of governance, the more likely it is for Taiwan to deepen its own sense of distinctiveness and separation from the Mainland.

People in Taiwan see that China's increasing material wealth is not translating into greater political freedom or a more open society. China's economic and political model, which is highly state-driven, is not something the general public in Taiwan seeks either to join or even emulate. The 1992 Consensus still may be relevant, however, if Taiwan's electorate decides this is something it would like to maintain in spite of growing animosity towards the dictatorial system of the Mainland. The 1992 Consensus is the closest thing to affirming the status quo, which is *de facto* separation and a detached seat of government in Taipei for the last seven decades.

What about the 1992 Consensus today and beyond? According to our elite interviews, the 1992 Consensus evokes strong views across the political spectrum in Taiwan. To critics in Taiwan it is just a slogan. The name is not well-remembered, but polling shows approval for *content* when asked about specifics within the agreement. DPP criticism, however, is causing public disenchantment with a One China policy to increase (see Chapters 6 and 7). To those from the Pan-Green side, the 1992 Consensus serves as the basis of KMT relations with the PRC. The 1992 Consensus most likely will cease as the foundation for the DPP government's policies. This situation could be problematic for the DPP, however, because the idea of One China as an alternative advocated by the Mainland is worse since it can be taken to mean that Taiwan is part of the PRC. In sum, the DPP and Mainland face the challenge of working out their own mutually acceptable new 'bridge' if the 1992 Consensus truly is repudiated by Taiwan. A senior aide to Tsai has indicated that the new DPP government would focus more attention on consolidating an island-wide consensus – so-called 'Taiwan consensus first' – as an important prerequisite. By implication, policy elites advising Tsai suggested it opens the door for the DPP government under Tsai to gradually accept the One China concept, if that is the emerging consensus of the general public over the course of the next four years. It also means that unless a clear majority favour the government to push for a more pro-independent line, Tsai, likewise, would tone down such calls as well.

Deepening business, trade and economic ties

Given its promotion of economic cooperation with the Mainland, ECFA can be seen as a long-term product of the 1992 Consensus. The PRC had been doing very well, economically speaking, and many

Taiwanese inferred that links should be expanded. By 2008, the DPP seemed out of touch with an upward economic trend on the Mainland that encouraged Taiwan to benefit from it as much as possible. The KMT under Ma came to power as a result.

What, then, are the emerging results of ECFA, Ma's signature policy? Signed on 29 June 2010, ECFA remains one of the most controversial initiatives of the Ma regime. Ma's proposal for closer economic linkages – through institutionalization of the three links and ECFA – should have brought the two sides closer together. Yet, by the end point of the Ma regime, the ECFA agreement became viewed as quite problematic in the eyes of most Taiwanese.

One unfavourable aspect, over and above ECFA itself, relates to declining trust in government in a general sense. Respondents in the elite interviews explained that many people became sceptical about the KMT government's statistics, most notably, data on benefits from the trade agreement with the Mainland. Public perception is that ECFA serves the interests of a few large business conglomerates and corporations that maintain close ties with the KMT. For example, even the increase in tourism (e.g. the agreement to allow Mainland tourists to visit Taiwan) rewards only a few large tourism companies. So donors and benefactors connected with the KMT are regarded as gaining from the agreement, with losses distributed among everyone else. ECFA therefore is associated with downward mobility, with limited material improvements for the majority on the island.

Another point of controversy arising from ECFA concerns its potential to enhance the Mainland's influence on Taiwan. Chinese companies certainly are now more visible on the island, setting up branches in Taipei and other locations. Many Mainlanders come to Taiwan and buy hotels and other assets. These acquisitions, however, create the danger of external control over the economy. Ma is perceived as too pro-PRC and that gets mixed together with anger over other issues. While Ma did not attend the 3 September 2015 military parade in Beijing, the former president of the KMT, Lien Chan, did. One interviewee said, humorously, that Ma is regarded as a 'running dog lackey' of the PRC.[2] Controversy ensued because of business interests on the Mainland and that hurt Ma's standing with the public. As one interviewee summed things up in a highly critical way: the Mainland is buying Taiwan. The concern from the interviewee suggests Taiwan's predicament is that with policies like ECFA in place, at some point Taiwan would become so heavily dependent on the Mainland that the economic and political costs of extricating the island from Beijing's orbit would be insurmountable. Economic integration, in short, would likely benefit the Mainland as its bargaining position becomes stronger vis-à-vis Taiwan.

Perceptions matter, but what does objective evidence say about ECFA? Data remains inconclusive on the benefits of closer economic integration with the Mainland. It may be too early to tell, as described by a credible *World Magazine* report, with the jury therefore still out on ECFA. At least so far, ECFA is good for some sectors and bad for others. Negative outcomes are clear for steel and petrochemical industries, but the deal works positively for some areas within the agricultural sector. Results are mixed regarding textiles and machinery. Among trade deals in general, ECFA therefore represents an anomaly, at least in the short term. The principal reason is that losses have been expansive, with gains being enjoyed rather narrowly. Trade liberalization normally works the other way around, albeit over the long term. Given its distribution of benefits and costs, short-term pain overshadows possible long-term gain from ECFA and makes the deal unpopular.

Consider those properties in tandem with a well-established trait of ECFA – its *degree* of impact. Statistics can be summed up as reporting an economic upheaval underway in Taiwan. Given the magnitude of redistributive effects, it becomes imperative for advocates to make the case for ECFA. Yet Ma fell short in explaining to the general public the intricacies of the trade deal. The general reflection from our interviewees was that ECFA, put simply, is not well-understood among Taiwanese. Nor did the government reach out sufficiently to small and medium enterprises, the manufacturing sector and agriculture to assure them of the long(er) term benefits of signing ECFA. For example, a frequently overlooked point is that ECFA helps Taiwan to stay competitive with Korea.

Ma, in spite of political dangers inherent in such a distribution of costs and benefits, did not address the needs of the net 'losers' affected by the agreement. The three-year waiting period should have been emphasized as delaying certain benefits. Yet the president remained very quiet and distant regarding ECFA.

One way to look at ECFA – or, for that matter, any economic agreement with Beijing that is realistic – concerns its inherent asymmetry. As a relatively small economy, Taiwan is quite vulnerable to arrangements involving comparatively huge partners. Thus, Taiwan cannot afford to play in games like ECFA.

A number of our respondents agree that given the public relations problem with ECFA, it is no surprise that its sequel, the Cross-Strait Service Trade Agreement (CSSTA), received such a strong pushback from the legislature. Even among KMT and other Pan-Blue coalition legislators, the CSSTA received criticism, while university student protestors and society at large held and communicated harsher views of the new deal.

One driver behind the growing divide between Taiwan and the Mainland, ironically, is a by-product of Ma's original intention to narrow the gap between the two sides and even to construct a Chinese consciousness, identity, and closer affinity with the Mainland. After all, improvements in material status can shape one's identity choice. This goal prompted him to open up tourism exchanges, whereby Mainland tourists could travel to Taiwan relatively freely. Greater people-to-people interactions presumably, over time, would allow the Taiwanese to realize that shared traditions, culture, and language are much greater than the perceived differences between the two peoples across the Taiwan Strait. Instead, with the increasing number of Mainland tourists, the consensus view from our elite interviews suggested that the general public in Taiwan began to realize that, in spite of commonalities, fundamental differences in values, especially political aspects, had crystallized.

Increased people-to-people exchanges have resulted in an interesting observation among Taiwanese: the more we interact with people from the Mainland, the less we like about China. It appears then that ideological factors have a stronger and much deeper impact on Taiwan's ideational choice, while self-interested, material factors play a more minimal role. Moreover, the shift is not purely generational, where the younger generation is more sceptical than the older one of closer ties with the Mainland. Some aspects of this growing divide may cut across age, background, education and socioeconomic status. Key differences include the political system and fundamental values in society. Along those lines, problematic areas highlighted by greater contact with the Mainland are freedom of the press, speech and religious practices, along with rule of law and political accountability. A seemingly irreversible trend is that people in Taiwan see themselves as distinct from Mainland Chinese in terms of values. Our interviewees pointed to the mass protest movement of 2014 as further evidence of the general public's sentiment and scepticism about the overall trajectory of the government's cross-Strait policy. Put simply, people increasingly posed this uncomfortable question to the KMT government: To what extent is ECFA (and closer economic relations with the Mainland) really benefiting society at large?

Gradual warming of ties across the Taiwan Strait in the years of Ma's presidency did not really bridge the identity or political gap. As one respondent put it, if former president Chen Shui-bian went to the extremes of creating unnecessary hostility and provocation towards the Mainland, Ma came to be seen as taking exactly the opposite position – rushing into détente with a general public unready to accept the associated political and economic arrangements. Public perception is that Ma neglected Taiwan's core interests, which would be met most effectively through consolidating consensus within Taiwan through an open, transparent and democratic process on how to best approach and negotiate with Beijing. Ma also failed to identify ways under which Taiwan's soft power might be able to influence China.

Public perception of Ma's cross-Strait policy is mixed, with much scepticism. Policies for closer economic integration (e.g. ECFA, institutionalizing people-to-people exchanges) had the right intentions from the get-go – that more regularized interactions between the two sides could help to bridge the differences, build trust and enhance mutual understanding. According to the policy elites we interviewed, an essential problem with Ma's cross-Strait policy is that he may have rushed into things without considering the public's attitude. The general sentiment (as seen in newspaper polls – from *United Daily News*) is that Ma went too far in reaching out to the Mainland at the expense of sacrificing Taiwan's democratic values. The public mood consequently became quite pessimistic about cross-Strait relations. Again, these are the consolidated views and voices of those we interviewed.

The Sunflower Movement of 2014

Scepticism about the policies of Ma's government is perhaps most visible with the younger generation, expressed dramatically through the Sunflower Movement in 2014. This student-based social movement does not focus primarily on Ma's position regarding Taiwan and the Mainland. As our interviewees explained, the Sunflower Movement is mainly about anger pertaining to other issues: expensive housing, static wages and lack of transparency in government. Student-centred opposition to the KMT government is much more about differences in wealth and position as they have developed under Ma. The Sunflower Movement, however, *does* tell politicians of all stripes to be careful about excessive closeness to China. All of this connects back to discussion of identity; young people increasingly are distant from parents and grandparents – they do not identify with the Mainland.

When it mobilized in March 2014, the Sunflower Movement shocked Ma and stands as a key turning point in Taiwan's public opinion about cross-Strait relations. University student groups and civil society organizations mobilized a mass protest movement that questioned the government's motivation for going forward with the CSSTA. University students led the protests, but these events also received widespread support and sympathy from the general public.

While the Sunflower Movement caused Ma simply to override the protesters, its significance should not be underestimated. The Sunflower Movement signalled the depth of dissatisfaction with the KMT because, in an ironic twist, it goes against pragmatism within the tradition of Chinese culture. The protests showed dramatically the general public's discontent with Ma's cross-Strait policies, most notably in connection with rising income inequality and declining standards of living for many Taiwanese. Elite interviews conveyed that a significant part of the electorate in Taiwan came to believe that Ma had been 'selling out' Taiwan's core interests in pursuit of a set of Mainland-centred policies that are good for a relatively small proportion of the public.

Disagreement exists over what will become of the Sunflower Movement. From a Pan-Blue point of view, the Sunflower Movement is *very* small, over-publicized, guilty of questionable tactics and quite likely to go away in light of the DPP victories in recent presidential and legislative elections. More positively, greater transparency is demanded by the Sunflower Movement and the DPP is likely to grant it, so that might be another reason for this entity to diminish or even disband. It also is possible that the Sunflower Movement *will* come back because it is critical of the DPP as well as the KMT. One observer predicted that participants in the Sunflower Movement probably would be disappointed regardless of what happens after the election. No matter what occurs in the near future, most respondents in our interviews indicated that young people will continue to be very suspicious of China. In addition, fringe groups such as Era of Change are much more extreme than the Sunflower Movement. Joining the Trans-Pacific Partnership, for instance, would mobilize anti-globalization activists.

Textbook controversy and colonial legacy

What about the controversy over textbooks – a companion piece, to some degree, of the Sunflower Movement? The dispute focuses on how to sum up the period of Japanese rule, and the colonial legacy's influence on Taiwan's identity choice. Taiwan experienced Japanese control for 50 years – the island therefore has known colonial status – and that is *very* important for understanding Taiwan today. The experience with Japan is rooted deeply in Taiwan. Valuable developments occurred in a range of domains – educational, medical science and so on – especially later in the period of rule by Japan.

Lessons learned from Japan include 'be law-abiding' and 'be a good citizen'. With Chiang's retreat and relocation of the KMT government to Taiwan in 1949, however, migrants from the Mainland did not share the positive experience regarding Japan – indeed, exactly the opposite. Chiang's regime did not understand the native Taiwanese. The KMT came in as a *foreign* party – not a national party. With the DPP's founding in 1986, genuinely Taiwanese people arose in opposition to the KMT. The party system therefore consists of indigenous versus refugee entities. This is the key point in understanding differences from a Pan-Green point of view.

As a senior DPP policy advisor explained, the use of the word 'governance' means that the regime during the Japanese era as just described is not viewed as something alien and harmful. The resulting focus today, from that point of view, should be on Taiwanese accomplishments in that period. Occupation, by contrast, refers to something from *outside* of Taiwan that parallels, at least to some degree, the very negative experience of the Mainland under the Japanese up to 1945.

For many of those with relatively positive views of Japan, the textbook controversy is regarded as a sideshow. Japan brings to mind organization, architecture and other positive legacies. Japanese influence lives on positively in Taiwan; former president Lee Teng-hui serves as an example of favourable, even warm, feelings towards Japan among Taiwanese. This is because Taiwan did not have an experience like that of the Mainland or Korea during Japanese ascendance. In sum, from one point of view, the textbook controversy is largely an unhelpful product of the media.

What, then, is the agenda for those mobilizing the textbook issue? One explanation for the origin of the dispute is that some Taiwanese despise *China* and therefore push for calling the Japanese era one of governance. Those more Sino-oriented refer instead to occupation. According to some observers, however, the controversy reflects the radical Green versus the radical Blue; upon reflection the textbook issue is too extreme and tends to drift into fanaticism. Thus, from a pragmatic point of view, the simple and correct summing up of history is that China handed Taiwan over to Japan in 1895. Japan, in turn, colonized Taiwan.

For other respondents, by contrast, the textbook controversy is a serious matter. One protester against reference to Japanese occupation in textbooks even committed suicide. There is a world of difference between using governance versus occupation when those words can signal such different visions of Taiwan. From a deep Green point of view, Taiwan needs to get rid of the term 'occupation' from the textbooks to diminish and perhaps even remove the KMT's Sinocentric influence. This is symbolic politics, but it constitutes a core element of the ideological factors that help shape what it means to be Taiwanese or of a distinct and emerging sense of Taiwanese identity.

China's rise, Taiwanese identity and the United States role

The subjects interviewed agreed that China's rise over the last 30 years is a dramatic development, and that the PRC's ascent causes both words and deeds that will continue to challenge the DPP government. Identified by some as a turning point in Sino-Taiwan relations is the visit to his alma mater, Cornell University, by President Lee Teng-hui in 1995 – notably the Mainland's reaction to it. The PRC shot missiles at Taiwan in retaliation for what came across as a frontal assault on Beijing's position with regard to cross-Strait relations, ultimately reined in only by US intervention.

China's continuing military buildup since that confrontation is not necessarily about becoming a world power. The PRC's goal is to control the region and not have to endure again the humiliation dealt out by the US in the cross-Strait confrontation 25 years ago. China may not have unlimited patience with Taiwan being outside of its authority. Successive landslide victories by the DPP in the 2016 and 2020 presidential and legislative elections suggest that Taiwan is moving further away from China in terms of its political identity and national consciousness, making it even less likely that Beijing would be able to achieve its long-sought unification and the 'great rejuvenation of the Chinese nation' by 2021, the 100th anniversary of the CCP's founding. The PRC eventually will react in some way.

Xi is raising the profile of China around the globe. The prior 150 years largely had been humiliating for the Mainland, so its leaders now seek a leading place in the world. The PRC's military modernization is especially salient. When the PRC recently staged an attack on a replica of Taiwan's presidential palace, this further stimulated fear of the Mainland among Taiwanese. Elite interviews confirmed that anxiety focuses on potential consequences of getting too close to the Mainland. This is a danger greater than that posed by a military assault itself – a threat to an independent identity for Taiwan.

Beijing's desire for enhanced standing and influence naturally carries over to relations with Taipei. While the PRC's military buildup is aimed primarily at the US, it affects Taiwan nonetheless. The Mainland is adamant in asserting the notion that the PRC is the only legitimate and representative government of the One China. Beijing's shifting position thus undermines public trust among the Taiwanese, namely, the changing line stimulates suspicion that the Mainland is not negotiating in good faith. Furthermore, the Mainland's hardening position does not take into account important changes in Taiwan. A separate seat of government is located in Taiwan and the island now is well-established as a fully functional democracy. Most notably, direct presidential elections took place for the first time in 1996 and Taiwan features legislative elections, rule of law, vibrant and active civil society groups and other characteristics associated with democratic government.

Consider the general public's views on China in particular. The PRC's uneven economic growth and recent dip in its financial market are red flags for Taiwan. Taiwan should not be putting all its eggs in the China basket. The Mainland's continuing military modernization is seen as a source of intimidation, bullying and coercion, rather than a manifestation of respected, legitimate power. In particular, the ongoing increase in deployment of short to medium range missiles in Fujian province off the coast of Taiwan shows that China is not negotiating in good faith. All of that points in the direction of greater suspicion among Taiwanese about the Mainland, even in comparison to just a few years ago, and a concomitant shift away from a Sinic identity.

According to a number of respondents in our interviews, China's rise may not be as peaceful as it claims. Consider the Mainland's ongoing tensions with Vietnam and the Philippines in the South China Sea, as well as its border disputes with India. The rise of China creates even more trouble for Taiwan, the US and Japan. Many respondents express genuine concerns about Taiwan being turned into Hong Kong. During his visit to the US in 2015, Xi discussed a range of issues, including disputed islands. China claims a historical case for control of various islands; Japan, the Philippines and Taiwan do not agree. The Mainland's basic goal is to delimit what it sees as excessive US influence from the region and take greater control in regional affairs. Moreover, the Norwegians experienced Chinese anger after selecting a dissident for the Nobel Peace Prize and that demonstrates the Mainland's hegemonic tendencies.

Divergent trends are evident. While economic relations are closer, political distance between people in Taiwan and the Mainland seems to be growing. The balance of power is trending towards China. As an interviewee pointed out, some travel-related issues are informative here and not that well-known outside of Taiwan. China's unilateral decision required Mainland-bound Taiwanese travellers to change their paper travel permit to a smart chip card. The policy was aimed to downgrade Taiwan's status to that of a special administrative region like Hong Kong and Macau. In spite of such impositions, Taiwanese identity persistently shifts in the direction of independence. Thus, the future of cross-Strait relations is more likely to look like crisis, rather than opportunity, management.

From the standpoint of some optimists who we interviewed, however, favourable changes on the Mainland are not ruled out as a possibility. China cannot keep its combination of dictatorship and aggressive foreign policy on track forever. Corruption is not without its corrosive effects and eventually must be addressed. Consider also the potential impact of Chinese students educated abroad. This is a form of diplomacy beyond the state. One interviewee suggested taking a look at the current issue of *Chinese Affairs* – the focus is on Mainland students in the US, Japan, etc. Many more of these students are returning to China than in the past. This poses a challenge because the regime does not tolerate organized dissent. Students who return home are likely to exercise a positive influence on the regime over time. The size and pace of this effect, in moderating dictatorship and coercive foreign policy, is the only question left.

From outside of the ROC–PRC dyad, the US is by far the most important influence. US leadership and credibility in the region is at stake, so Washington is expected to maintain a keen interest in developments unfolding between Beijing and Taipei. Discussion starts naturally with the Taiwan Relations Act (TRA) in 1979. When reflecting on the TRA, it becomes clear that political values and shared interests between the United States and Taiwan are much more closely aligned than sometimes perceived. Notwithstanding the lack of formal diplomatic ties, the TRA is the next best thing to *de facto* recognition. By law, the Act guarantees US security support for Taiwan, regardless of the political party in control of the White House and/or Congress.

Endorsed and applied by every US administration for four decades, the commitment embodied in the TRA is unlikely to change. The US goal is to control, not resolve, the Taiwan Strait problem. The US prefers the status quo – an equilibrium in which power remains balanced. As long as Taiwan does not appear to provoke the PRC, coercion from the Mainland is expected to prompt a strong defensive US reaction and presence across the Taiwan Strait.

Some of the policy elites we surveyed in Taiwan argued that, to preserve credibility and leadership in the Asia-Pacific region, the US needs to *increase* its commitment to Taiwan. The TRA is important, but strengthening bilateral ties should go beyond intermittent arms sales.

The military balance across the Taiwan Strait is in China's favour, so Taiwan needs to maintain credible deterrence. The United States can help Taiwan develop indigenous weaponry and improve its defensive capabilities. Likewise, more training of military cadets and officers (e.g. at West Point, Naval War College, Army War College, National Defense University) would increase Taiwan's military means, skill sets and expertise. Some ongoing training programmes began in recent years, but they should be expanded. Taipei applied to be an observer in US naval and military exercises in the Pacific region (eg RIMPAC in Hawaii since 2000), but Washington has not taken this up, owing to political sensitivities, its preference to maintain strategic ambiguity, and to avoid being roped into any unnecessary conflict in cross-Strait relations. Observers in Taipei point out that US view may change as a result of recent upgrades in US–Taiwan relations and in light of China's staging of military exercises near the Taiwan Strait with increasing frequency. US policy is followed very closely in Taiwan and limitations such as those preceding are well-understood. As an expert on US–Taiwan relations pointed out, the key question in US–Taiwan relations therefore is this one: What can Washington do for Taipei to help it feel more confident in future dealings with Beijing?

What does the US, in turn, want from Taiwan? Respondents in our interviews explained that Washington needs Taipei's assurance that no Unilateral Declaration of Independence (UDI) will occur. The US does not have the power to bring the CCP and DPP governments together for dialogue to affect change. Cross-Strait negotiations are the prerogative of the governments in Taipei and Beijing, so assertive US influence would not be appropriate. The best role for the US is to help ensure regional stability. So long as Taiwan holds up its end of the bargain – no unilateral changes to the status quo – Washington should be able to honour its commitments under the TRA.

While in principle the DPP can count on the US honouring the TRA if the Mainland, without provocation, attacks Taiwan, one interviewee pointed out troubling features of a RAND Corporation report from September 2015. Entitled *US/China Military Scoreboard*, this report advised against US carrier groups getting closer than 2,000 kilometres. Other data points in the same direction regarding a potential US pullback from Northeast Asia. A September 2015 survey from the Chicago Council on Global Affairs reveals that the public does not seem to approve of US use of force in support of Taiwan across a wide range of scenarios. About 40 per cent of Americans surveyed do not endorse the use of force in any context related to Taiwan. Elites respond a bit more favourably about Taiwan's security, but still generally are disposed against US use of force. Public opinion therefore may point towards the rise of a worrisome isolationism in the US that could put Taiwan in great jeopardy.

Some interviewees in Taiwan expressed further concerns about President Obama in particular, and the Democratic Party in general, with regard to maintaining a commitment to Taiwan. Discussions related to the potential 'Finlandization' of Taiwan implied that Washington is not trusted as much anymore; worse yet, Taiwan may become a mere pawn in ongoing, high-stakes negotiations between Washington and Beijing. For some policy advisors in Taipei, then-Secretary of State John Kerry in particular was not perceived as friendly towards Taiwan.

Notably, the pacifist wing of the Democratic Party is seen as quite willing to give up on Taiwan altogether. Obama is perceived as soft and maybe even weak. In particular, Obama knows that Americans right now would *not* want to go to war on behalf of Taiwan in spite of obligations from the TRA. Obama therefore possesses little room for manoeuvre in dealing with Xi and prefers that Taiwan avoids trouble with the Mainland.

Consider also the financial crisis of 2008 as an example of an important trend line that points away from an active US foreign policy *per se*. The PRC came out of the financial calamity from a few years ago relatively unscathed, while the forecast for US economy in the near term is not good in comparison. The US is in a crisis of confidence that shows no signs of ending. Furthermore, the PRC is the US's greatest creditor. Beijing does not favour Washington's continuing engagement in the region. At this point in history, the US needs China more than the reverse.

The fluctuation in US leadership in the region raises a degree of uncertainty in cross-Strait relations. Policy elites surveyed in Taipei recognize that their strategy would be to remain low-key in foreign policy and eschew dramatic change, maintaining pragmatic connections with Japan, the US and even China and, in a word, preserve the status quo. Taiwan must hope that the PRC, under these conditions, will respect its distinct identity and the realities of a separate political entity in Taipei.

One idea articulated by a number of interviewees in Taipei is for Taiwan to diversify trade and even its set of allies. In pursuit of greater security, the argument behind this option is that Taipei currently is too embedded in the triangular relationship with Washington and Beijing. For example, Taiwan should make an effort to get Japan to support its entry into the newly minted Comprehensive and Progressive

Agreement for Transpacific Partnership and other international entities. Taipei should broaden its 'New Southbound Policy' and deepen its links with South Asia, Southeast Asia and Australasia, a priority that policy advisors close to Tsai are pushing during her tenure. At the same time, if it goes in that direction, Taiwan must be prepared for PRC-initiated punishment, which could include loss of diplomatic links with countries, for instance, in Central and South America and the Pacific islands.

One interviewer asked, in the context of possible efforts towards economic diversification, about comparison of Taiwan with Canada. Both Taiwan and Canada live next door to an overwhelming neighbour. Reference to the Canadian effort to diversify trade and investment links through greater contact with Europe in the 1970s, which ultimately failed to shift the economy significantly away from the US, came to the fore. For Taiwan, a comparable attempt at economic diversification would be seen as quite likely to end up the same way.

From a Pan-Blue standpoint, the preceding illustration from Canadian history responds effectively to much of the criticism directed at KMT policies that have emphasized economic exchange with the PRC. Like Canadians at times vis-à-vis the US, the Taiwanese public is drifting into wishful thinking about transcending relations with the Mainland. Taiwan, as the saying goes, 'cannot live with China and cannot live without it'. It therefore is not realistic to see India, Southeast Asia or anything else as an alternative to building on economic exchange with China.

According to an interviewee, part of the problem with the KMT's engagement of the Mainland, however, had been that the opposition effectively lumped other domestic policy shortcomings under the Ma administration with his approach to cross-Strait relations. So the general attitude is thus quite negative. This led, in turn, to multiple problems. It set a high bar for the government to explain satisfactorily the benefits and importance of its cross-Strait economic policies. The public, however, may not fully realize what they are voting for or against at any given time. Very little international news is available through the media and the public is not well-informed about policy at that level. ECFA is a prime example. So, too, is CSSTA. A KMT policy advisor observed bluntly that if the university student leaders from the Sunflower Movement had questions and doubts about such government policies, they should have lobbied to engage directly with officials or requested parliamentary debate on the administration's cross-Strait policies rather than staging largely unhelpful public sit-ins, blockades and taking over government buildings.

Reality dictates that Taiwan must engage in closer economic interactions with the PRC. Tangible benefits accrue from working with the Mainland, as opposed to closing off Taiwan's market to the world's second largest economy. Taiwan can play a key role in the Greater China market. It also can use its advantage of a more developed service industry and IT sector as a regional hub for research and development. All of the other countries in the region are deepening ties with the Mainland; shunning this opportunity would further isolate Taiwan's international status and relevance. In fact, Taiwan became able to sign Free Trade Agreements (FTAs) in the region with New Zealand and Singapore only because the relations between China and Taiwan had stabilized and become less adversarial.

Reaping the fruits of cross-Strait economic integration may require years, but it is an essential step to take. Ma's administration followed that path from start to finish. In the short to medium term, the forces of globalization and closer economic interconnectedness mean that some sectors in Taiwan (e.g. agriculture, labour unions) will bear the brunt of stiff competition from the Mainland. Jobs will be lost. Over the long run, however, such structural changes in Taiwan's economy will help it move up the value chain and become more competitive in the region. Close advisors to the KMT acknowledged that the Ma administration is partially at fault for not being better at (re)allocating resources to those affected adversely by ECFA, along with not explaining sufficiently the bigger picture and imperatives of economic cooperation with the Mainland.

Tsai's presidency and cross-Strait relations

With the ongoing importance of the Mainland in mind, consider the initial signals coming from the Tsai presidency, along with a DPP-controlled Legislative Yuan, and their implications for cross-Strait relations. Tsai's speeches – both on the campaign trail, during her visit to Washington, DC in June 2015 as a presidential candidate, and beyond – place great emphasis on upholding and maintaining the status quo. Tsai's message of reassurance to Washington and Beijing casts against type; she is making the case that her presidency will not be like that of Chen Shui-bian. The Tsai government does not intend any provocation of the Mainland. Consider, for example, the Travel Agency Association (TAA). The TAA asked Tsai while on the campaign trail about limiting travel from the Mainland. Tsai gave the politically astute answer: "no".

Elites interviewed in Taipei predicted that Tsai will not declare independence and this is understood and accepted as the truth even by many on the Mainland, even if Beijing does not publicly disclose such thinking. Likewise, the DPP government will not do anything radical, such as changing the formal name of the country, even if the party commands a strong majority in the legislative branch. Continuity will be notable – for example, Tsai will participate in the celebration of the ROC's National Day. Our interviewees further explained that the Taiwanese electorate are more sophisticated than in the past and understand themselves, already, to be the ROC and not the PRC. Young people, in particular, feel that Taiwan is independent in all but formal terms. The basic response, in light of the status quo, is: "Why bother with independence?"

Even with a negative public perception of Ma's cross-Strait policies, it is highly unlikely that Tsai will dismiss publicly the 1992 Consensus. It is quite possible that, even if she also does not endorse formally the 1992 Consensus, the president will continue to affirm the content and principles in her speeches as president. Her advisors note that Tsai may try to repackage the ideas and the spirit of the 1992 Consensus in a new form.

Views are mixed about DPP priorities, with divisions across partisan lines. From the Pan-Green side, the government should make security its first priority. Its supporters see the policies of Ma as putting Taiwan directly and dangerously into China's orbit. When asked by an interviewer "Is the book *While England Slept* a good comparison?", Pan-Green adherents quickly said "yes".[3] Thus, by the next presidential election, Taiwan should seek to reverse its current situation on security by *demanding* that the PRC respect co-existence. Taiwan is democratic – the effective status quo of being recognized as a country is what Taiwan and the DPP wants. Taiwan might even seek formal independence via a referendum someday.

While Tsai remains aware of the PRC's concerns, along with preference for the status quo among leadership in the US, interviewees knowledgeable about Tsai's policy priorities explained that she still believes that Washington will sell arms to Taiwan. This is because President Tsai sees her record of reassuring the US about the stabilizing nature of a potential DPP government as being well-established. Worried about provoking China, Ma halted arms deals with the US during the last four years of his tenure. The result is very limited Taiwanese military capability as the DPP begins its time in office. Critics of the KMT's policy assert that Taiwan must protect itself and that arms sales are important in political and symbolic terms. It is *good* to purchase arms from the US, although weapons systems are *very* expensive. Arms sales help to maintain the status quo and keep close relations with the US. The TRA can be cited in favour of arms sales that effectively *reinforce* the status quo rather than threaten it. The basic idea here is peace through strength.

Those more Pan-Blue in orientation opined that the Tsai administration will not depart very far from the status quo. Tsai may not have a choice but to continue key aspects of Ma's cross-Strait policies. In saying that she would not make any unilateral changes to the status quo, Tsai effectively is reaffirming the core values of the 1992 Consensus. Thus, changes in Mainland policy can be expected, but within limits. No major party, whether the KMT or DPP, is likely to sustain much beyond 50 per cent support for any of its ideas at the stage of implementation. This is a problem embedded within the political system and therefore it is reasonable to expect minor alterations at most. Attitudes expressed from the Mainland, however, are likely to become stronger. Tsai is very Taiwan-centric, so Xi is likely to be displeased with the island's choice of a new government. There could be a 'face issue' with the DPP's victory and association with the idea of independence. All of that could strengthen the position of hawks on the Mainland because the military will pressure the leadership to be more assertive with Taiwan. In sum, the status quo, but perhaps a bit more negative than now, can be expected for cross-Strait relations.

Subjects stated that Beijing is observing cautiously and distilling the implications of a Tsai presidency. If it reaches out to Tsai, this would be a clear signal from the PRC that it is amenable to building ties, trust and open communication with the DPP government. Tsai has been touting the notion of consolidating Taiwan's consensus first, a theme she put forward in her first presidential bid back in 2012. Thus there is an opportunity for Tsai here; according to her policy advisors, if she can really deliver on her promise to find bipartisan support and consolidate Taiwan's consensus on managing relations with the Mainland, then it would give her much needed political capital in dealing with Beijing. Tsai could end up negotiating with the Mainland from a position of strength.

Interesting to ponder, as a possibility for the DPP government in Taipei, is the 'Nixon goes to China' scenario from 1972. Only the staunchest sceptic of communism – and Nixon's career met that description – could make the visit to Beijing and open up relations with China without arousing suspicion from the American public. As a DPP president, the general public in Taiwan can be assured that Tsai will not sell out Taiwan's interests in dealing with Beijing.

Interestingly, Tsai possesses the potential to be like Nixon with regard to opening up China, namely, great credibility on the issue in terms of representing Taiwan assertively in any negotiations that might ensue. But will it happen?

This scenario can occur, but our respondents stipulated that it would happen with the precondition that Tsai is able to convince hard-liners in the DPP that it is safe to pursue a *rapprochement* with the Mainland. Tsai had been able to ride a wave of anti-Ma sentiment to the presidency, but the deep Green faction advocating formal independence makes life difficult for the DPP once in power. Hard-liners oppose a peace deal and see pursuit of anything like that as a sign of weakness. Tsai is parsimonious with political capital and that is likely to continue. Silence about China is optimal from the standpoint of domestic politics and that can happen if the KMT's implosion is sustained in years to come and effective opposition remains absent.

Another obstacle to significant negotiations identified by subjects could come from the Mainland. Tsai is seen by Beijing as quite ideological and possibly more difficult to deal with than the last DPP president, Chen Shui-bian, regarded by Beijing as a 'politician' who could be incentivized to cooperate. Tsai is well known and disliked by Beijing as the chief architect of the former KMT President Lee Teng-hui's cross-Strait policy. She came up with the term 'special state-to-state' relationship in describing cross-Strait relations for Lee. Xi could very well come out and simply denounce Tsai – some on the Mainland already see her as arrogant – making the noted Nixon-style scenario impossible for the foreseeable future. Thus, a more feasible story line may be that the *Mainland* will be the one to originate talks, if they do occur at all. Given Tsai's statements about the PRC not accommodating Taiwan's views, however, a Beijing-initiated negotiation also seems improbable for at least the near future. In response to Tsai, Xi simply reaffirmed the idea of one country with two systems.

One further reason that the Nixonesque scenario is not likely any time soon follows on from the circumstances of Tsai's first presidential term. Great pressure exists to focus on economic challenges at home because DPP supporters have emphasized problems such as housing, food safety, social welfare for a rapidly ageing population and pension reform. Tsai recognized that priority even before the election by announcing a new economic policy on 22 September 2015. While Tsai eventually might offer a trade of no independence in return for no invasion, concerns exist in the DPP that economic osmosis is very far along already and possibly irreversible.

Over and above results directly from the election of 2016, what is the likely future of Taiwan's party system after the election? Pan-Green supporters worry about a 'scorched earth' approach from the KMT in at least the short term. As DPP advisors warned, the KMT will 'raise hell' in ultra-partisanship and claim that the DPP is destabilizing Taiwan. The DPP therefore will experience difficulty in governing because career administrators overwhelmingly are from the KMT. One interviewer relayed an anecdote about President John F. Kennedy describing his dealings with the State Department as being like punching a feather pillow and ending up getting hit by it and the interviewee agreed that governing is likely to be just that way for the DPP. Tsai, however, still can succeed because of being highly educated, with a doctorate, and knowledgeable about trade negotiations.

What advice might be given to the KMT in light of its poor electoral performance in 2016? It needs to move towards the centre and become more Taiwan-focused. The 'old guard' within the KMT leadership has prevented the younger generation from rising in its ranks, so the party needs a reshuffle. There is a great need for renewal of the leadership and the coalition is incoherent at present. It would be wise to *purify* the leadership, according to an interviewee familiar with the inner workings of the KMT. Any potential unifying figure must be relatively young and charismatic and embrace a new sense of Taiwanese identity emerging in local politics.

Leadership change could produce a recovery if carried out with skill and foresight. But the KMT is unlikely to learn quickly from its loss in the election and heavy in-fighting is a problem. Our interview respondents suggested that at least a decade will be required to accept the necessary insights from the historic losses of 2016 – maybe more. The KMT practices 'old people' politics. It even could be 20 years or longer before the KMT comes back. Problems within the KMT, which reinforce the idea of a realignment towards the DPP being in progress or already achieved, are illustrated by the ill-fated presidential candidacy of Hung Hsiu-chu and its connection to KMT in-fighting, along with persistence of the People First Party.

Hung Hsiu-chu did not even mean to run and merely filled a gap in leadership for the KMT.[4] Hung had been the only candidate available, evoking a comparison with the highly unsuccessful Bob Dole in the US presidential election of 1996. She lacked experience in administration and failed at fundraising. Hung is a local, not national, personality, and too identified with unification. Her candidacy gave the appearance of a party insider who had come into the leadership role via connections rather than merit. Consider also the candidacy of Hung in the context of evolving Taiwanese identity. As a result of seeming to endorse the common interpretation of One China, she dropped to 13.67 per cent in the polls. The KMT candidate made her party appear out of touch with fundamental underlying public sentiments and thereby facilitated realignment of partisanship towards the DPP.

Hung's unsuccessful candidacy resulted from in-fighting between Ma and party leaders. Ma failed, in this instance and others, with management of *intra*party politics and that brought on the decline of the KMT. For example, Ma had a falling out with Wang Jin-pyng of the Legislative Yuan that became quite public and mutually destructive in 2013. Ma even filed a graft-related lawsuit against Wang. While Wang *was* bad, Ma aggravated the situation by making it so public. The president gambled on linking up with the PRC to obtain greater prosperity and divert attention from other problems, but that increasingly became unpopular.

What about charges that, put simply, 'Ma is stupid'? One Pan-Blue supporter asserted that Ma's persona at times is just an act. He is "pretending to be a pig in order to eat the tiger". In other words, his strategy and tactics vis-à-vis the Mainland are much more sophisticated than many imagine. Again, these are the views and voices of those we interviewed.

Persistence of People First, a very Blue offshoot party, is problematic for the KMT as it seeks to rebuild support. James Soong, a second-generation Mainlander with great affection for China, is the standard-bearer for People First. Soong opposes abolition of Taiwan's status as a Chinese province and sees himself as the *true* voice of the KMT. He wants to protect People First from disappearing, which would produce additional support for the KMT. As one person colourfully put it, Soong is protecting his "chicks" in the Legislative Yuan. Critics, however, point to Soong's age as a problem that prevents him from relating effectively to today's electorate. The basic reaction from young people often is "who is James Soong?". People First therefore faces an uncertain future. KMT and People First would seem to have an incentive to join forces after the major DPP victory of 2016. Otherwise, People First may live on in a very limited and ineffective way while drawing support away from the KMT, to the detriment of both parties.

Serious problems beset the KMT, so the DPP therefore might appear to be poised to stay in power a very long time as a result of realignment among voters. Others, however, see the jury as still out on the subject of a stable shift in partisanship. The 2000 election and initial DPP victory in the presidential race did not last at all – definitely not a critical election – and thus it is important not to overreact this time. KMT support declined in the last eight years and loss of the presidency and Legislative Yuan could signal potential realignment. Furthermore, civil society movements against the KMT have gained momentum over the years. The critical mass of society seems, however, to be *independent* rather than DPP in partisanship. Thus, the best answer on realignment still is 'maybe'. To build on its success and solidify a realignment that may be underway, the DPP will need to be strategic and not move towards socialism – instead, expect it to be centrist and try to gain trust from the public.

What about being Taiwanese, Chinese or both? Our interviewees had many interesting thoughts. Inhabitants of the island are trying to figure out what those terms mean now. Consider the meanings attached to Taiwan and being Taiwanese: What does 'I am Taiwanese' mean to you? According to one respondent: "It is my country and I love it." This interviewee also notes that "my family has been on the island since *before* the KMT". Taiwan is equated with freedom.

Taiwan faces a dilemma. Its identity is complex now. Along one dimension, citizens have the choice of identifying as Chinese, Taiwanese or both. The other dimension shaping the mindset is unification versus independence. About 80 per cent of Taiwanese say they are for the status quo. Designations as Chinese or Taiwanese are flawed, however, because they are too encompassing and the status quo holds multiple meanings depending on their sense of identity. For one respondent, at a personal level, "Taiwan is Taiwanese". Academically, he adds that "Taiwan is Taiwanese, but also not Chinese". Taiwanese people differentiate the Chinese culture and people from their government. Quite recently identification as Taiwanese is taken to mean that one has been *born* in Taiwan. A generational change towards a sense of being Taiwanese is clear to see.

What is the status quo and how does it play into the future? The Taiwanese people say that they like the status quo, but there is variation in what this means. As one interviewee humorously observed, it brings to mind chaos or quantum theory! The basic meaning that commands some agreement is functional, *de facto* as opposed to *de jure* independence.

With one interviewee, a *China Quarterly* article (Huang and James, 2014) became a topic. The article had identified youth as not being ideological. While youth are economically pragmatic, they also are disposed towards independence and that will impact significantly upon the likelihood of maintaining the status quo.

Some new developments are positive and others mixed from the standpoint of Taiwan. So the situation corresponds to one of the half full and also half empty glass. The rise of city-to-city contacts is a positive thing. The persistent status quo is good in political terms, but bad economically. Consider the business community. Executives are very concerned about the future of Taiwan. Recent years have seen a major exodus from Taiwan of executive talent. The Mainland is very nationalistic. The communist leaders at the top now are very bright and seek control of Taiwan through one means or another.

Analysis and synthesis

General characteristics

Findings from the research interviews with policy elites in Taipei between 2015 and 2016 present an interesting puzzle: if more Taiwanese support the status quo indefinitely in cross-Strait relations, how and why do people in Taiwan increasingly identify themselves as distinct from Mainland China? Policy elites reflect on three key factors shifting Taiwan's public opinion, particularly with regard to the island's sense of distinctiveness from the Mainland.

For one, more than half a century of separation (over 70 years since the inconclusive end to the Chinese Civil War) means that people in Taiwan are growing less attached to the Mainland. The symbolic attachment and longing for "returning to the motherland" are waning with the inevitable demographic shift in Taiwan. During the Ma presidency, the KMT government sought to deepen and broaden cross-Strait ties and interactions, in the hopes that increasing people-to-people exchanges would lead to political *rapprochement* and a greater sense and appreciation of the shared "Chinese" traditions and culture across the Taiwan Strait. (As one interviewee had summed it up, "the more we [in Taiwan] interact with people from the Mainland, the less we like about China"). The interactions with Mainlanders crystallized the clear gaps in political culture, values and systems, including freedom of speech, freedom of the press, religious tolerance and acceptance, the rule of law, and political accountability. Scepticism grew as a result of more contact. This growing divide cuts across age, socioeconomic status, ethnic background and education. In other words, it is not simply a cohort-related issue, where the younger generation is more sceptical of closer ties with the Mainland than the older generation.

Second, China's policy inadvertently plays an important role in shaping Taiwan's sense of distinctiveness. What Beijing does (or does not do) is also an important and determining factor. Beijing's policy receptiveness (or lack thereof) towards Taipei and on cross-Strait relations shapes Taiwan's self-image and identity. For over two decades, both Beijing and Taipei adhered to a neither legal nor binding consensus. The 1992 Consensus worked, as long as Taipei and Beijing agreed to honour the principal points of the agreement: both sides of the Taiwan Strait understand that there is One China and that each side would interpret that differently. This unique arrangement is something the general public and the government in Taipei initially accepted. At a minimum, it captures the political reality that separate entities exist across the Taiwan Strait.

In recent years, however, the Mainland has been more adamant in asserting the notion that Beijing is the only legitimate representative government of the One China, using material force, threats and coercion when necessary. These actions undermine public trust in Taiwan about the Mainland and encourage belief that the latter is not negotiating in good faith. Beijing's insistence on One China continues to squeeze and paralyse Taiwan's international space, even in functional areas of cooperation such as disaster relief, public health, aviation safety and criminal investigations. The Mainland also ignores the fact that a separate seat of government is located in Taipei and that the island has evolved and become a fully functional democracy. All of this has led to a more sceptical and pessimistic attitude in Taiwan about the Mainland and a growing sense of separation from Beijing's orbit.

Third, and finally, government policies in Taipei with regard to cross-Strait relations can impact upon Taiwanese identity as well. Former president Chen Shui-bian and his DPP administration from 2000 to 2008 went to the extremes of creating unnecessary hostility and provocation towards the Mainland. Chen's proposals and attempts to put on a plebiscite and alter the status quo in favour of *de jure* independence failed. Ma's presidency reversed most of Chen's course of action and took cross-Strait policies to the exact opposite position. Ma increasingly looked like someone rushing into a détente with the Mainland, which prompted the electorate in Taiwan to question the government's motivation and take issue with the opacity in its negotiations with Beijing.

From observing and analysing the political developments in Taiwan over the last decade and a half, the general public's preference and sense of identity have become more apparent: the two extreme ends of the political spectrum (e.g. unification and declaration of *de jure* independence) increasingly are marginalized. Voters instead favour stability and predictability. Tsai's government seemed to have tapped into this public sentiment during the election campaign. She proposed to forge greater cohesion and consensus within the Taiwan electorate about the nature of the status quo. The basic components of a Taiwanese consensus are that Taiwan is a *de facto*, separate entity that is self-governing under the rule of law, democratic principles and ideals. These traits are what make Taiwan and its inhabitants distinctive from, but not a threat to, the Mainland.

Findings from the elite interviews indicate that Taiwanese identity does not neatly co-vary along strict ethnic or racial lines. In fact, ethnic identification – whether the individual migrated from the Mainland in the 1940s or grew up on the island – is but one aspect of Taiwan's complex and changing identity. A majority of those living in Taiwan identify themselves as Han Chinese, but the study of Taiwanese identity has revealed a more fine-grained breakdown of such sub-ethnic groups as the Holo, Hakka, Mainlanders, and the original inhabitants of the island, who are Austronesians in origin. When identity is expressed in political terms, these ethnic divisions become less salient as distinctive markers. Those supporting eventual unification in Taiwan in the Pan-Blue camp draw adherents from each of these various sub-ethnic groups on the island. Likewise, those in the Pan-Green coalition represent a similar and diverse make-up.

Internal versus external identity forces

Simplifying identity politics on the island to just Mainlanders (*Waishengren*) and Taiwanese (*Benshengren*) thereby belies the fact that the process of localization (Taiwanization) has become an increasing trend in recent years, an observation reflected in the elite interviews from this chapter. Put simply, more than seven decades after the Chinese Civil War, the reality of a divided Chinese nation, broadly speaking, has cultivated a distinct sense of increasing self-awareness and self-identity for those making a living on the island of Formosa. National identification for a substantial majority of Taiwan's population is becoming more pragmatic: they agree with Taiwan independence if there is no military threat from China and are likewise open to a political union if the Mainland becomes similar to Taiwan in political, economic and social conditions.

These characteristics, moreover, are central to Taiwanese identity. Protection of labour rights, civil liberties, freedom of speech and religion, and the rule of law exemplify important achievements in Taiwan's democratization. All of these traits reflect the political culture and values organically developed and cultivated on the island since martial law was lifted. Taiwan's highest court and government became the first in Asia to recognize same-sex marriage in 2019 – a further reflection of Taiwan's deepening commitment to human rights as a core value of its emergent identity. The label of being Taiwanese reflects this trend and draws wide-ranging support that cuts across and draws from different ethnic lines and party identification.

At the same time, exogenous and broader structural factors contribute to this growing sense of distinctiveness and pragmatism in Taiwanese identity. First and foremost is China's economic modernity and rapid ascent in regional and global affairs, all of which have considerable effects on Taiwan's identity formation. The vast economic opportunities of the consumer and labour markets on the Mainland are powerful incentives that draw Taiwan closer into the Chinese leadership's orbit. China's increasing material capabilities, especially its armed forces, further deter the nationalistic Taiwanese from formalizing their independence-leaning campaigns.

Despite China's economic and military advantages and superiority, however, Taiwan has not capitulated. Ongoing resistance speaks volumes about its unique identity, as well as the salience of such non-material, ideological factors as the rule of law, protection of basic human rights and individual freedoms, democratic elections, and a culture of political accountability that have bound a collective sense of identity on the island. For the Taiwanese electorate, any meaningful *rapprochement* needs to be premised on seeing measurable progress in these areas on the Mainland. The 'one country, two systems' formula and model can work only if and when the Mainland converges with Taiwan on values. This is perhaps one of the key reasons why ongoing social unrest in Hong Kong matters greatly even beyond the fate of the former British colony. There are unintended consequences for the political future of cross-Strait relations as well, whereby Beijing's approach towards curtailing the civil liberties of Hong Kong becomes a harbinger for the Chinese leadership's tolerance of political autonomy and dissent across the board. In short, what the Mainland does or does not do in regard to repression of dissent would further determine the rate in which the distinct sense of Taiwanese identity grows and deepens on the island.

What about the US role in cross-Strait relations? This is another major determinant shaping and affecting Taiwan's identity formation. A sustained level of support from the White House and Capitol Hill can strengthen the island's defence capabilities and economic vibrancy. Doing so could increase Taiwan's self-confidence vis-à-vis the Mainland. Taipei's leaders then would enter into any negotiations with Mainland counterparts from a position of strength, knowing full well that political backing from Washington will be sustained.

Sudden or even gradual reversal of such support could alter Taiwan's identity in significant ways. If the US follows through on Trump's pledge to reduce its military operations abroad, then Taipei cannot count on Washington to intervene, should cross-Strait relations escalate into military conflict. Without a security guarantor like the US, Taiwan would be entering into any negotiation with the Mainland from a weakened position. If US support diminishes, the national identification preferences for Taiwan's electorate could see a dramatic shift (or return) towards a more favourable view of Sinicization and possibly even some form of political union with China. The geostrategic reality of living next to a potential economic and military juggernaut without any real sense of the US as a security guarantor would alter Taiwan's political calculus and sense of identity.

Taiwan's identity thus has shifted towards increasing pragmatism in recent years. In synthesizing the research interviews, the findings point to a consistent view where the island's inhabitants increasingly see themselves as Taiwanese. Interviewees identify with the democratic values of a free and open society that stand in stark contrast to Mainland China and provide a beacon of hope for Hong Kong. Thus we see a definite bias towards Ideological Ideation and value-based motivations, not personal gain.

Just as internal developments and democratization over the decades have helped foster a distinct sense of being Taiwanese, there are equally powerful and salient forces from beyond the island that shape and affect the politics of identity formation. Taiwan's self-image and identity also are by-products of the role and influence of the US and China, as well as the state of their bilateral relations. Interestingly, in *The China Choice: Why America Should Share Power*, Australian scholar and former deputy secretary in the Department of Defence in Canberra, Hugh White, observes that neither China nor the US 'can hope to win a competition for primacy outright, so both would be best served by playing for a compromise' (2013: 66). Within the context of Northeast Asian security, White therefore prescribes a unique set of security arrangements and through a policy proposal that he terms a 'Concert of Asia'. Within this Concert, Washington and Beijing should treat each other as equals and demarcate two clear spheres of influence. The strategic consideration behind White's logic is that if a balancing coalition against China's rising power is impending, then it is quite possible that Washington can retain a leading role in the Asia-Pacific, with critical support from those around the region alarmed by China's disruptive rise. White (2013: 66) opines that

> Asia's strategic alignments over the next few decades are going to be much more complicated than a simple 'with us or against us' ... [East Asian countries] will not sacrifice their interests in peace and stability, and good relations with China, to support U.S. primacy unless that is the only way to avoid Chinese domination.

More recently, Han and Paul (2020: 1) explain that the key factors explaining the absence of intense hard balancing in the region, either by or against China, include (1) 'deepened economic interdependence China has built with the potential balancers, in particular, the United States, Japan, and India'; and (2) 'the grand strategy of China, in particular, the peaceful rise/development, and infrastructure-oriented Belt and Road Initiative'; and 'any radical changes in these two conditions leading to existential threats by the key states could propel the emergence of hard-balancing coalitions'. Would the two sets of conditions identified by Han and Paul (2020) be about to change in the post COVID-19 world? The results would likely have further implications for Taiwan's identity evolution and cross-Strait relations.

To a large degree, the preceding analysis and logic from White reflect the current security landscape in the Asia-Pacific region. From Taipei's vantage point, as well as that of a number of capital cities in Northeast Asia, Washington and Beijing are important partners for different reasons; the former a significant security guarantor while the latter is arguably the most essential trading partner. Forcing Taipei to choose one side or the other becomes problematic and may unduly complicate relations with these two strategic powerhouses in the Asia-Pacific, a position that would undermine its emerging preference for pragmatism in managing cross-Strait relations.

Summing up

Multiple waves of interviews for elites from the government, academe and media of Taiwan point towards a complex and evolving identity for Taiwan. A wide range of issues that combine material and ideational aspects can be identified in connection with a sense of self, with abstract, ideological factors exerting the most influence. Interviewees confirm that forces on and beyond the island have impacted upon how people see themselves. A range of identities can be identified along the way, with an increasing movement among upcoming age cohorts in the direction of a sense of being primarily Taiwanese. At the same time, an identification with Han Chinese customs and practices persists in tandem with a desire to keep at least some distance in institutional and economic terms. All of this leads effectively into the next chapter, which looks at survey data to obtain breadth that will complement the depth given by interviews.

Notes

1. For example, an interviewee initiated a discussion of the wave-based theory of democratization from Huntington (1991).
2. This epithet had been a standard in *The People's Daily* from the Maoist era.
3. Authored by John F. Kennedy prior to his time as president of the United States, the book condemns the failure of leadership in the UK to take action to deter aggressions by Nazi Germany that culminated in the Second World War.
4. Note that party chair Eric Chu replaced Hung as the presidential candidate at the KMT Special Convention on 17 October 2015.

6

Popular Reflections (Survey I)

Overview

This chapter reports and assesses popular reflections on the basis of evidence gathered during an online survey in 2015. The contents of the survey permit assessment of Taiwanese voters' participation and identity formation, along with their views about cross-Strait relations and the role of the US in Northeast Asia. Evidence gathered through the surveys strongly corroborates the patterns from elite reflections and interviews reported in the preceding chapter while also offering data on some aspects that have been covered less so far.

This chapter provides empirical support for the theoretical approach of analytic eclecticism and systemism described in Chapter 4. As shown in that theoretical chapter, the issue of Taiwanese identity, the rise of China, cross-Strait relations and the US presence in Northeast Asia cannot be satisfactorily and effectively explained with one single theoretical paradigm. Several prevailing International Relations paradigms – realism, liberalism and constructivism – would lead the dynamics of cross-Strait relations in their respectively distinct directions. Empirical evidence presented in this chapter, together with material presented in the preceding and next chapter, is part of the effort to unite inter-paradigm ideas and evidence to produce improved explanations of what goes on across the Taiwan Strait.

Work in this chapter on survey results for popular reflections unfolds in three following sections. The second section conveys basic traits of the survey and sample. The third section offers analysis and synthesis by linking elite interviews with surveys on issues that pertain to the political economy of China's rise, cross-Strait relations, Taiwanese identity and US activity in Northeast Asia. The fourth and final section sums up the contributions of the chapter and sets the stage for the second survey that follows in Chapter 7.

Basic traits of the survey and sample

Conducted by Frank C.S. Liu of the Institute of Political Science at the National Sun Yat-Sen University between 20 November and 14 December 2015, the online survey collected 824 valid responses.[1] The distribution of respondents in the sample includes 38.2 per cent from northern Taiwan, 19.3 per cent from central Taiwan, 30.8 per cent from southern Taiwan and 2.5 per cent from eastern Taiwan. Demographic data on gender and age also reveal a range of respondents: 40.9 per cent are male, while 59.1 per cent are female, with 35.3 per cent in their 20s, 26.5 per cent in their 30s, 17.8 per cent in their 40s and 21.4 per cent in the age groups above those cohorts. The majority of the respondents are single, 69.5 per cent, while 27 per cent are married.

Validity for online surveys is an ongoing matter of contention. This study is no different in that its collection method is open to question. Data obtained through online surveys do tend to skew the sample towards the younger age cohorts. In this particular case, respondents under 50 have been more likely to participate in the survey, in all probability due to a greater degree of comfort with technology witnessed in other contexts as well. For several reasons, however, this distribution should not cause significant problems for our analysis.

First, the skewness is in a direction that points towards the future. On the one hand, people over 50 have a higher likelihood of pro-Mainland or even pro-unification views. On the other hand, these generations are gradually diminishing on the island. Thus, the older age cohorts are unlikely to significantly influence the formation of the new Taiwanese identity among younger generations of citizens. At the same time, the higher age groups are present to a degree sufficient to reveal their views, which continue to exert influence in the short-to-medium term.

Second, the age-related challenge to representativeness is not unique to our survey. For instance, there has been a recent debate in Taiwan among major survey agencies and TV stations on whether to allow mobile phone numbers to be included in the randomized pool to draw interviewees for opinion polls in presidential elections (Yeh et al, 2019). Use of a traditional landline is more likely to be tied to the older generation of voters, which potentially creates a selection bias that is opposite to what online surveys might encounter. In a way, online polls, like this one, may serve as a balance to what traditional surveys fail to capture. Moreover, as Hsu (2018: 93) points out, 'internet and social media have helped the rise and construction of Taiwan identity'. In this day and age, the internet is playing an increasingly dominant role in popular participation. Researchers must find ways to capture empirical data through online platforms, such as the one through which this poll was conducted.

Third, and finally, the Taiwan National Security Survey Data gathered by Emerson Niou of Duke University, to be discussed in greater depth in Chapter 7, relies upon a traditional telephone survey method. Data in that chapter serves as an interesting comparison to the online survey data, the primary focus of this chapter's analysis. The combination of elite interviews in the preceding chapter, online surveys in the present chapter, and traditional telephone surveys in the chapter to follow provides a comprehensive set of empirical evidence to assess the ongoing relevance of findings from prior academic research. The mixed methodologies and data are a reflection of the analytic eclecticist approach used in this research project.

Before continuing with the main focus on Taiwanese identity, a brief presentation of the descriptive data can help to present a fuller picture of reflections obtained from the Taiwanese public. This data includes responses to questions about items such as perceptions about Chinese culture, identity, economic prospects and travel etc., which can prove revealing in various ways.

Figure 6.1 reveals that 74 per cent of the respondents have not visited the Mainland in the past five years, whereas only 26 per cent have done so. Furthermore, the two top-ranked reasons for the respondents to visit the Mainland are for tourism – no. 1 (score 847^2) and business/investment – no. 2 (score 274) in Table 6.1. The natural question that arises is this one: why have well over a majority of those surveyed not visited the Mainland?

One reason might be that, since the proportion of respondents in their 20s and 30s is substantial, most of those surveyed are too young to hold high positions in well-established businesses. The lack of substantial business ties to the Mainland in the younger generation, moreover, is likely to affect the nature of a uniquely Taiwanese identity among such voters. Those who have been to the Mainland are about three times more likely to visit for tourism rather than business or investment reasons.

Next on the list from Table 6.1 are academic, non-government or cultural exchanges (no. 3–266) and study (no. 4–176). These activities, on average, would be either neutral or point towards younger people in terms of involvement. In addition, and perhaps a reinforcing point

Figure 6.1: Have you been to Mainland China in the last five years, excluding Hong Kong and Macao?

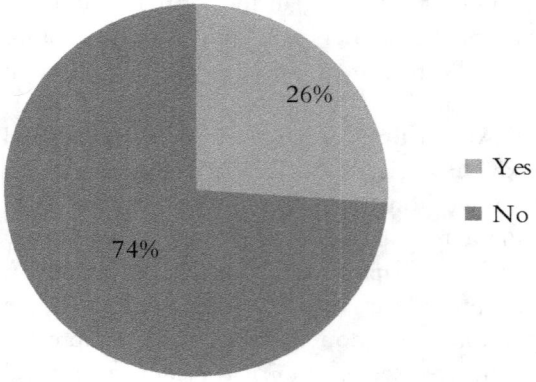

Table 6.1: What was your main purpose to visit Mainland China?

	Score*	Overall rank
Tourism	847	1
Business or investment	274	2
Academic, non-governmental or cultural exchanges	266	3
Study	176	4
Government or political activity	47	5
Total respondents	216	

Note: * Score is a weighted calculation. Items ranked first are valued higher than the following ranks, the score is the sum of all weighted rank counts.

Source: Liu (2015)

about patterns of activity for younger age cohorts in the sample, note the low number for government or political activity – no. 5 (score 47 in Table 6.1).

Most respondents, as revealed by Figure 6.2, believe the standard of living is better in Taiwan (62 per cent) than Mainland China (6 per cent) at the time of interview. Note, however, the high degree of uncertainty about whether that will persist – about one-third claim not to know (32 per cent).

Reinforcing the preceding point, Figure 6.3 shows that about a quarter (26 per cent) believe that the margin would be reversed in ten years' time. According to the graphic, slightly more respondents believe

Figure 6.2: Do you think the standard of living is better in Taiwan or Mainland China now?

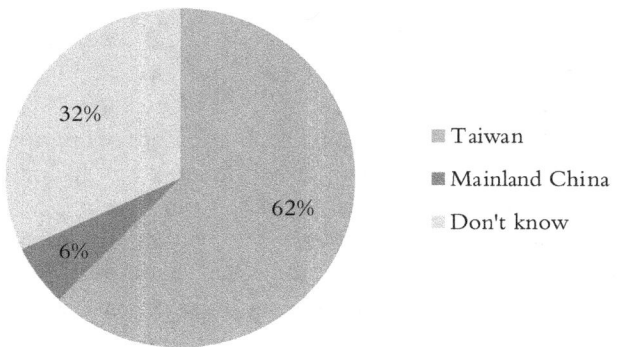

Figure 6.3: Do you think the standard of living will be better in Taiwan or Mainland China in ten years?

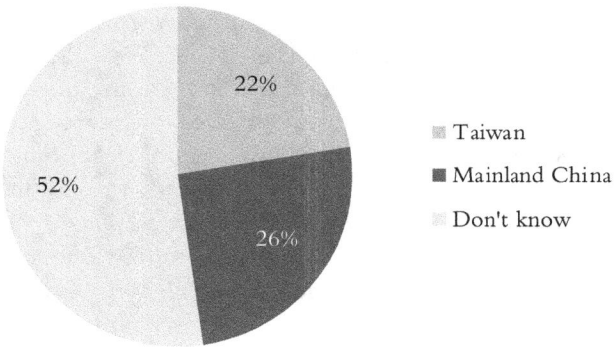

that the standard of living will be better in Mainland China (26 per cent) than in Taiwan (22 per cent) within a decade. Uncertainty is also noteworthy; 52 per cent of respondents claim not to know whether the Mainland or Taiwan will have a higher standard of living ten years later. This belief is in line with experience because change has been rapid and invites caution about forecasting the political economy of Northeast Asia. However, the fact that more people think that the standard of living will be better a decade from now for Mainland China in comparison to Taiwan than vice versa further deepens the mystery of why the Taiwanese people are reluctant to develop closer political ties and forge an identity that is closer to the Mainland Chinese. A desire for separation persists in spite of the widely accepted possibility for a good or even better standard of living on the Mainland. One possible explanation provided by Lepesant (2018: 70) is that young Taiwanese believe the elders took all the benefits of the 'economic miracle', leaving their generation only the problems to solve and they tend to view Taiwan as facing many limits and threats, such as a 'sluggish economy and mounting Chinese pressure'. This point will be addressed more at a later point in the chapter.

Moreover, consider Figure 6.4, which shows a continuum of opinion about China's economic rise as a threat or opportunity for Taiwan. Possible answers range from a very serious threat (0) to a very good opportunity (10). More respondents believe China's economic rise poses a threat (44.66 per cent of the respondents are in the threat direction, i.e. categories 1–4) to Taiwan than presenting an opportunity (34.22 per cent in the opportunity direction, i.e. categories 6–10). Slightly over one-fifth (21.12 per cent) of the respondents remain neutral (i.e. category 5) – interestingly enough, the highest percentage for any point along the continuum.

While more people see China's economic rise as a threat than an opportunity to Taiwan, a good number of respondents in Taiwan would be willing to wait and see what the Mainland would do in order to obtain a clearer vision. A prosperous economy on the Mainland alone does not necessarily make China less threatening to people in Taiwan. What matters more is whether China's economic prosperity can translate into tangible benefits to people in Taiwan. Recall that one interviewee in the previous chapter stated that public perception about ECFA is that it only "serves the interests of a few large business conglomerates and corporations that maintain close ties with the KMT". For example, increases in tourism rewards only a few large tourism companies. Moreover, increased economic power might encourage assertiveness and even aggressive policies in the near abroad. This could include activities on both land and at sea. Thus, what the Mainland does in connection with Taiwan matters more than the rise itself, which helps to explain the dispersion of answers in Figure 6.4.

Attention turns from material to ideational issues in Figure 6.5, which focuses on opinions about language use. The pie chart reveals that 64 per cent of respondents agree they should speak more native dialects or languages, such as Taiwanese, Hakka, or one of the Aboriginal options. This relatively high proportion suggests that language is a very essential part of cultural and social formation. The survey suggests that a majority of people in Taiwan, especially younger generations, prefer speaking more local dialects – or at least claim such a position. About one-third of respondents (33 per cent) offer

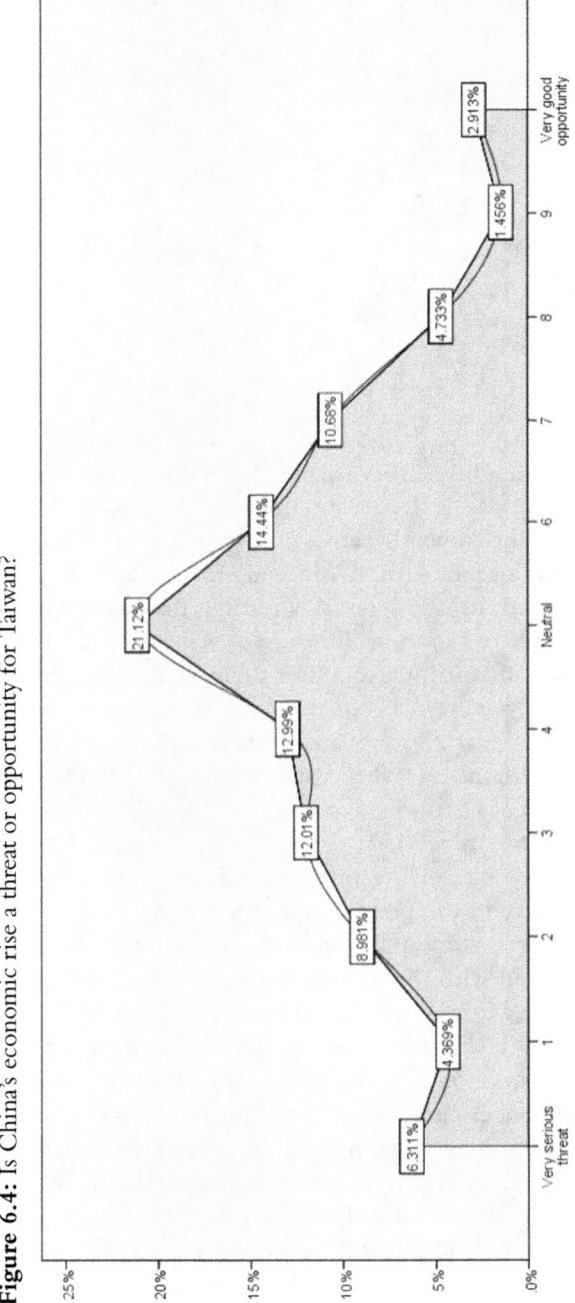

Figure 6.4: Is China's economic rise a threat or opportunity for Taiwan?

Figure 6.5: Do you think you should speak more native dialect or language, such as Taiwanese, Hakka or aboriginal language (November 2015)?

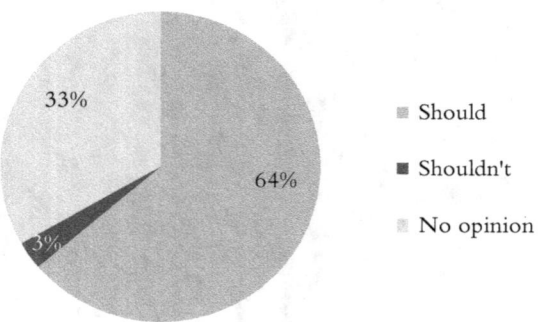

no opinion. Only a very small percentage (3 per cent) of respondents clearly oppose a departure from the exclusive use of Mandarin, which points towards active construction of a unique cultural and social experience that is different from the Mainland. This social reconstruction, if it persists, is leading in the direction of a different identity shared among Taiwanese. An indicator is that politicians in Taiwan like to mix together their Mandarin Chinese and one or several Taiwanese dialect(s) to show that they are different from the Mandarin-speaking-only mainlanders.[3] Note that many politicians from the Mainland 'who could speak only Mandarin, such as James Soong and Ma Ying-jeou, had to learn Taiwanese in order to campaign for electoral office' (Hsu, 2018: 96).

Although many Taiwanese see China as the centre for economic opportunity in the present and increasingly in the future, others still want to keep some political distance and, in particular, do not want to be united with the Mainland. Figure 6.6 shows the distribution of answers to a question about what respondents hope for regarding the cross-Strait relationship: 38 per cent of respondents prefer maintaining the status quo for now and decide later; 24 per cent prefer immediate independence; 22 per cent prefer maintaining the status quo for now and independence later; 12 per cent prefer maintaining the status quo indefinitely; 3 per cent prefer maintaining the status quo for now and unification later; and only 1 per cent prefer immediate unification. The status quo in general, regardless of its specific meaning for any given person, enjoys vastly more support than any other option. This is consistent with Lepesant's (2018: 75) observation that 'no matter

Figure 6.6: Do you wish the status of Taiwan and Mainland China to be unification, independence or status quo?

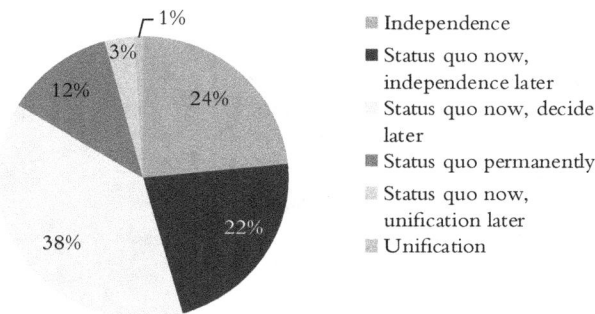

how the question of unification is looked at, the groups of potential supporters are shrinking'.

These numbers suggest that the overwhelming majority of Taiwanese are quite unsure about what kind of future cross-Strait relations they would like to experience. In particular, most Taiwanese see neither independence nor unification as an immediate option. This may not be entirely bad news for Beijing with regard to policy planning. Put simply, what Beijing does – most notably, the approach towards cross-Strait relations as well as development of its own political system – will have some bearing on how people in Taiwan see the future of cross-Strait relations.

What, then, does the concept of the status quo itself signal to respective respondents? As shown in Figure 6.7, for those who answered in any one of the following ways – maintaining status quo for now and decide later, maintaining status quo for now and independence later, maintaining status quo indefinitely, or maintaining status quo for now and unification later – 33 per cent think of the status quo as 'no unification, no independence, and no war'; 28 per cent as 'Taiwan as an independent sovereign state'; 26 per cent as 'ROC as an independent sovereign state', and 13 per cent as 'two Chinas, one on each side (mainland China and Taiwan)'. Taken together, these results once again confirm that the status quo can be associated with any number of meanings among contemporary Taiwanese. This range of beliefs can be traced to abeyances built into the 1992 Consensus or, for that matter, ambiguities that persist in public statements from leaders about the character of Taiwan in relation to the Mainland.

Figure 6.8 summarizes views from the survey about cross-Strait relations in particular. The pie chart reveals that most respondents

Figure 6.7: How would you describe the current status quo in the Taiwan Strait?

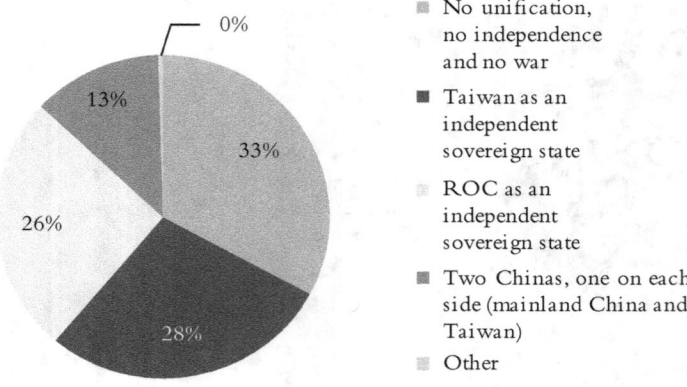

- No unification, no independence and no war
- Taiwan as an independent sovereign state
- ROC as an independent sovereign state
- Two Chinas, one on each side (mainland China and Taiwan)
- Other

Figure 6.8: How would you describe cross-Strait relations?

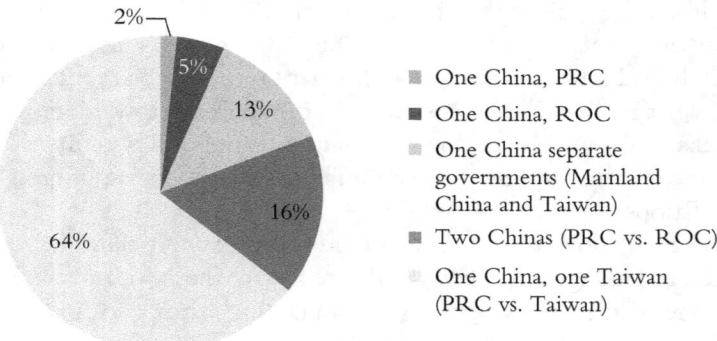

- One China, PRC
- One China, ROC
- One China separate governments (Mainland China and Taiwan)
- Two Chinas (PRC vs. ROC)
- One China, one Taiwan (PRC vs. Taiwan)

(64 per cent) believe there is one China and one Taiwan; 16 per cent think there are two Chinas (PRC vs ROC); 13 per cent think there is only one China consisting of two parts – Mainland China and Taiwan; 5 per cent think there is only one China – the ROC; and 2 per cent think there is only one China – the PRC. The results here reinforce the preceding chapter's analysis of beliefs about cross-Strait relations. Across the board, whether among policy elites or the general public, most Taiwanese offer very little explicit support for the 'one country, two systems' approach or the 1992 Consensus. The majority of Taiwanese view themselves as increasingly distinct from the One

Figure 6.9: Do you consider yourself Taiwanese, Chinese, both or other (November 2015)?

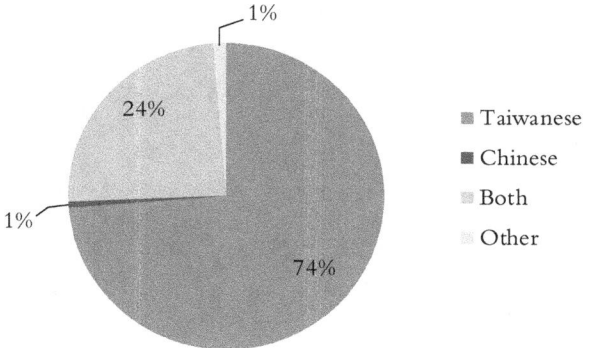

China identity – interestingly enough, the same perception (64 per cent) that are open to the use of multiple languages.

Figure 6.9 shows the distribution of responses to a direct question about self-designated identity: 'Do you consider yourself Taiwanese, Chinese, both or other?' (November 2015). Data in response to this query, perhaps, is the single most important to appear in this chapter. A significant proportion of those on the island see themselves as Taiwanese instead of Chinese. When asked about their identity, 74 per cent of the respondents perceive themselves as Taiwanese, 24 per cent self-identify as both Taiwanese and Chinese, and only about 1 per cent feel either Chinese or something altogether different from the two main options.

Figure 6.10 displays a bar graph that intersects the preceding categories of identity with whether a person has visited the Mainland. The figure reveals that knowing whether the respondent has been to the Mainland is informative about their self-designated identity in a limited way. While each category features a majority that has not visited the Mainland, the difference is by far the most visible for those who identify strictly as Taiwanese.

For those who identify as Taiwanese, what makes them think or feel that way? Table 6.2 lists the top five stated reasons: (1) eating Taiwan's rice and drinking Taiwan's water (growing up and being raised in Taiwan); (2) traditional Chinese; (3) democratic system; (4) freedom of expression, assembly, and religion; and (5) Taiwanese dialect. These reasons reflect the importance of Taiwan's unique socialization process, of which a sense of belonging to the island and democratization are

Figure 6.10: Cross-tabulation of identity and whether been to the Mainland

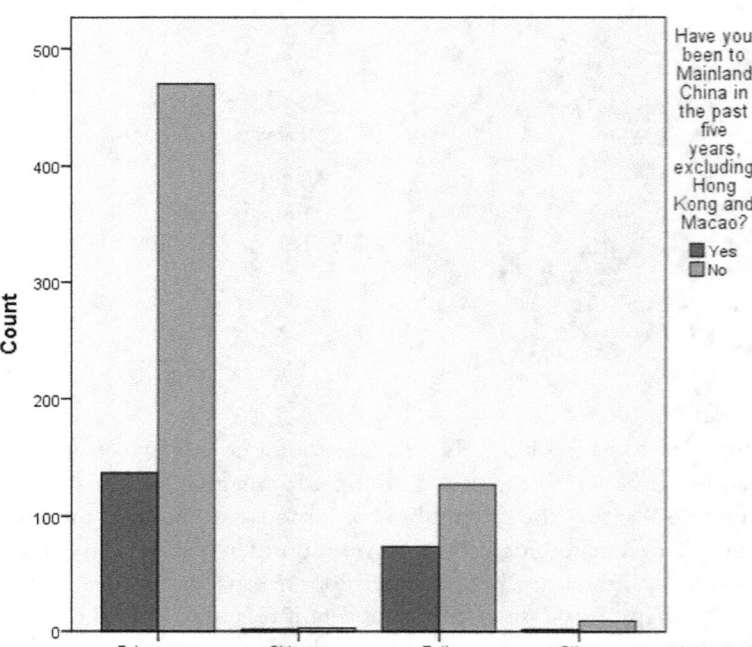

both critical parts. Note the presence of both material and ideational elements across the categories. And many of the top five listed factors are intangible cultural factors rather than tangible institutional factors, such as democratic institutions and specific types of freedom. This further illustrates the shift from materialist to postmaterialist priorities through self-expression values (Inglehart, 2016).

Within Table 6.2, the first two items on the list combine to tell an important story about evolving identity. First on the list is growing up in Taiwan – something soon to be possible for all but a small proportion of those who emigrate as adults to Taiwan. The second item, traditional Chinese, conveys a key point about culture. The Chinese culture clearly is important to at least some and perhaps many respondents who do not want to unify with the PRC. Such respondents clearly want to maintain a hybrid culture, within which a Chinese element continues to be welcome.

Figure 6.11 shows a continuum of positions on the subject of Mainland tourists visiting Taiwan. The range of opinions is from very much agree (0) to very much oppose.[4] The figure reveals that

Table 6.2: What makes you think or feel you are Taiwanese?

	Score*	Overall Rank
Eating Taiwan's rice and drinking Taiwan's water	6486	1
Traditional Chinese	6316	2
Democratic system	5843	3
Freedom of expression, assembly, and religion	5093	4
Taiwanese dialect	5043	5

Note: * Score is a weighted calculation. Items ranked first are valued higher than the following ranks, the score is the sum of all weighted rank counts.

Source: Liu (2015)

the number of people who are in favour of more Mainland tourists coming to visit Taiwan is slightly higher than the number opposed. Among respondents, 40.74 per cent (categories 1–4) support increased Mainland tourism, whereas 34.26 per cent (categories 6–10) are against it. However, a significant number of people – about 25 per cent appear in category 5 – remain neutral. Once again, a wide range of opinion is manifested on a subject related to contact with the Mainland – at 25 per cent, neutrality is the modal category.

Many people, it can be inferred, are taking a 'wait and see' approach in regard to tourists from the Mainland and probably other associated issues as well. Post-election statistics show that the number of Mainland tourists decreased significantly since Tsai won the election in 2016. Taiwan's tourist industry has expressed ongoing concerns about the decline, fearing a cooling down of the island's tourism, which in turn could lead to a decline in its economy.[5]

One especially interesting question to consider is what role tourism to Taiwan by the Mainland Chinese has played in cross-Strait relations during the PRC's rise. On the one hand, people seem to recognize the importance of contributions made by tourists from the Mainland to Taiwan's economy; on the other hand, as one interviewee reported in Chapter 5, "the more we interact with people from the Mainland, the less we like about China". This assertion draws attention to a truly ironic point of contention between Taiwanese perceptions about their economic future and political identity. To some extent, 'Chinese tourists have only reinforced existing group boundaries between Taiwan and the Mainland' (Lepesant, 2018: 80). The tension that exists between autonomy and prosperity also may account for why answers

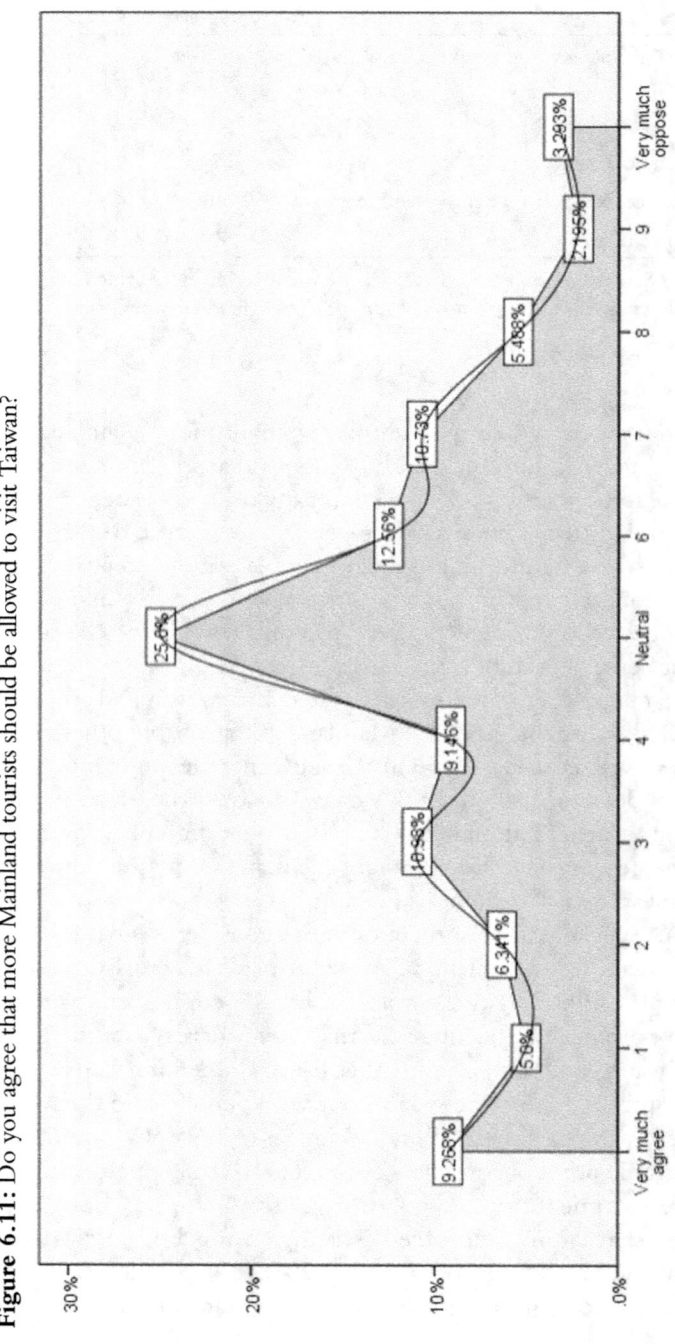

Figure 6.11: Do you agree that more Mainland tourists should be allowed to visit Taiwan?

Figure 6.12: Do you know what the '1992 Consensus' entails?

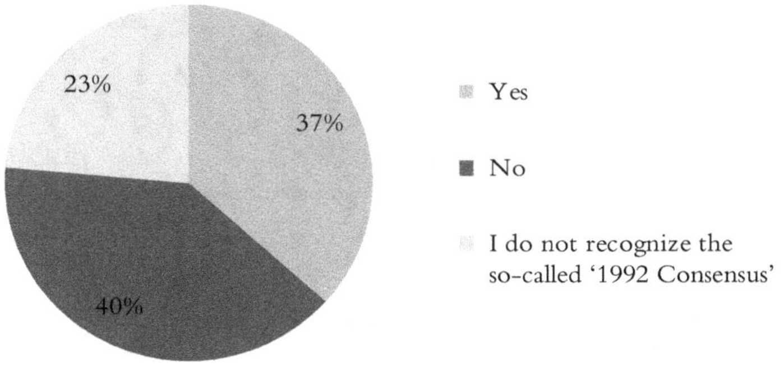

- 37% Yes
- 40% No
- 23% I do not recognize the so-called '1992 Consensus'

to questions with numerous categories tend to produce a relatively even distribution across them.

The 1992 Consensus represents an important identity-related legacy of negotiations involving the ROC and PRC. We saw growing scepticism reflected in elite views of the 1992 Consensus detailed in Chapter 5. What does Figure 6.12 say about mass views of the 1992 Consensus? About 23 per cent of respondents do not recognize the 1992 Consensus; 40 per cent do not know what the 1992 Consensus is; and 37 per cent know what the consensus is. Along the political spectrum, the first category probably picks up purely Green opinion, with the second and third categories including a more diverse set of positions from those in the middle through to Blue.

Figure 6.13 summarizes responses for a question that focuses on the 1992 Consensus in greater depth with regard to dispositions about its presumed contents. When further pressed about which part(s) of the 'one China with different interpretations' do you agree, 49 per cent of the respondents agree with the 'different interpretations' part of the 1992 Consensus, while only 7 per cent agree with the 'one China' part. Note further that 14 per cent agree with the entire statement and 30 per cent refuse to recognize the entire statement. This distribution of responses points once again to the ambiguity inherent in the 1992 Consensus from its inception onward. Furthermore, the majority of people believe that the long-standing consensus should be the basis of neither cross-Strait economic nor political negotiations.

Figure 6.14 shows a continuum of opinion about political unification for the ROC and PRC. Categories range from absolutely impossible (0) to 100 per cent possible (10). The figure reveals that the majority of respondents are not optimistic about a possible future political unification of Taiwan and Mainland China. Among respondents, 44.42

Figure 6.13: Of the two parts of the '1992 Consensus' – 'one China with different interpretations', which part do you agree with the most?

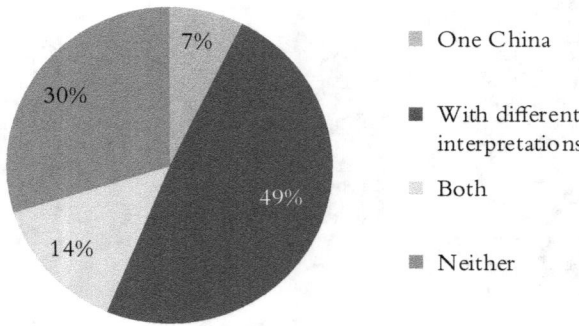

per cent are leaning in the direction of a future political unification not being possible (i.e. categories 1–4), while 36.17 per cent believe it could happen in the future (i.e. categories 6–10). Note that the peak of the distribution, as with other such continua, is reached at the neutral midpoint (i.e. category 5). Although this distribution of responses may look troublesome to a PRC in search of unification, it could also be viewed as an opportunity for the Mainland to put forward concrete initiatives that would improve its chances in the future.

Consider this situation in light of what has been learned about Brexit, a process of secession that can be informative in this context of irredentism for the PRC relative to Taiwan. The departure of Great Britain from the EU in 2020 is a movement away from an institution that in an objective sense virtually guaranteed greater prosperity over the long term. The victory of the 'Leave' side in the referendum, even in the face of likely economic costs, can be explained due to the *emotive* or identity-related elements that adversaries on the 'Remain' side did not take sufficiently into account (Guibernau, 2011). Leadership in the PRC may be in the process of making the same error – 'banking', it might amusingly be said, too much on economic factors that favour integration and simultaneously underestimating the emotional appeal of Taiwanese identity that is preserved best through autonomy.

Figure 6.15 displays a range of positions on the likelihood of US assistance in defending Taiwan from 0 to 100 per cent. Respondents' expectations about whether a firm US commitment to defend Taiwan, if a military conflict broke out in the Taiwan Strait, are the most scattered for a response to any question in the survey. Figure 6.15 shows that, when categories below and above 50 per cent are combined,

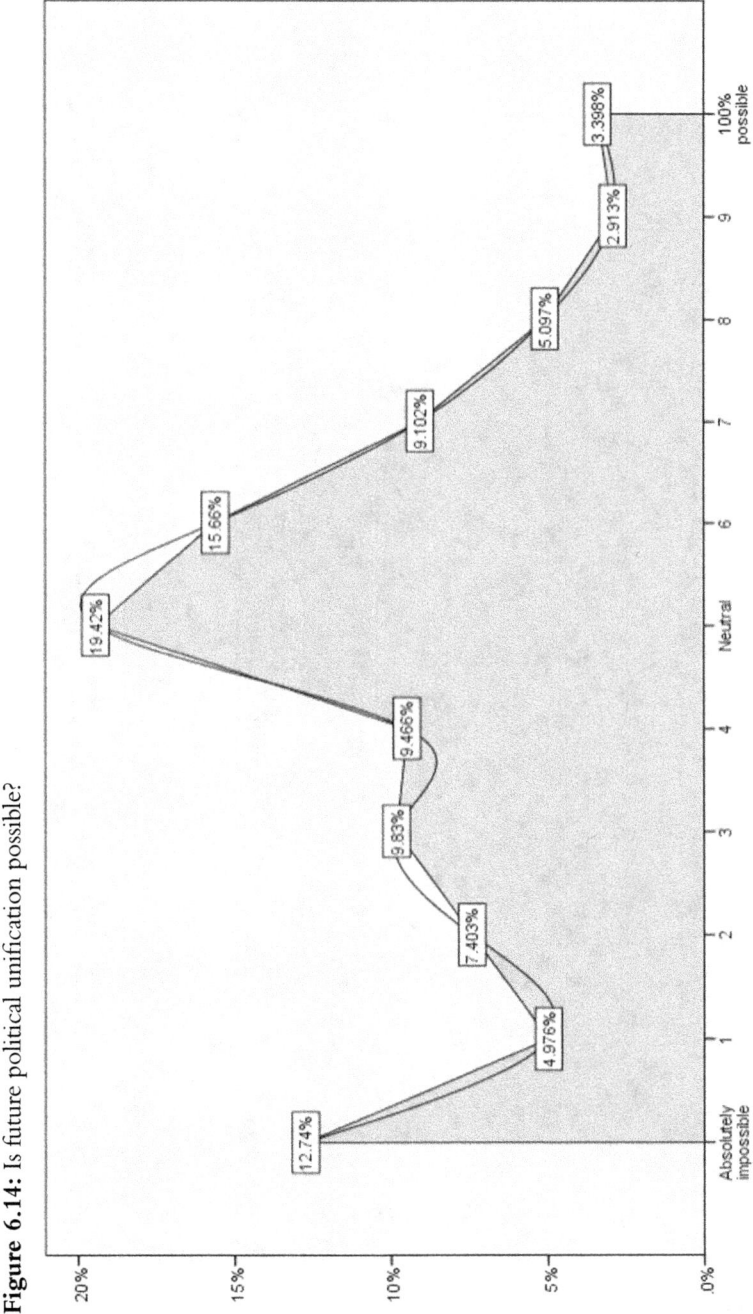

Figure 6.14: Is future political unification possible?

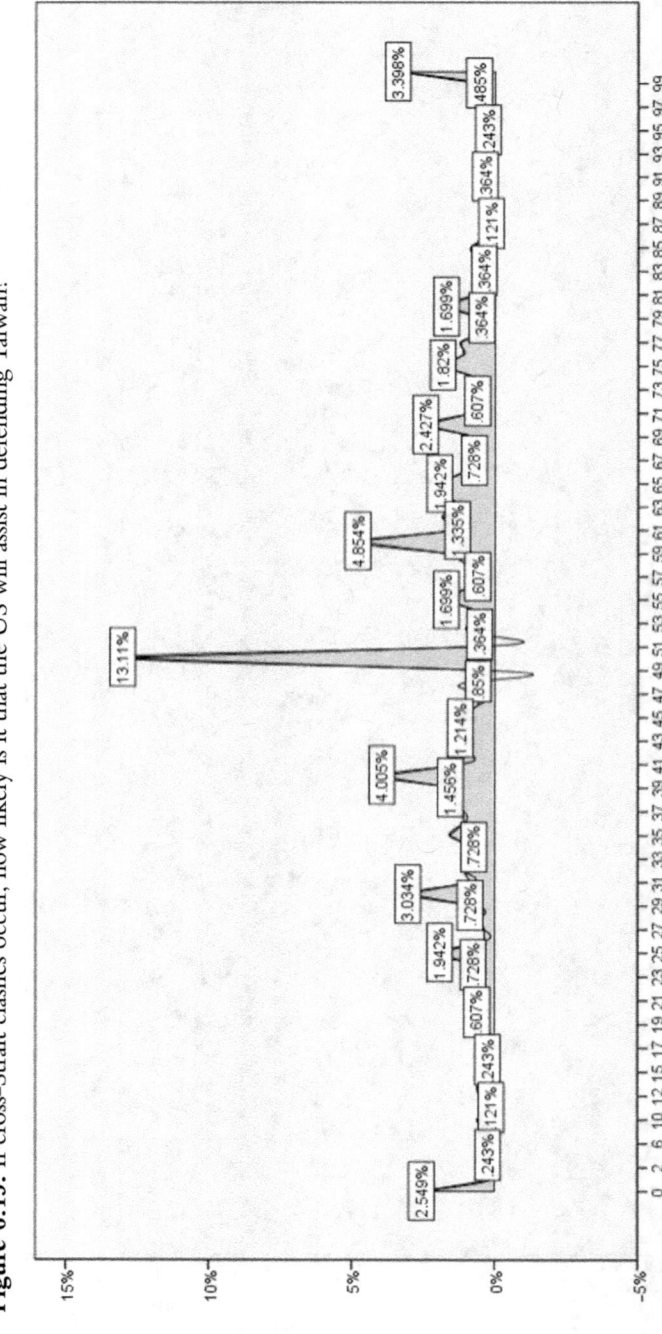

Figure 6.15: If cross-Strait clashes occur, how likely is it that the US will assist in defending Taiwan?

Figure 6.16: Do you agree or disagree that our culture is the traditional Chinese culture?

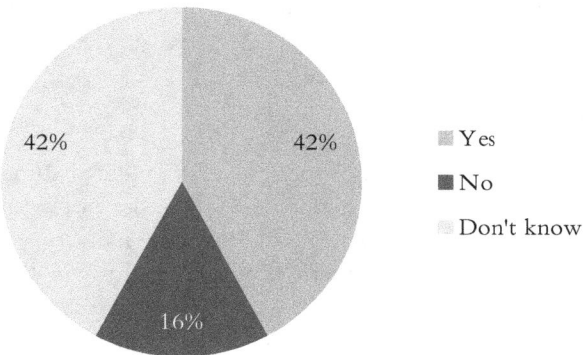

respectively, 39.4 per cent of the respondents believe that the US would not assist in defending Taiwan, whereas 47.4 per cent believe that it would. And 13.11 per cent are neutral on this question. This pattern of responses once again points towards uncertainty among Taiwanese about the intentions and likely actions of the US, a longstanding patron.

Finally, consider Figure 6.16, which shows results from an inquiry about the nature of Taiwanese culture in connection with the Chinese one. When asked if 'our culture' is the traditional Chinese variety, answers split evenly between those who agree and those who disagree – 42 per cent for each side – while 16 per cent do not know. While one bloc of respondents have questions about whether their culture is the same as the traditional Chinese one, the other bloc seems to think there is clear connection between these ways of life. It is very interesting to note that, if culture is measured by traditional Chinese characters, customs and holidays, cultural relics, and the like, many would find that Taiwan has preserved more traditional Sinic ways than the Mainland itself. Astute observers of comparative politics, such as Almond (1956), Verba and Almond (1965) and Chilton (1988), maintain that individuals can be (1) socialized into their culture but also (2) produce and reproduce culture. Clearly, the sense of Chinese culture has been evolving among the Taiwanese. Such changes, we believe, are linked to the dynamics of identity. This could be a clear sign of what Inglehart (1990) refers to as a 'a cultural shift'. On the one hand, people in Taiwan have preserved many similarities in culture with the mainland Chinese, with whom they share a common ancestry. On the other hand, the Taiwanese people's cultural values have been changing because their first-hand experiences have changed. If this shift in culture has an 'emphasis on self-expression values', such a cultural shift could lead to potential institutional changes further down the road (Inglehart and Welzel, 2001: 2).

Analysis and synthesis

Along with the most recent polls, the online survey suggests some dramatic and possibly even alarming trends that create the potential for escalated conflict. First, the newly formed Taiwanese identity – a self-image that differs from the dominant Chinese version on the Mainland – has been consolidated in recent years. Second, in spite of continuing economic and societal contact across the Taiwan Strait, the two sides are not moving down a clear path of political integration, a point underscored by elite reflections as well in Chapter 5. This section provides a possible explanation from a theoretical perspective and then begins to link the evidence from elite interviews and the online survey to each other.

From the standpoint of theory, Taiwan's identity change should be placed in a broader context of the political sociology literature, particularly in regard to associated issues of socialization and modernization (Lipset, 1959; Inglehart, 1981, 1990). In his seminal work, Lipset (1959) introduced the connection between economic development and democratic transition. Since then many studies have been done to further refine that causal mechanism (see Putnam et al 1994; Przeworski and Limongi, 1997, for example). Inglehart (1981: 882) tested the 'socialization hypothesis' and showed that after a period of 'sharply rising economic and physical security', people, especially younger groups who have been 'shaped by different experiences in their formative years', tend to show substantial differences in their 'value priorities'. For example, in 1949 when post-war reconstruction had just begun in Germany, ' "Freedom from Want" was the leading choice by a wide margin' for German citizens; however, by 1958, ' "Freedom of Speech" was chosen by more people than all other choices combined' (Inglehart, 1981: 883). These examples show that when people reach a certain level of material economic security, their priorities may shift to post-materialist values. These post-materialist values are linked to the rise of the 'new class' and higher likelihood of political change (Inglehart, 1981: 892, 894).

Although modernization is not linear, it has followed some generalizable patterns. For example, Inglehart and Welzel (2001: 2) put particular emphasis on the role of 'human development', of which identity is a critical part, and argue that 'modernization is evolving into a process of human development, in which socioeconomic development brings cultural changes that make individual autonomy, gender equality, and democracy increasingly likely, giving rise to a new type of society that promotes human emancipation on many fronts'. In general, Taiwan's democratization process has followed closely what the modernization theory has predicted. As Taiwan gradually moves from a materialist to a postindustrial society, a clear shift in cultural values can be detected in the form of a changing identity for the Taiwanese people.

Taiwan's cultural lineage to the Chinese culture is undeniably strong, but there have been clear signs of changes in cultural values, particularly in certain political values and identity. Gries and Su (2013: 74) point out that, with regard to the causes and consequences of how Taiwanese look at China, knowledge remains limited. According to Wang and Liu (2004: 574–576), survey data imply that cultural and political and identities may be incongruent in the Taiwanese context and some residents may regard themselves as politically Taiwanese and culturally Chinese. A decade ago, 43 per cent of those surveyed on the island identified as both Chinese and Taiwanese, with four multiple identities already in place: 'Taiwanese nationalist identity, the pro-Taiwan identity, the mixed identity, and the China identity' (Wang, 2004: 302; Wang and Liu, 2004: 576). Recent polls indicate that about three-quarters of the population identify themselves as Taiwanese (including the survey conducted in this project – 74 per cent), a two-decade high, so the island's identity may be converging towards some degree of consensus.

Several recent studies suggest that cross-Strait economic convergence, as evidenced by Taiwan's increasing dependence on Mainland China, has not led to any significant spillover into the political realm. On the contrary, economic convergence has led only to stronger political divergence between the two sides (Clark, 2007; Li, 2014a). China's recent favourable policies for Taiwan, such as the 31 Preferential Policies (31PP), have not helped either. In fact, these policies have made Taiwan even more alarmed about China's rise and Taiwan's dependence upon it. S. Lin (2016) argues that consolidated national identity has allowed the Taiwanese to separate their preferences regarding Taiwan's economic policy towards China from their preferences on Taiwan's future political status.

Particularly during the Ma Ying-jeou administration, Ma's pro-Mainland efforts to nurture human, economic and cultural rapprochement with the Mainland 'failed to enhance the appeal to Taiwanese youth of a possible unification with "the mainland"'

(Lepesant, 2018: 74). There are several possible reasons. First, many people in Taiwan have inferred that Mainland China's economic policies are intended to make the Taiwanese believe that 'Taiwan was doomed if it did not hasten the liberalization of trade in goods and services' with the Mainland. Second, 'this discourse was based on both the use of the fear of Taiwan's regional marginalization and the pride that could stem from a revived Chinese economic domination of the world'. And finally, 'the promised brighter future did not materialize' for many Taiwanese (Lepesant, 2018: 77–78). The result is that many in Taiwan see economic integration with the Mainland as a 'threat to Taiwanese employment' and a way of creating inevitable dependency on China (Lepesant, 2018: 78).

No longer can the complexity of the Taiwan issue be explained by economic factors alone. In particular, 'in spite of Taiwan's deepening economic integration with mainland China after Ma came to office in 2008, only a minority of the Taiwanese public holds favorable views toward China, and an increasingly substantial proportion even identifies themselves as Taiwanese only and Taiwan as a completely separate state from China' (Chen, 2017: 5). Social aspects, such as identity, also must be taken into consideration. The standard explanation for evolving Taiwanese identity in recent decades is, in a word, democratization (Wang, 2004: 293; Li, 2014a: 132).

Looking at this development from a broader perspective, Inglehart (1981), for instance, argues that as the middle class moves from materialism to post-materialism, values change for the 'new class' as it goes through a shared socialization process. New identities may be formed during this experience. Inglehart and Welzel (2001: 2–3) further explain that

> cultural emphasis shifts from collective discipline to individual liberty, from group conformity to human diversity, and from state authority to individual autonomy, giving rise to a syndrome that we call self-expression values. These values bring increasing emphasis on the civil and political liberties that constitute democracy, which provides broader latitude for people to pursue freedom of expression and self-realization. Rising self-expression values transform modernization into a process of human development, generating a society that is increasingly people centered. This reflects a humanistic transformation of modernity.

We believe this 'humanistic transformation of modernity' is the basis of Taiwan's identity change. Taiwan's economic and political transformation in the past several decades seems to have followed very closely a conventional pattern of modernization. As the middle class gradually emerged in the 1980s and 1990s, Taiwan began to experience an increased desire for political transformation in the direction of democracy. Democratization in Taiwan, in turn, helped to fuel the socialization process that created the new Taiwanese identity, which differs from that of the Mainland. At the same time, however, China has taken a different path, which can be characterized as rapid economic growth from state capitalism coupled with sustained rigidity in its political system. This route, in turn, has created a different socialization process as compared to the one found in Taiwan over the last few decades. Several recent moves by Beijing, such as the removal of presidential term limits in 2018 that could enable Xi Jinping to extend his rule, and the passing of a wide-reaching national security law in 2020 that further undermines the autonomy set out in Hong Kong's mini-constitution, have deepened the divergent paths of socialization in Taiwan and on the Mainland.

Thus, the story of identity for Taiwan is one of movement towards a more complex range of designations. For example, research from Zhong (2016) suggests that the majority of Taiwanese people do not identify with the Mainland state, although they still associate themselves with the Chinese *nation*. In recent years, systematic de-Sinicization and Taiwanization processes have occurred in Taiwan. Some are government-led efforts, such as modifying history textbooks to emphasize the Aboriginal culture, language and history, promoting local dialects, changing 'China Post' to 'Taiwan Post', and the like. Other processes are citizen-led efforts, such as putting 'Republic of Taiwan' stickers on passports, preference for local dialects over Mandarin Chinese, and so on (Lynch, 2006; Liu and Li, 2017).

Scholars such as Brown (2004) have argued that identity does not come from a social vacuum. Identity is formed and solidified on the basis of mutual experiences. Such common background could include the interaction of individuals who share the common social and/or cultural environment, for example, shared history or political experience. When social experiences change, identity can change too. People in Taiwan have gone through several major changes in social experience – from the annexation by Japan in the 1890s, to the return of Taiwan to the ROC in the 1940s, and to the White Terror Era following the 28 February incident in 1947. National identity in Taiwan has gone from resistance to Japanese occupation to being Chinese again after Taiwan's return to the ROC, all the way through to opposing the Mainland Chinse after the 28 February incident and beyond. Perhaps the most notable recent change in common social experience is Taiwan's gradual democratization, not least in its increasingly vibrant electoral process. The island has truly evolved into a multiparty democracy.

Taiwan's popular elections and multiparty political system have created a unique social experience that is vastly different from that of Mainland China. The consequence of the formation of the democratic social experience in Taiwan is the creation of a unique Taiwanese sense of self that is different from the dominant Han Chinese identity of the Mainland. This perhaps explains why an increasing number of people in Taiwan identify themselves as Taiwanese instead of Chinese – despite beliefs that, in relation to the Mainland, (1) the future prosperity of Taiwan may not be as great; and (2) Taiwan may be highly and even irreversibly dependent. Evidence suggests that, in spite of such challenges, the unique Taiwanese identity will continue to deepen and consolidate. For example, through an executive order, Taiwan's Ministry of Education has been instructed to significantly reduce the coverage of Chinese history and increase the coverage of Taiwanese history in the high school history curriculum. Note that 'the time ratio of Taiwanese history to Chinese history to world history is 1:1:2' (Chiung, 2018: 54). In addition, and perhaps a warning about the future, several statues of Sun Yat-sen and Chiang Kai-shek, who were symbols of the Chinese identity, were vandalized in early 2017.

Taiwan's democratization has enabled the construction of a new Taiwan-centred historiography that emphasized the two diverging historical trajectories of Taiwan and China, the promotion of competing political discourses and the emergence of several forms of Taiwanese nationalism (Wang, 2005: 69–70, cited in Lepesant, 2018: 66). So we have seen the construction of a unique 'Taiwan experience', which includes the shared 'economic miracles', 'political successes (constitutional government reformation)' and a 'modern democratic nation unifying both moral culture and material civilization' (Maehara, 2018: 90). During both the Lee Teng-hui and Chen Shui-bian administrations, the government in Taiwan tried to: (1) introduce a truly representative regime limited to Taiwan (Mengin, 1998: 34); (2) build a new collective national memory and narrative centred on Taiwan; and (3) turn Taiwan into a 'globalized multicultural island nation' (Lepesant, 2018). All of these are aspects of a concerted effort to create a unique Taiwan-centred socialization experience and identity.

We now turn to the linkage between the elite interviews conveyed in Chapter 5 and this chapter's survey of public opinion. What can be said on the basis of this information, which takes both individual and aggregate form, about Taiwanese identity? Recall in the discussion earlier, when asked 'do you consider yourself Chinese, Taiwanese, both or other', 74 per cent considered themselves Taiwanese, 24 per cent both, and only 1 per cent Chinese. The results here stand in stark contrast to the Mainland's nationalistic attachment to Taiwan.[6] And even with the KMT and the Pan-Blue coalition's efforts to retain Sinicization in Taiwan, the numbers from the survey tell a remarkably different story about how far Taiwanese identity has solidified.[7] Even more significant is the fact that until quite recently, as one interviewee pointed out, identification as Taiwanese had been taken to mean that one had been born in Taiwan. This is a clear indication that a generational shift towards what it means to be Taiwanese has occurred.

During elite interviews in Chapter 5, several individuals made revealing comments about their views about the evolving Taiwanese identity. One person summed things up as follows:

> 'He is not sure how to identify himself and still hesitates to reply when asked "where are you from?" The answer could be Chinese, Taiwanese or something else – and the question seems increasingly difficult to answer. Prior to the age of 40, he had been considered by the ROC government to be from a province in China, where his family lived previously. However, in 2000, President Chen changed this policy; the government removed "belonging" to a location on the Mainland from birth certificates. Thus legal identification for this second generation Mainlander shifted to a place in the northern part of Taiwan. He added that his son already sees himself as Taiwanese, with reasons for this self-identification being traced to peers and school textbooks.'

Another interviewee commented that:

> 'Movement toward a Taiwan-centered identity is true especially of younger age cohorts. While cultural identity is a hybrid of Taiwanese and Chinese, political identity is Taiwanese. A supermajority of younger people – 80 to 90 per cent in survey results – identify as Taiwanese and only about 10 per cent respond as Chinese. It is natural for the older generation to have closer sentiments about

unification or to support maintaining cordial relations with the Mainland. This demographic in Taiwan's population, however, is dwindling.'

The preceding interview material highlights the impact of time itself. As the flight of the ROC in 1949 from the Mainland to Taiwan recedes, identification with a separate, post-Mainland way of life becomes pervasive. Only a small fraction of Taiwanese possess any memory of the ROC as an entity on the Mainland. This shift happened incrementally over time with the emergence of an environment which nurtures the identification with a Taiwanese nation or a 'Taiwanese first' identification (Lepesant, 2018; 74, 77). With the passing of time and gradual diminishing of the pro-Mainland generations, the trend is expected to continue towards an island-centred sense of the world among Taiwanese.

Elite interviews and survey results are thus highly consistent with each other. Combined, the empirical data suggest the following observations. The dominant identity in Taiwan has clearly shifted from a Chinese or mixed Chinese-Taiwanese identity to Taiwanese. Such shifts can be explained by two factors. On the one hand, democratization in Taiwan has gradually created a sociopolitical environment that is vastly different from that of the Mainland. In turn, people in Taiwan see themselves as different from the Chinese on the Mainland. On the other hand, there has been a clear and managed social engineering process on the part of the government in Taiwan. Taipei gradually has re-engineered the social and political environment to foster a Taiwanese-centred identity and environment. One interviewee stated that "whoever is in power in Taiwan can shape popular perceptions". Popular views about how people in Taiwan and on the Mainland are different from each other thereby solidify the unique Taiwanese identity over time.

According to one interviewee, "democratization is driven internally, not by the PRC, as Taiwan is the only ethnically Chinese democracy. The political system stands as one of Huntington's Third Wave success stories – very little violence in process of democratization". From the Taiwanese public's perspective, the Taiwanese people expect the Mainland to 'affirm the existence of the ROC's democratic values and system of governance'. To some extent, the stories about China and Taiwan have become a perfect 'social and political laboratory' to demonstrate how a Chinese society functions under different political systems (Mahbubani, 2020: 99).

Despite the Mainland's efforts to further strengthen economic and social ties across the Taiwan Strait, increased people-to-people exchanges have resulted in an interesting observation among Taiwanese, as one interviewee observed:

> 'The more we interact with people from the Mainland, the less we like about China. Moreover, the shift is not purely generational, where the younger generation is more skeptical than the older generation of closer ties with the Mainland. Some aspects of this growing divide may cut across age, background, education and socio-economic status. Key differences include the political system and fundamental values in society. Along those lines, problematic areas highlighted by greater contact with the Mainland are freedom of the press, speech and religious practices, along with rule of law and political accountability. A seemingly irreversible trend is that people in Taiwan see themselves as distinct from Mainland Chinese in terms of values.'

One scholar observes that increased human contacts have not bridged the gap separating the two populations – they have only emphasized the differences in 'values, world visions, behaviors, divergences in language, centers of interest and life styles that create a "we Taiwanese" identification distinct from a "they Chinese" identification' (Lepesant, 2018: 78–79).

Recent events in Hong Kong have not made things easier for the future of Taiwan under the 'one country, two systems' model. China's hard-line approach curbing civil liberties in Hong Kong has further eroded the chance to maintain a democratic Taiwan, should Taiwan and China return to a unified structure under the 'one country, two systems' model. With increasing scepticism among the Taiwanese electorate about China's political arrangement with Hong Kong, one of Tsai's pithy campaign slogans – 'Today's Hong Kong, Tomorrow's Taiwan' – may have captured what is at stake for Taiwan in the 2020 presidential election. Beijing's heavy-handed approach to the Hong Kong crisis yielded a number of unintended consequences that have reverberated across the Taiwan Strait and injected a new sense of unpredictability into cross-Strait relations.

Summing up

As one interviewee stated in Chapter 5, 'China's policy plays a determining role in shaping Taiwan's sense of distinctiveness. What Beijing does (or does not do) is also an important and determining factor. Beijing's policy receptiveness (or lack thereof) toward Taipei and on cross-Strait relations shapes Taiwan's self-image and identity'. If China wants to win over Taiwan, reverse recent trend lines in Taiwanese identity, and demonstrate its commitment to becoming a responsible stakeholder in the region, it will need to exercise greater prudence in its dealings with Taiwan. Recent unilateral decisions to suspend issuing individual travel permits to allow Mainland residents to visit Taiwan, to increase the circling and fly-over of fighter and bomber jets in Taiwan's air space, and to continuously squeeze out Taiwan's international participation in the World Health Assembly to fight COVID-19, all undermine China's outreach to 'win the hearts and minds' of Taiwan's electorate. These responses also raise an important point. One can recognize the influential role that an ascendant China plays in Taiwanese identity in affecting both ideological and interest-based motivations. Certainly, a richer and more powerful Mainland generates opportunities for people's personal and household economic gain. But the more powerful China is also less restrained and more likely to take actions that fuel the factors driving people to see themselves as exclusively Taiwanese. It also puts more of a strain on the triangle of China, the US and Taiwan.

The current dynamic in the Taiwan Strait illustrates the clear lack of trust in the trilateral US–China–Taiwan relationship. Beijing has been reluctant in accommodating Taipei's demands for more international space such as representation in the World Health Assembly and the International Civil Aviation Organization. Beijing does not believe Taipei's reasons to enter these international agencies or organizations are purely technical. Allowing Taiwan to be accepted into these functional institutions could open the floodgate of a 'spillover' into bigger political institutions further down the road (Mitrany, 1975). In Beijing's defence, that is likely Taipei's true purpose. Such concessions on Beijing's part would be hard to take back once given and be seen by the domestic audience in Mainland China as a weakness of its leaders. There also is distrust between Taipei and Washington. Having been sold out once when Washington switched diplomatic recognition from the ROC to PRC, Taipei is acutely aware that the US–ROC relationship is a derivative of the US–PRC relationship. The US cares about Taiwan only because China cares about Taiwan. The distrust between the US and China has only intensified in recent years, most evidenced by the recent trade war between the two countries and the nosedive of bilateral relations since COVID-19. Taiwan remains the red line and the most important strategic piece on the US–China chessboard.

The complexity of the Taiwan issue shows that interest-driven choices have certainly played a role in Taiwan's domestic politics. However, evidence presented in this chapter shows that idea-driven choices have clearly taken shape in Taiwan. A new Taiwan-centred identity different from that of the Mainland Chinese has been formed and solidified over time in Taiwan. This Taiwanese identity is the result of both a natural emergence and deliberate reconstruction of a unique experience centred on Taiwan's socialization process in the preceding decades. This trend line is both consistent with the interviewees discussed in Chapter 5 and a second set of empirical analysis based on a different survey in Chapter 7. We now hone in on the group of people who identify only as Taiwanese through a layered empirical approach in the next chapter.

Notes

1. Professor Frank C.S. Liu has graciously granted the authors use of his Cross-Strait Opinion data, for which we are highly appreciative.
2. The score is a weighted calculation. Items ranked first are valued higher than the following ranks, the score is the sum of all weighted rank counts.
3. This brings to mind the sustained example of multilingual communication in Canada, where it is a standard practice to use both English and French. More specifically, no candidate for prime minister would be viable without at least a functional ability in these official languages of Canada.
4. Note that the direction of the continuum is *opposite* to what appears in Figure 6.4. This assists in identifying any response set that might occur, with respondents simply checking the first or last answer available for any question. No response set has been detected for this survey.
5. For detailed discussions, see Li and Zhang (2017).
6. Chinese nationalism has been on the rise in recent years, especially for matters related to national sovereignty and integrity. See, for example, Weiss (2019) and Chen et al (2019).
7. Beijing's views and positions regarding the KMT is a good case in point about the construction and re-construction of identity. During China's war with Japan, the CCP worked closely with the KMT to fight against the common Japanese intrusion. The CCP maintained a relationship of amity with the KMT. During the Chinese Civil War, the CCP fought against the KMT. The Chinese Civil War eventually led to the KMT's defeat and fleeing to Taiwan. The CCP-led government in Beijing and KMT-led government in Taipei remained foes throughout much of the 1940s and 1980s. Things started to change in the 1990s as a *rapprochement* across the Taiwan Strait started to occur. The rise of the pro-independence DPP propelled the return to a relationship of amity between the CCP and KMT. Today, Beijing largely views the KMT and a KMT-led government in Taiwan as friendly. This is a classic example of what Wendt (1992) describes as the social construction of identity. The CCP's relationship with the KMT has been constructed and reconstructed (Li, 2014a) as a friend (Sino-Japanese War), a foe (Chinese Civil War through the 1980s) and back to a friend (since the 1990s).

7

Factors Influencing Identifying Only as Taiwanese: A Layered Empirical Approach (Survey II)

Overview

People in Taiwan increasingly view their identity as separate and different from those on the Mainland. The Taiwanese sense of self in the new millennium is complex, dynamic and relational (Liu, 2016). Cross-Strait relations play a crucial role in influencing how the people of Taiwan view themselves and their relationship with the PRC (Kastner, 2016). In Taiwan, many citizens now feel they have the choice of identifying as Taiwanese, Chinese or both, rejecting the notion that their past dictates their present (van der Horst, 2016; Green, 2017). Furthermore, we saw in Chapters 5 and 6 that a wide variety of factors influence elite and mass identity formation in Taiwan. In particular, the qualitative and quantitative empirical analyses discussed in this study thus far demonstrate that there has been a significant shift in identity formation; Taiwan's democratization process now plays a major role in affecting the preferences of those who see themselves as Taiwanese (Friedberg, 2005).

What is it to be Taiwanese? This is the question that Jacobs and Kang ask in *Changing Taiwanese Identities* (2018). We start this chapter with an even stronger question, *what is it to be only Taiwanese?* Our focus here is on the factors that influence someone to identify as exclusively Taiwanese. We are especially interested in building on the survey results of Chapter 6 by examining individual characteristics and contextual conditions that influence identity in Taiwan in addition to the critical factors democracy and the US. In this chapter, we are interested in how beliefs about cross-Strait relations influence an individual's ideational formation as exclusively Taiwanese (Callahan, 2010; Kastner, 2016; Liu, 2016; Li and Zhang, 2017). This focus reflects a priority given the rapid rise of China across a variety of domains, but most especially in the economic domain (Chen, 2014; Mearsheimer, 2014a). Doing so can help us gain greater analytical clarity and insights into how and why a 'Taiwanese only' identity has evolved on the island.

This chapter unfolds in six additional sections. The second section reviews our theoretical approach. The third section describes the Taiwan National Security Survey Data and the variables developed to address these questions. The fourth section conducts multivariate statistical analyses with a focus on Proportional Reduction of Error (PRE) to explore critical questions about factors influencing Taiwanese identity. In doing so, we focus on Taiwanese–Mainland relational issues, such as the 1992 Consensus. We then determine how the model used to explain ideational issues operates with political issues such as the performance assessment of President Tsai Ing-wen. In addition to stacking our layered model we present logistic analyses of three dependent variables and include a wide array of diagnostics. The fifth section explains the novel type of methodological approach we employ to analyse our systemist perspective and implements a preliminary set of stacked, layered analyses. The sixth section provides analysis and synthesis of the statistical results. The seventh and final section sums up the accomplishments of the chapter.

Theory

As discussed in Chapter 4, our theoretical perspective combines analytic eclecticism and systemism. Thus, our corresponding empirical approach needs to be both layered and comprehensive, looking at the impact of multiple levels and categories of factors on different choices. Systemism facilitates combining variables across paradigms and disciplines to construct a coherent whole. The systemist perspective emphasizes the desire to avoid *ceteris paribus* clauses through dynamic model specification across different layers of levels of factors influencing behaviour. Our theoretical approach is inclusive, going beyond paradigmatic boundaries and borders and notably incorporating individual factors, Taiwanese issues, and the nature of the relationship between Taipei and Beijing.

With this systemist approach in mind, we continue looking into the matrix of factors driving mass ideational choices in Taiwan. In this chapter, we focus on how beliefs about cross-Strait relations have developed in response to the rapid rise of China. Specifically, we ask how critical factors, especially those that relate to the rapidly changing dynamic of cross-Strait relations, influence the likelihood of someone in Taiwan claiming to be Taiwanese-only, and not a blend of Taiwanese and Chinese, and not Chinese.

We view identities in Taiwan as layered, reflecting multidimensional complexity (Kastner, 2016; S. Lin, 2016; Lin, 2019). In the US, an American might identify as Italian-American for example (or Jewish-American, or African-American, etc). But they, and citizens in their community, are unlikely to identify as Jewish but not American (there are of course exceptions, such as possibly the Jewish people in Monsey, New York; Freedman, 2000). Unlike the common formation in the US, however, Taiwanese identities are not so immutable (He, 2014; Schafferer, 2016) and might include those who identify as Taiwanese economically, Chinese culturally, and anti-Chinese politically (Chen, 2014). As one Taiwanese said,

> 'I was told at school I'm Chinese. Young people are told they're Taiwanese. Their education tells them to be wary of China – that the country's backwards and disorderly and that it threatens us. But we're all Chinese by blood. However, we taught our daughter to be whoever she wants to be'. (Quoted in Rob, 2018)

These ideational layers mean that linear-oriented empirical approaches to unpacking identity formation might lead to the wrong understanding of how the ideational process works and how the people of Taiwan see themselves. While the earlier chapters focus on the role of democracy (see also Muyard, 2018) and the US, this chapter seeks to expand the range of factors found affecting Taiwanese ideation.

Looking at the influence of these layers on identification as Taiwanese-only, we are especially interested in answers to the following questions:

1. *How do views of the 1992 Consensus influence identity?* The 1992 Consensus between Mainland and Taiwan constituted an agreement on the existence of a single China but this consensus turned out to mean different things on either side of the Strait. We explore whether beliefs about whether Taiwan should be independent or be a part of China represent factors that drive ideational decisions (Brown, 2004; Shirk, 2007).
2. *How do views of independence from the Mainland and the possibility of war after independence affect Taiwanese ideation?* Peoples' expectations

vary dramatically regarding the probability of Taiwan's independence from the Mainland and the consequential likelihood of war. We examine whether these beliefs influence individual's sense of who they are (Legro, 2007; Kastner, 2015).
3. *Is Taiwanese identity truly an elemental identity or is it driven by strategic calculations based on personal gain?* Do people identify strategically as mixed Taiwanese and Chinese or Chinese when they face possible personal gain from economic interactions with the Mainland? That is, are identities driven by self-interest?
4. *How does Taiwan's potential gains or losses from the Mainland's economic rise influence Taiwanese-only identification?* The rise of China and growth in cross-Strait relations can both provide gains for Taiwan or provide greater ability for China to manipulate and undermine Taiwan. What do people think about these dynamics and how do those beliefs influence their identities?
5. *To what extent do standard demographic factors influence Taiwanese identification?* Gender and education are often seen as critical to identity formation. In Taiwan, many point to generational dynamics and the role of age in explaining variation in Taiwanese identity (Wang, 2017), although there also have been studies that suggest some generational models may be misidentified (Zhai, 2019).
6. *How do all of the factors discussed vary in their influence of ideational choices versus political assessments?* National identity is an abstract concept. Do the relationships found in understanding Taiwanese identity influence more concrete political assessments such as evaluations of President Tsai's performance?

Data analysis will respond to these questions and build upon the initial sense of theorizing gleaned from the academic literature and depicted graphically in Figure 4.2 from Chapter 4.

Taiwan National Security Survey Data

To explore answers to the preceding questions we analyse the Taiwan National Security Survey Data, a poll of approximately 1,000 Taiwanese adults conducted in 2017 by Emerson Niou (see also Wang, 2017).[1] These telephone interviews were conducted by the Election Study Center of the National Chengchi University in Taiwan. This dataset complements the online surveys conducted by Frank C.S. Liu of the Institute of Political Science at the National Sun Yat-Sen University, which were introduced in Chapter 6.

For all variables in this chapter, we code as missing those observations where the response was 'Decline to Answer'. In the following, we specify for each variable how we handled responses such as Depends, Indifferent and Don't Know. In our diagnostics we added back into the models observations we identify as dropped and employ alternative variable coding schemes. Text quoted in the variable descriptions represents translations of the Taiwan National Security Survey Data codebook by a native Taiwanese speaker.

Dependent variables

We employ three dependent variables: (1) *Identify Only as Taiwanese*, (2) *Identity Choice* and (3) *Disapproval of President Tsai*. These variables are summarized across their number of observations, mean, standard deviation, minimum and maximum in Table 7.1.

Identify Only as Taiwanese. Respondents were asked, 'In our society, some call themselves as "Taiwanese" and some call themselves as "Chinese" while some say they are both. Do you consider yourself as Taiwanese, Chinese, or both?' If a respondent answered 'Taiwanese' the variable was coded 1, if they answered 'Both', 'Chinese', 'Hard to

Table 7.1: Variables contributing to Taiwanese identity

Variable	Observations	Mean	Standard deviation	Min	Max
Identify only as Taiwanese	1,075	0.50	0.50	0	1
Support 1992 Consensus	1,075	3.49	1.33	1	5
Probability of future success of Taiwanese independence	1,020	3.24	2.75	0	10
Mainland economic ties	1,075	1.51	0.74	1	3
Mainland leverage	1,075	3.27	1.35	1	5
Pocketbook	1,075	2.38	0.49	1	3
Probability of war if independence	1,075	3.15	1.36	1	5
Taiwan's economy	1,075	2.72	0.47	1	3
Age	1,075	48.26	14.31	20	101
Education	1,075	4.84	1.41	1	7
Gender	1,075	0.50	0.50	0	1
Identity choice	1,054	0.53	0.57	0	2
Disapproval of President Tsai	1,075	3.61	1.21	1	5

tell', 'Indifferent' or 'Don't know' the variable was coded 0. Exactly 50 per cent of the sample identified as Taiwanese. The 50 per cent figure reflects the 'ambiguous' attitude some claim Taiwanese have towards their national identity (Yeh, 2014), yet it is higher than some assert (18 per cent, Mearsheimer, 2014a: 30) and lower than others expect (67 per cent according to Election Study Center, NCCU, 2020; 74 per cent according to the Institute of Political Science at the National Sun Yat-Sen University Survey in Chapter 6 and 90 per cent, quoted in Rob, 2018; see also Chen et al, 2017).

Identity Choice. Respondents were asked, 'In our society, some call themselves as "Taiwanese" and some call themselves as "Chinese" while some say they are both. Do you consider yourself as Taiwanese, Chinese, or both?' If a respondent answered 'Taiwanese' the variable *Identity* was coded 0, if they answered 'Both' the variable was coded 1, if 'Chinese' a 2. Observations that included 'Hard to tell', 'Indifferent' or 'Don't know' were dropped (see the Diagnostic sub-section for more on this issue). Of the 1,054 respondents, 50.7 per cent identified as Taiwanese, 45.5 per cent as both and 3.8 per cent as Chinese.

Disapproval of President Tsai. Respondents were asked, 'How satisfied are you with President Tsai's performance?' The variable *Disapproval of President Tsai* was coded 1 if 'Very satisfied', 2 if 'Satisfied', 3 if 'Depends', 'Indifferent', 'Don't know', 4 if 'Dissatisfied' and 5 if 'Very dissatisfied'. Disapproval of the president averaged 3.61, with category 4/Dissatisfied as the modal value.

Layered variables

Drawing on our Systemism theoretical approach, we employ an empirically layered method to build our understanding of how key factors interact to contribute to our understanding of these three critical dependent variables. This analytical approach incorporates a wide range of factors that focus especially on cross-Strait relations along with other critical factors beyond democratization and the relationship with the US. In doing so, we will draw on the following variables, also summarized in Table 7.1.

Support 1992 Consensus. Respondents were asked, 'Do you support the claim that Taiwan and China should interact because of the 1992 Consensus?' Respondents who answered: 'Completely oppose' were coded 1, those who responded 'Opposed' 2, answers that included 'Depends', 'Indifferent' and 'Don't know' 3, 'Support' 4 and 'Completely support' 5. The average answer is 3.49, suggesting respondents lean towards support. We expect that those who more strongly oppose the 1992 Consensus and the One China concept are more likely to identify only as Taiwanese (Wu, 2016).

Probability of Future Success of Taiwanese Independence. Respondents were asked, 'On a scale of 0 to 10 to indicate the probability of future success of Taiwanese independence, with 0 being the least probable and 10 being the most probable, how would you rate the probability?' The mean answer is 3.25 with 0 being least probable and 10 being most probable. Note that 55 observations were dropped that indicated 'Depends', 'Indifferent' or 'Don't know'. We reanalysed our models dropping this variable, and thus including those 55 observations, with results being essentially the same (not shown).

Mainland Economic Ties. Respondents were asked, 'Within our society, some people suggest that we should strengthen the economic and trade relations with the Mainland, while some suggest that we should diminish such relations. Which do you agree with more?' Answering 'Strengthen economic and trade relations with the Mainland' was coded 1, responses that included 'Depends', 'Indifferent' or 'Don't know' as 2, the answer 'Diminish economic and trade relations with the Mainland' as 3. The average answer was a 1.51, reflecting a position between don't know and strengthen ties.

Mainland Leverage. Respondents were asked: 'If someone says, "If Taiwan overly relies its economy on the Mainland, in time the Mainland will use its economy as a political leverage against Taiwan." Do you agree or disagree with this statement?' The variable Mainland Leverage was coded 1 if the answer was 'Completely disagree', 2 if the response was 'Disagree', 3 if the answer was 'Depends', 'Indifferent' or 'I don't know', 4 if 'Agree' and 5 if 'Completely agree'. People on average were between I don't know and agreeing with a mean of 3.27.

Pocketbook. Respondents were asked: 'If the cross-Strait relations become strained, do you think the economy in your household will become better, worse, or have no effect?' If respondents answered 'Better', the variable *Pocketbook* was coded 1. If they replied, 'About the same' or 'Depends', 'Indifferent' or 'Don't know', the variable is coded 2, and the answer of 'Worse' resulted in a 3. The variable *Pocketbook* has a mean of 2.38, suggesting most people have a household-based, economic connection to the Mainland economy.

Probability of War if Independence. Interviewers were told to inquire of respondents about their level of agreement with the statement, 'If Taiwan declares independence unilaterally, will the Mainland attack Taiwan?' Those who responded, 'Absolutely not' were coded as a 1, 'No' a 2, answers of 'Depends', 'Indifferent' or 'Don't know' a 3, 'Yes'

4 and a response of 'Absolutely yes' led to a 5 for this variable. The mean answer was a 2.72, approaching the answer that it depends.

Taiwan's Economy. Respondents were asked: 'If the cross-Strait relations become strained, do you think Taiwanese economy will become better, worse, or have no effect?' The variable *Taiwan's Economy* captures the impact of the Mainland's economy on Taiwan's national standing, as opposed to household economic health like the variable *Pocketbook*. If respondents answered 'Better', the variable *Taiwan's Economy* was coded 1, 'About the same', 'Depends', 'Indifferent' or 'Don't' know' is coded 2, 'Worse' is a 3. The variable *Taiwan's Economy* has a mean of 2.7, suggesting people strongly believe Taiwan has a vigorous economic connection to the Mainland economy, a dynamic shown to have substantial influence on Taiwanese identity choices (Chen, 2014).

Age, Education, Gender. Respondents were asked, 'Which Republic Year were you born in?' The variable *Age* is 106 minus their response. Age ranges from 20 to 101 with a mean of 48 and a standard deviation of 14. Respondents were asked, 'What is your highest degree of education attained?' The variable *Education* was coded 'Illiterate or never enrolled' 1, 'Elementary school' 2, 'Junior high school' 3, 'Senior high school' 4, 'Junior college' 5, 'University' 6, 'Graduate school or above' 7. *Education* ranges from 1 to 7 with a mean of 4.8, between senior high school and junior college. Gender was coded 1 if male and 0 if not male. Fifty per cent of the respondents identified as male.

Methods and data analysis

Proportional reduction of error

As we noted in Chapter 4, which presents our initial stage of theorizing, systemism encourages thinking innovatively beyond the standard multivariate approach that attempts to isolate the independent effect of one variable while holding the others constant. We anticipate in many situations that it would be impossible to meet the *ceteris paribus* assumptions of independence necessary to employ a multivariate analysis. Instead we create an empirical process that draws on the statistical diagnostic Proportional Reduction of Error (PRE) to help illustrate the layered, multidimensional dynamics driving identity formation.

For a binary variable like *Identify Only as Taiwanese*, where the values are yes/no (1/0), statistical significance can be misleading. This concern is not unique to analysis of Taiwan. For example, imagine an academic study that finds that college-educated Americans are more likely to say 'yes' they know the movie *Star Wars* than non-college-educated Americans. Imagine also, however, 98 per cent of Americans are familiar with *Star Wars* and respond 'yes' to the question about whether they know the movie. In this hypothetical, no fancy statistical model is needed to predict whether someone from the US likely knows about *Star Wars*. Guessing the modal value 'yes' is going to lead to the right answer 98 per cent of the time, which represents an extraordinary level of accuracy for a prediction. Even if variables in a statistical analysis are statistically significant, the variables and the model can provide only minimal explanatory power because simply by choosing 'yes', one is able to get it right 98 per cent of the time. The predictive power of categorical and especially binary variables is thus not just a function of statistical significance. We also need to focus on the explanatory power of our models given the distribution of the dependent variable. Put simply, it is what a model buys you in explanatory power that is key.

PRE explains the percentage of the explained variance from a model beyond simply choosing the modal value (Gartner, 2011). Ranging from 0 to 100 per cent PRE captures how much of the remaining variation the model explains after choosing the modal value. Thus in our *Star Wars* example, the variable education might be statistically significant, but given that 98 per cent of the public knows about *Star Wars*, the model is unlikely to explain any additional variation beyond that captured by the highly skewed modal value and have a PRE of 0.

An empirical analysis employing PRE works well in tandem with a systemist approach to Taiwanese identity, where multiple layers and categories of factors interact together to encourage and discourage ideational choices (Chen, 2014; Pan, 2015). For binary variables like *Identify Only as Taiwanese* that are close to 50/50 (a coin toss), additional explanatory power is especially important because guessing the modal value provides little predictive power, making PRE particularly important.

Factor layering

Focusing initially on *Identify Only as Taiwanese*, our layered approach applies PRE in two ways. First, we conducted bivariate analyses of each of our explanatory variables on *Identify Only as Taiwanese*. We then noted the PRE for the analysis with each variable and sort them from largest to smallest. The results are presented in Table 7.2.[2]

The results in Table 7.2 provide interesting insight into the variables' explanatory power for identifying those who identify as Taiwanese

Table 7.2: Bivariate PRE values for *Identify Only as Taiwanese*

Support 1992 Consensus	32.2%
Probability of future success of Taiwanese independence	31.3%
Mainland economic ties	30.9%
Mainland leverage	24.5%
Pocketbook	23.4%
Probability of war if independence	16.1%
Taiwan's economy	16.1%
Age	6.7%
Education	4.1%
Gender	0.0%

only. We see that, for the variables *Support 1992 Consensus*, *Probability of Future Success of Taiwanese Independence* and *Mainland Economic Ties*, each variable explains about 30 per cent or more of the variance remaining after choosing the modal value of *Identify Only as Taiwanese*. In other words, if you were to obtain one piece of information to help you predict if someone in Taiwan identified as Taiwanese, the best information for informing your prediction would be their assessment of the 1992 Consensus, followed by their estimate of Taiwan being able to become independent in future and the national importance of ties with the Mainland. And, with just one variable, the improvement in your ability to predict those who identify exclusively as Taiwanese would be substantial, as PRE scores of thirty percent would be high values for an entire model, let alone for just one variable. Part of the reason for these figures is the knife-edge, 50/50 distribution of those who select Taiwanese as their identity. The other reason is the strong explanatory power that each of these factors possesses in predicting those who see themselves as just Taiwanese.

Two other striking observations can be made about the contents of Table 7.2. One is that, while self-interest does play a role, the variable *Pocketbook* – how connected people see their own economic circumstances tied to cross-Strait relations – is in the middle of the variable list in terms of explanatory power for capturing who claims Taiwanese identity. Perhaps even more interestingly, the personal variables, *Age*, *Education* and *Gender*, explain comparatively little of the remaining variation. The weak power of *Age* and *Education* are especially noteworthy given the generational and educational perspectives many use to view Taiwanese identity formation.

A layered analytical approach

We next use these PRE values to sequence our model layering, starting with the variables that provide the greatest explanatory power, *1992 Consensus*, and working towards *Gender*, the weakest. In doing so, we can estimate the marginal gain in PRE. That is, each time we add a variable we can see what, if any, additional explanatory power we gain in our multilayered approach over the previous model and what we would gain predicting the modal value of the dependent variable (without holding any of the variables or their parameters constant or equal). While not a general evaluation, as the results are sequence specific, the approach exemplifies our story of how layers of factors combine and stack together to influence identity choices in Taiwan.[3]

We begin with the 1992 Consensus. As the Consensus may not be as widely known as some of the other factors we analyse, and because it connects so critically to our elite interviews, we spend substantially more time introducing it and explaining our expectations than we will for the other variables (see also Chapter 6 and especially Figures 6.12 and 6.13).

Talks began in Beijing in March 1992 and Hong Kong in October 1992 (Su and Cheng, 2002). The talks concluded that there is 'One China'; however, the phrase's definition is different for each entity (Xu, 2001). While the ROC and PRC have engaged in military confrontations since 1949, Taiwan had yet to institute a statute that indicated it is not a part of China. Indeed, Taiwan maintained a 'Three No's Policy', meaning, 'no contacts, no talks, no compromises'. The lack of an independence statement and/or law, however, made the Consensus negotiations possible. In 1991, Beijing established the Association for Relations Across the Taiwan Straits (ARATS) and Taipei established the Straits Exchange Foundation (SEF) for cross-Strait negotiations regarding technical matters that impacted upon both sides.

During March 1992, the SEF and ARATS negotiated cross-Strait notarized documents and the tracing of, and compensation for, lost registered mail. Talks continued to be used for the resolution of issues such as maritime smuggling. During this time, both sides agreed to adhere to the one-China ideal. However, Taiwan highlighted that under the one-China policy each side was able to speak for itself and this emphasized its sovereignty. Meanwhile, the Mainland insisted that the issues discussed during the talks were regarding the internal affairs of one country. Thus, despite efforts to resolve mutual issues without discussing the one-China policy, it inevitably was discussed (Xu, 2001).

Also referred to as the One China Consensus, the term 1992 Consensus was coined by Chi Su, the Minister of the Mainland Affairs council (MAC), in 2000 (Su and Cheng, 2002). It was previously referred to as 'one China, different interpretations' in Taiwan (Wu, 2016). The Consensus was negotiated in Hong Kong from 28 to 30 October 1992 by the ARATS and SEF after the international condemnation of the Tiananmen crackdown (Wu, 2016). Negotiations included both oral and written 'formulas' for expressing the mutual adherence of the One China principle. After the talks, no agreement was made. Subsequent negotiations via letter and telephone, however, led to the arrangement of oral statements that pledged agreement to the one-China policy (Xu, 2001). But each party clearly had its own interpretation of One China. The CCP view both Mainland China and Taiwan as being One China with the aim of unification. The KMT, the ruling party from 1949 to 2000 and 2008 to 2016, indicated that while both the Mainland and Taiwan are 'One China', 'China' refers to 'the Republic of China' and not 'The People's Republic of China' (see also Kan, 2014; Wang et al, 2018). This conceptualization was reflected in statements made by the ARATS and SEF.

On 1 August 1992, the following statement was adopted by the National Unification Council on the meaning of 'One China' (Kan, 2014: 49):

> Both sides of the Taiwan Strait agree that there is only one China. However, the two sides of the Strait have different opinions as to the meaning of 'one China.' To Peking, 'one China' means the 'People's Republic of China (PRC),' with Taiwan to become a 'Special Administration Region' after unification. Taipei, on the other hand, considers 'one China' to mean the Republic of China (ROC), founded in 1911 and with de jure sovereignty over all of China. The ROC, however, currently has jurisdiction only over Taiwan, Penghu, Kinmen, and Matsu. Taiwan is part of China, and the Chinese Mainland is part of China as well.

On 3 November 1992, the following statements were made about the interpretation of 'One China':

> Taipei's SEF: On November 3, a responsible person of the Communist Chinese ARATS said that it is willing to 'respect and accept' SEF's proposal that each side 'verbally

states' its respective principles on 'one China'. (Kan, 2014: 50–51)

> Beijing's ARATS: At this working-level consultation in Hong Kong, SEF representatives suggested that each side use respective verbal announcements to state the one China principle. On November 3, SEF sent a letter, formally notifying that 'each side will make respective statements through verbal announcements.' ARATS fully respects and accepts SEF's suggestion. (Kan, 2014: 51)

It is clear from the preceding quotations that, depending on their perspective, people can see the concept of One China as meaning very different futures for Taiwan (Funnell, 2018).[4] At the same time, despite claims repeated by the Mainland, the Taiwanese people increasingly do not feel connected to the concept of global China (Wang, 2018) and the 1992 Consensus. Recall in Figure 6.13, when asked about the agreement with which part of the 1992 Consensus, 49 per cent of the respondents agreed with the 'different interpretations' part the most and only 7 per cent agreed with the 'one China' part; while 14 per cent agreed with 'both' and 30 per cent agreed with 'neither'. Given the importance of the 1992 Consensus in cross-Strait relations, its unusual status as a 'success', and its framework for coordinating operations between Taiwan and the PRC, it is not surprising that it possesses strong explanatory power.

Layering models

We can see in Table 7.3, Model A, that both the Proportional Reduction in Error (PRE) and the predictive impact that the 1992 Consensus has on the likelihood of identifying exclusively as Taiwanese. Specifically, values of the variable *Support 1992 Consensus* explains 32.2 per cent of the variation remaining after predicting the modal value of *Identify Only as Taiwanese*. The addition of *Probability of Future Success of Taiwanese Independence* and *Mainland Economic Ties* in Models B and C add 7.8 per cent and 5.4 per cent respectively to our ability to predict identity. The PRE difference captures the additional, marginal explanatory power of the variables beyond what was explained by the previous model. Thus, the explanatory power captured by the PRE for these factors is lower than we saw earlier in Table 7.2 because in Table 7.2 each independent was examined by itself, while now the variables stack on top of the previous model. That means the variable reflecting success of independence is included with the variable measuring attitude

Table 7.3: Layered PRE impact on *Identify Only as Taiwanese*

Specification	PRE	PRE gain
Model A		
Support 1992 Consensus	32.20%	
Model B		
Model A + Probability of future success of Taiwanese independence	40.00%	7.80%
Model C		
Model B + Mainland economic ties	45.40%	5.40%
Model D		
Model C + Mainland leverage	45.80%	0.40%
Model E		
Model D + Pocketbook	47.60%	1.80%
Model F		
E + Probability of war if independence	47.20%	-0.40%★
Model G		
Model F + Taiwan's economy	47.40%	-0.20%★
Model H		
Model G + Age, education, gender	48.00%	0.40%★

Note: ★ Percentage taken off the previous highest figure (e.g. Pocketbook for last three calculations)

towards the 1992 Consensus and economics is included with variables capturing views on both the Consensus and independence.

When stacked onto the previous model, the variables *Mainland Leverage* and *Pocketbook* each add a small amount of additional explanatory power in Models D and E. Both Model F, which adds the *Probability of War if Independence* and Model G, which includes the variable *Taiwan's Economy* to the previous model, actually decreases the PRE from what it achieves in Model E. That is, the explanatory power is higher without the addition of these variables – they negatively impact the model's predictive power. Finally, inclusion in Model H of the personal variables to the model adds a small amount to the PRE. We can see that stacking six of the layers expand our ability to predict who will identify only as Taiwanese beyond the modal value of the variable (again sequencing matters, so it does not mean that the addition of these variables using another sequence would result in the same contribution to the explanatory power). With a PRE of

Table 7.4: Multivariate analysis of *Identify Only as Taiwanese*

	Coefficient	Std. Err.	z	P>z
Support 1992 Consensus	-0.478	0.066	-7.24	0
Probability of future success of Taiwanese independence	0.145	0.030	4.81	0
Mainland economic ties	0.629	0.119	5.28	0
Mainland leverage	0.270	0.060	4.53	0
Pocketbook	-0.493	0.156	-3.17	0.002
Age	-0.011	0.006	-1.81	0.07
Education	-0.163	0.062	-2.63	0.008
Gender	0.098	0.150	0.65	0.513
_cons	1.868	0.700	2.67	0.008
N (observations)	1020			
Log likelihood =	-539.017			
LR chi2(8) =	335.73	Prob > chi2 = 0.0000		
PRE	49.2%			

48 per cent, we can explain almost half of the variation remaining in *Identifying as Taiwanese* after selecting the variable's modal value – 48 per cent is a comparatively high PRE.

Table 7.4 provides a standard multivariate model. The model has an impressive PRE of 49.2 per cent (dropping the factors that decreased explanatory power, see the diagnostic section for models with their inclusion). Analysing the responses of the 1,020 people in the sample, we see that support for the 1992 Consensus decreases the likelihood of identifying solely as Taiwanese – or conversely, opposition to the Consensus, which recognizes one China, increases likelihood of seeing oneself exclusively as Taiwanese. People who can personally gain from improved economic connections with China and older people are also less likely to Identify Only as Taiwanese. The remaining variables (except *Gender*) – *Probability of Future Success of Taiwanese Independence*, *Mainland Economic Ties*, *Mainland Leverage* and *Education* – all are correlated positively with *Identifying as Taiwanese*. That is, those who see a greater probability of Taiwanese independence, those who preferred Taiwan to have reduced economic ties with the Mainland, those who feared Chinese leverage resulting from economic engagement, or those who had greater educational attainment, were more likely to identify only as Taiwanese.

Financial gain does not have an automatic connection to the question of whether factors that draw from identity versus interest influence the ideational process. Economics can cut both ways on identity, reflecting both ideational benefits and fears (Chen, 2014; Chiang et al, 2014, 2019). Ma's push for ECFA, for example, benefited a number of large corporations eager to tap into China's cost-effective production base and vast market opportunities. This economic arrangement, however, squeezed out the small and medium enterprises in Taiwan, with limited capital to move into the Mainland market. Similarly, those with limited economic mobility to seek new job prospects in China were stuck with stagnant wages in Taiwan, leading to increasing levels of frustration and scepticism about the boundless opportunities that ECFA and Ma's pro-*rapprochement* policies had promised. Indeed, our *Pocketbook*, *Mainland Economic* and *Mainland Leverage* variables suggest conflicting beliefs. This is consistent with the evidence presented in both Chapters 5 and 6 that many interviewees and survey respondents do not believe that ECFA is apolitical and it has benefited people across Taiwan equally. By and large, sectors, businesses and locations that are more closely associated with the KMT have benefited more (also see Lepesant, 2018).

Diagnostics

We conducted extensive diagnostic analyses of the final model to make sure that the results were robust to other modelling and empirical choices (all diagnostic results are available from the authors). The bottom line – regardless of a multitude of alternate modelling and empirical approaches, the results presented in Table 7.4 and our narrative for the factors that explain identifying solely as Taiwanese are especially strong, consistent and clear. Our diagnostics included:

- The model in Table 7.4 was reanalysed using the ordinal variable *Identity Choice* and employing an ordered logit procedure. Results in Table 7.5 are very similar, with a PRE of 42.5 per cent and equally strong model fit measures. All variables, once again except for *Gender*, are statistically significant with coefficients similar to the bivariate model presented earlier.
- We checked the Variance/Covariance matrix to make sure no variables had abnormally high covariance indicating that they were

Table 7.5: Ordered logit analysis of *Identity Choice*

	Coefficient	Std. Err.	z	P>z
Support 1992 Consensus	0.469	0.065	7.18	0
Probability of future success of Taiwanese independence	-0.124	0.029	-4.22	0
Mainland economic ties	-0.672	0.121	-5.57	0
Mainland leverage	-0.278	0.057	-4.89	0
Pocketbook	0.408	0.149	2.74	0.006
Age	0.015	0.006	2.48	0.013
Education	0.126	0.059	2.13	0.033
Male	-0.046	0.143	-0.32	0.749
/cut1	1.665	0.674		
/cut2	5.619	0.713		
N (observations)	1006.000			
LR chi2(8)	337.500		Prob > chi2 = 0	
Log likelihood	-660.791			
PRE	42.5%			

possibly capturing different versions of the same structural dynamic, which is not an issue here.
- Concerns specific to particular variables were reanalysed. For example, the variable *Pocketbook* might not represent self-interest but could rather reflect increased contact with Mainland people, which would influence pro-China identities through contact theory (Wu et al, 2014). To control for that possibility, we included in a diagnostic analysis a measure of visits to the Mainland, which was not statistically significant nor did it affect the variable *Pocketbook*'s impact.
- Returning to Table 7.4, the variables *Probability of War if Independence* and *Taiwan's Economy* were not included because in the layering it was shown they added negative PRE. These variables were added to a diagnostic model and reanalysed. Results were the same as those presented.
- The analysis in Table 7.3 was reanalysed, dropping those who identify as Chinese (making the dependent variable a choice between Taiwanese or both Taiwanese and Chinese), with similar results as those presented.

Political evaluation

Identity is an amorphous concept. Evaluations of politicians, however, represent more concrete attitudes, especially if they are tied to the act of voting. On the one hand, studies have found that, in Taiwan, attitudes can form independently across a range of critical issues (Lee et al, 2018). On the other hand, party and national identification are jointly endogenous, influencing each other: 'Taiwan's electoral and party politics are not only reflective of social cleavage, but also constructive in shaping ordinary people's party identification and national identity' (Lin, 2019: 69). There are thus multiple and sometimes conflicting layers of dynamics that influence Taiwanese identity.

To assess the robustness of our layered model of factors that influence ideational behaviour, we employ a model similar to that presented earlier in Table 7.4 to predict an individual's assessment of President Tsai Ing-wen's political performance. In particular, we examine how the variables that provide such substantial explanatory power for understanding who identifies exclusively as Taiwanese perform in an analysis of the disapproval of President Tsai. By applying the model we used to explain identity to support for the president, especially this president and her strong views on identity, allows us to double check to make sure that factors such as the wording on our identity question and other issues are not driving our results. Thus this second analysis meaningfully explores the robustness of our earlier results. It also expands the scope of our analysis beyond the abstract self-conception of identity to include the more concrete evaluation of the country's most prominent and controversial politician.

By aligning with a mixed Chinese and Taiwanese identity, the KMT cut itself off from those who saw themselves as exclusively Taiwanese (Batto, 2019). The DPP was one of the main parties to fill the void left by the KMT's political decline. While the DPP was both influenced by changing Taiwanese identities and affected people's identities (Li and Zhang, 2017), much of the attention has focused on President Tsai. President Tsai was elected on 20 May 2016 with 56.15 per cent of the vote (Tung, 2016). In many ways her victory was 'unprecedented' (Lin W., 2016). She is the first woman to be elected President of Taiwan and represents the DPP, which is a member of Taiwan's Pan-Green Coalition. President Tsai initially opposed the 1992 Consensus and supported Taiwanese independence. Her policy positions have become more in sync with the ambiguity of the status quo, although under this president's tenure, relations with the Mainland have been tenuous.

Table 7.6: Multivariate analysis of *Disapproval of President Tsai*

	Coefficient	Std. Err.	z	P>z
Support 1992 Consensus	0.172	0.051	3.34	0.001
Probability of future success of Taiwanese independence	-0.197	0.025	-8.02	0
Mainland economic ties	-0.444	0.091	-4.88	0
Mainland leverage	-0.258	0.048	-5.34	0
Pocketbook	0.637	0.128	4.97	0
Age	-0.007	0.005	-1.55	0.122
Education	0.169	0.048	3.51	0
Gender	-0.138	0.117	-1.18	0.238
N (observations)	1,020			
Log likelihood =	-1329.492			
LR chi2(8) =	328.710	Prob>chi2 = 0		
PRE	15.30%			

President Tsai has successfully pushed a progressive agenda including LGBTQ rights while also increasing defence spending.

Table 7.6 displays the ordered logit, multivariate analysis results of applying the model in Table 7.4 on *Disapproval of President Tsai*.[5] The model largely shows that variables have a parallel effect on disapproval of the president as they had on identity formation. *Support 1992 Consensus*, *Pocketbook* and *Education* are positively connected to disapproval. Once again, *Gender* plays no role, while *Age* is just barely insignificant. Views on independence, economic ties and leverage have significant negative effects on her evaluation. Statistics suggest good model fit; the PRE is 15 per cent. Overall, the political model and its variables perform similarly to the identity model, although the explanatory power of the political model to predict beyond what is gained beyond choosing the modal value (4/dissatisfied) is considerably lower than the identity model.

Analysis and synthesis

It is an understatement to say that identity in Taiwan is a big deal. Firing up the crowd at a DPP rally, Taiwanese public figure Chen Li-hung stated 'I was born in Taiwan. I grew up in Taiwan. So why did the teachers in school tell me I am still Chinese? Since my youth, I have felt that I am not Chinese, *I am Taiwanese!*' (Frisch, 2016, emphasis added). A declaration of Taiwanese identity represents a powerful message capable of mobilizing the DPP party faithful.

It is important to understand how this seemingly elemental claim about sense of self differs so dramatically from that of other national identities. For example, take an American perspective. Imagine prior to the presidential election 2020 President Trump going to a rally to whip up his supporters not by shouting "Make America Great Again" but by simply stating "I am American". In the US, such a claim would be vacuous. Everyone at the rally would identify as an American. Some might claim to be Italian-Americans, Evangelical-Americans, Jewish-Americans, Cuban-Americans or a African-Americans, but it is the word that modifies American that reflects their ideational choice – not simply the statement of American identity (and of course the same would be true for President Biden during the election – claiming that he is an American would neither be controversial nor mobilize his followers). Not so in Taiwan. Taiwanese identity is not just the embrace of a country, but represents the embrace of a distinctive vision of a people's journey forward into the future.

A major reason that Taiwanese identity remains controversial and worthy of study is that the ROC is not giving in easily to the PRC's goal of unification (BBC, 2019). Recognizing the layered nature of Taiwanese identities, the PRC uses direct strategies such as promoting Chinese culture and the idea that being 'Taiwanese' betrays it (Stockton, 2002); using its foreign policy and its massive economy to isolate Taiwan globally and to have Taiwan's country status downgraded and sovereignty abated (Pan, 2007; Blanchard and Yu, 2017); and by supporting pro-China groups within Taiwan (Lee and Pomfret, 2019). Indirectly, it is the rapid rise of the Mainland's power, regional and increasingly global leadership, technological prowess and, most of all, economic ascent that amplifies the status of the Mainland and the potential benefits of enhancing cross-Strait relations for Taiwan and its people (Keller and Rawski, 2007). At the same time, China's unrestrained use of its accumulating material power and capabilities to coerce Taiwan has also produced the unintended and opposite effect of further widening the political gap. This cross-Strait dynamic, in turn, profoundly influences how the Taiwanese people view themselves.

Focusing on the influence of cross-Strait relations on identity formation among Taiwanese people, and attempting to move beyond topics such as democracy and US activity that were examined in Chapter 6, we asked six questions: (1) How does the 1992 Consensus influence identity? (While this was surveyed in Chapter 6, here we examine in particular the explanatory power on identity formation that the Consensus wields.) (2) How do views of independence and war affect Taiwanese identity? (3) Is Taiwanese identity based on personal gain? (4) How do Taiwan's potential gains or loses affect identity? (5) To what extent do demographic factors influence Taiwanese identification? (6) How do all of these factors vary in their influence on identity formation versus political assessments?

We have employed, in this chapter, a layered empirical approach that is consistent with our systemist perspective and its goal of minimizing exclusive reliance on *ceteris paribus* clauses through model specification across different levels of factors influencing behaviour. We analysed the Taiwan National Security Survey Data, a survey of approximately 1,000 Taiwanese adults conducted in 2017. Multiple methods, three different dependent variables and extensive diagnostics suggest the reported results are robust.

We find that beliefs about policies and actions regarding cross-Strait relations play the critical role in identifying who views themselves as Taiwanese versus those who see themselves as both Chinese and Taiwanese or Chinese. The same dynamic applies to the political evaluation of President Tsai. Specifically, we obtain the following results:

1. *Support 1992 Consensus.*
   a. The most influential factor in our models. Identification as Taiwanese is greatly affected by one's perspective on the 1992 Consensus. Those who reject the 1992 Consensus are much more likely to Identify Only as Taiwanese and those who accept the Consensus much more likely to identify as both Chinese and Taiwanese or as Chinese. Critically, this position explained a large percent of the variation remaining in *Identify as a Taiwanese* after choosing the modal value. This finding is important. It means that those who reject the one-China approach for Taiwan reject personally as well. *We thus demonstrate a clear connection between preferences over national policy and choices regarding individual identity.*
   b. Those who reject the 1992 Consensus are more likely to rate President Tsai's performance higher.
2. *Probability of Future Success of Taiwanese Independence.*
   a. Those who believe that the likelihood of the 'future success of Taiwanese independence' is higher are more likely to Identify Only as Taiwanese. This variable explained a substantial percent of the variation remaining in *Identify as a Taiwanese* after choosing the modal value.
   b. Higher levels of the belief of independence also translated into stronger support for President Tsai.

3. *Mainland Economic Ties.*
   a. Those who oppose stronger economic ties with the Mainland are more likely to Identify Only as Taiwanese. This variable explained a substantial percent of the variation remaining in *Identify as a Taiwanese* after choosing the modal value.
   b. Those who oppose stronger economic ties with the Mainland are more likely to support President Tsai.
4. *Mainland Leverage.*
   a. Those who are concerned about the ability of China to translate its ascent into leverage against Taiwan were less likely to Identify Only as Taiwanese.
      i. Looking at both Mainland Economic Ties and Mainland Leverage, a number of the respondents see the rise of Mainland China's economy as a threat (providing leverage over Taiwan) and not a benefit (providing gain to Taiwan).
   b. Those who are concerned about the ability of China to translate its ascent into leverage against Taiwan are less likely to disapprove of President Tsai.
5. *Pocketbook.*
   a. Those who believe they personally gain from increased interaction and improved cross-Strait relations are less likely to identify only as Taiwanese.
   b. Those who believe they personally gain from increased interaction and improved cross-Strait relations are more likely to disapprove of President Tsai.
6. *To what extent do standard demographic factors influence Taiwanese identification?*
   a. Standard demographic factors like gender, age, and education play little role (just age) on identity although both *Age* and *Education* are negatively correlated with the likelihood of identifying exclusively as Taiwanese.
   b. Those with more education are less supportive of President Tsai. Neither *Age* nor *Gender* affect assessment of the president.

What does all of this mean? The findings in this chapter reinforce the pattern from Chapters 5–6. In particular, this empirical chapter shows that *Taiwan identities are heavily based on relational conceptions of the Mainland and Taiwan*. And, that abstract ideological factors, such as views on whether there are one or two Chinas, are more important than personal gain. The results presented are robust.

The implications of a cross-Strait-driven identity versus one shaped solely by personal gain are important. In particular, a cross-Strait-driven identity formation process means that people are less influenced by the potential economic gains generated by a rapidly ascending China than the growing evidence of China's anti-democratic nature resulting from the policies China's government employs to foster those economic gains. In particular, some events, such as the handling of COVID-19, vividly highlight the differences in democratization and governance between Taiwan and the PRC.

We also find that standard factors that influence identity, such as age, education, gender and self-interest, play a smaller role in the identity formation process than beliefs about policies and cross-Strait relations. This challenges standard generational explanations for identity change and suggests that it is not youth, but rather a political perspective that rejects the two-state-one-system notion that is most critical for explaining who identifies as exclusively Taiwanese. Remember, the correlation of age and the other variables never exceeded standards of concerns. Thus, while young people may be more likely to embrace the full array of ideological factors that shape Taiwanese identity, it is not age itself but the belief in these ideas that drives the Taiwanese ideational formation process.

Summing up

Policy matters. The results of data analysis carried out in this chapter suggest a close connection between policy and identity. The key policy we examine here, the 1992 Consensus, has the greatest impact on people's choice of identity. We have examined how cross-Strait relations influence both individuals' identities and their domestic political assessments, recognizing also that identities, evaluations and elections influence cross-Strait relations (He, 2014). Taiwanese people's understanding of the 1992 Consensus or the one-China concept is at least in part determined by how Beijing ensures the integrity of the 1992 Consensus. The one country, two systems model currently implemented in Hong Kong and Macao is the touchstone of Taiwan's future under the one country, two systems framework.

This study also showed further support for the greater influence of ideology over self interest in influencing ideational behaviour. Positions on intangible concepts explained significant amounts of the unexplained variance, while variables capturing personal advantage had considerably less influence.

What are the policy implications of these results? For Taiwan, they suggest that claims that demographics by themselves will enable rapid and widespread change in identity might be overstated (perhaps similar to how US election analysts overestimated the pre-2020 election impact of the growing Hispanic population on electoral politics). Instead, policy makers need to make clear the values and ideology that underly people's decision to embrace an exclusively Taiwanese identity. For China, it is clear that the prospect of personal gain is insufficient for many Taiwanese to counterbalance the negative results of the Mainland's aggressive policy to isolate and threaten Taiwan. Our results suggest that China can neither buy Taiwanese identities nor bully the Taiwanese people into identifying with the Mainland.

Studies show, that dyadic conflict tends to reinforce nationalistic thinking (Momesso and Lee, 2019). This dynamic appears to create a feedback loop across the Taiwanese Strait – nationalism leads to stronger identity with Taiwan, which causes more conflict, which increases the spirit of national identity. Thus, domestic factors that encourage a mutual, soft power, détente-like approach might be required to break the mutually powered conflict spiral.

The current great power competition between the US and China will also influence the status quo in Taiwan and its people's identities. The Mainland has repeatedly threatened both parts of the country (most notably Quemoy and Matsu) and poised a potential existential threat to Taiwan, which in all cases was defended and supported by the US. Many of those efforts, such as during the Korean War, occurred before the ascent of China and its status as a global superpower. The policies that emerge from the simultaneously economically robust and politically conflictual relations between the US and China will clearly affect Taiwan and, as our results show strongly, influence Taiwanese identities.

There are few places in the world where saying 'I identify with the governing institution' represents a contentious claim. Taiwan is clearly one of those places. 'I am Taiwanese' reflects more than just an identity, it is a powerful statement reflecting an ideologically influenced vision of a nation and its future that flies in the face of the world's second most powerful country. Taiwanese identity represents a complex, dynamic concept that blends political, sociological, anthropological, economic and psychological influences. We have examined the explanatory power of a wide array of factors reflecting this blended structure to explain who identifies exclusively as Taiwanese. We found that alignment with a set of cross-Strait ideological policies is much more influential than individual interest for capturing who identifies as exclusively Taiwanese. Thus those who claim to be Taiwanese identify with a distinctive story driving Taiwan's future trajectory.

Notes

1. See Niou (2017). Professor Emerson Niou has graciously granted the authors use of his Taiwan National Security Survey data collected by the Election Study Center of the National Chengchi University, Taipei, Taiwan under the auspices of the Program in Asian Security Studies (PASS) at Duke University, for which we are highly appreciative. All variable coding and analyses were conducted by us.
2. Note we do not present the statistical models' results (although they are available from the authors) as these bivariate regressions are under-specified; they are missing the other variables we think may be important and thus their coefficient estimates are biased. Rather, we use the PRE generated by these analyses to order the layering we conduct in constructing our more complete multivariate models.
3. That is, the parameter estimates are not meaningful during the stacking process until the final model. Only the final model is complete and does not suffer from missing variable bias. As the sequencing of model construction influences PRE scores, with a different sequence leading to different PRE values, the specific values of the scores are less important than whether or not the addition of the variable explains more of the remaining variation. Thus the stacking process (as opposed to our final model) illustrates our story but does not test it.
4. For additional informative quotations, see Kan (2014).
5. As a reminder, respondents were asked, 'How satisfied are you with President Tsai's performance?' A response of 'Very satisfied' meant the variable *President Tsai's Disapproval* was coded 1 if 'Very satisfied', 2 if 'Satisfied', 3 if 'Depends', 'Indifferent', 'Don't know', 4 if 'Dissatisfied' and 5 if 'Very dissatisfied'.

8

A New Vision of Taiwanese Identity, the Rise of China, Cross-Strait Relations and the United States in Northeast Asia

Who is it that can tell me who I am?
(King Lear in William Shakespeare, *King Lear*)

Who am I? I am myself and I'm looking for myself.

I'm thinking of myself, looking at myself and getting to know myself.

I'm questioning myself, hating myself but also loving myself.
(Wu Hsing-Kuo, 'A Taiwanese Actor's Personal Response to King Lear')[1]

Overview

This study has focused on Taiwanese identity, the ascent of China, cross-Strait relations and the role of the US in Northeast Asia. An ensemble of methods has been applied in order to learn more about how these items theoretically and empirically impact upon each other. Our method thus draws on the broad-brush approach often employed to think about confusing and conflicted identities and their fundamental ideational questions, such as those posed by King Lear and Wu Hsing-Kuo. The significant difference in time and location for the preceding questions reinforces the point that issues of identity are global and immanent.

What, then, can be said about Taiwanese identity in connection with the ascent of China, cross-Strait relations and US activity in Northeast Asia? A look back at preceding chapters will set the stage for the tasks that remain to be carried out. All of this works towards a sense of where identity stands among the ideal points identified in Table 1.1, which include primarily ideology- or interest-based, along with gradations in between.

We began in Chapter 2 with a historical overview of Taiwan from early times, with emphasis upon the period after the KMT migration in the late 1940s and especially the years in the new millennium. This material created a context for research on our basic question about identity, while also providing a basic background to those who are specialists in neither Taiwan nor Northeast Asia.

Chapter 3 reviewed academic literature on the evolving Taiwanese identity and factors seen shaping its evolution to obtain a baseline model for elaboration through further research. This chapter demonstrates that there is a long, historical dynamic driving Taiwanese identity. Most critically, however, recent and dramatic improvements in China, especially economically, have created disequilibrium in the Taiwanese ideational process, requiring new efforts to capture these shifting systems and to reconcile them with past dynamics.

Chapter 4 organized insights from existing academic studies – a wide range of scholarship that reflects analytic eclecticism as opposed to paradigmatic boundaries – into a new, systemist graphic representation of cause and effect to capture the array of influences on Taiwanese identity. In doing so we make two key points. First, the structure underlying national ideational processes is too complex to be captured in a standard, 'A $\rightarrow$ B' causal argument and regression-style equation. More like a dynamic social-network movie, the factors shaping the Taiwanese ideational process are literally all over the map. Second, we focused on three factors: cross-Strait relations, the ascent of China and the US as key blocks within the ideational system and then delineated subfactors such as the 1992 Consensus, the Sunflower Movement, party dynamics between the KMT and DPP, and others as critical by themselves and through their linkages. Together, these factors created a far-ranging matrix of causal factors for us to examine empirically through multiple methods of data collection.

Empirical elaboration for the baseline of knowledge got underway in Chapter 5, which analysed multiple waves of elite interviews that took place in Taiwan. These interviews were striking in their frank and honest nature of both the complexity and opaqueness of Taiwan's identity, the political import captured by the simple statement, 'I am Taiwanese', and the multitude of factors shaping and being shaped by identity issues in Taiwan. The interviewees also explained that the tremendous rise of China simultaneously changed everything and changed nothing. That is, the power of the Mainland and the pressure it could impose were clear and influential. At the same time, the transformation of identity in Taiwan was a process driven by a host of factors, generational, democratic and ideological, that China did not influence.

Chapters 6 and 7 reviewed the results from multiple, independent surveys of public opinion in Taiwan and identified further connections. Flowing from the findings in Chapter 5, Chapter 6 focused on the role of the US and the influence of democratization on Taiwanese identity. Both factors, along with age and generational dynamics, were found to strongly influence who included Taiwanese as a part of their notion of self. Employing a different dataset and empirical method, Chapter 7 expanded on the results shown in Chapter 6 by looking at how views on the 1992 Consensus, the likelihood that Taiwan declares independence, personal gain from business with China and individual characteristics affected those who claimed to be only Taiwanese. We found that factors like the view of the 1992 Consensus played a huge role in capturing Taiwanese identity, but not so much factors that reflected those who stood to gain from improved relations with the Mainland or standard socioeconomic factors like age, gender and education level.

This final chapter will unfold in five additional sections. Using the knowledge gained from the empirical analyses in Chapters 5-7, the second section reviews the contents of Figure 4.2, which in Chapter 4 synthesized what has been learned so far from the academic literature on Taiwanese identity, cross-Strait relations, the rise of China and US activity in Northeast Asia. The third section elaborates upon the systemist graphic to provide an updated sense of what is to be believed about cause and effect. Drawing on the results of our multimethod empirical research, the fourth section assesses this elaborated vision of Taiwanese identity, cross-Strait relations, the rise of China and US involvement in Northeast Asia. Suggestions for future research appear in the fifth section. The sixth and final section offers a few final thoughts on the project as a whole.

A review of what is known so far

While no review of the four interlocking subject areas – Taiwanese identity, cross-Strait relations, the ascent of China and the role of the US in Northeast Asia – could claim to be complete, the contents of Chapter 3 reflect an extensive search through the literature (and draw on the historical dynamics laid out in Chapter 2). Conceptual location of relevant items also is made somewhat easier because many expositions focus on two or even more of these four interwoven features (Taiwanese identity, cross-Strait relations, ascent of China and the role of the US). Thus Figure 4.2, which offered a graphic summary of cause and effect gleaned from the academic literature, may be regarded as representative of what has come before. This graphic represents our 'theoretical baseline'; replicated as Figure 8.1, it will be elaborated on through the accumulation of findings from interviews and surveys reported in the preceding chapters.

Figure 8.1 contains 16 variables in its depiction of cause and effect, four of which play generic roles. Six variables are initial and thus set pathways in motion – one micro and three macro from within Northeast Asia, with two located in the international system. The graphic features two convergent variables – one at the macro level and the other at the micro level. There are three terminal variables in the figure – two micro and one macro. As a reminder of a few basic points of notation, initial and terminal variables appear, respectively, as an oval and an octagon. A convergent variable takes the form of a parallelogram, while a divergent one appears as a diamond. A hexagon corresponds to a nodal variable.

From the standpoint of systemism, calling back to the ideal types of connection displayed in Figure 4.1, the graphic summary of cause and effect looks comprehensive. Figure 8.1 includes macro–macro, micro–micro, micro–macro and macro–micro connections, along with linkages back and forth between the system and its environment. In a strict sense, however, the figure remains incomplete because one variant from among the four leading back and forth between the system and its environment does not appear. More specifically, there is no link from the micro level of the system to the environment. Nevertheless, this figure and its conceptualization stands as relatively complete in comparison to many models encountered through the study of politics, which tend to leave out at least one basic type of connection altogether (James, 2019a; 2019b).

Looking over the results and syntheses of our elite interviews, multiple statistical analyses and historical evaluation, what did we

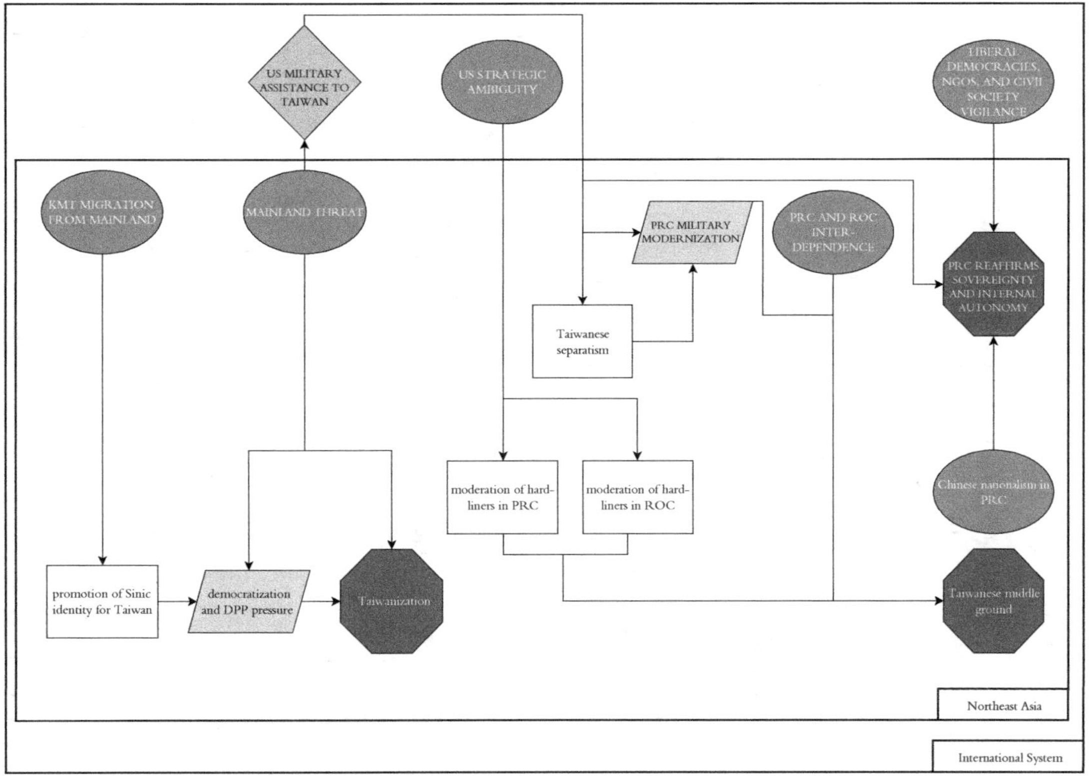

Figure 8.1: Cause and effect for Taiwanese identity, the rise of China, cross-Strait relations and US influence in Northeast Asia

learn about the complex system shaping Taiwanese identity? The short answer is, we learned a lot! And, drawing from the approach outlined in Chapter 4, we also developed graphical methods to communicate our synthetic results.

Elaboration

Figure 8.2 displays a revised model that reflects the results from the elite interviews and public opinion surveys reviewed in Chapters 5–7. Consider the profile of the diagram in terms of variables. The elaborated Figure 8.2 now includes 26 variables. The pathways entail four initial and two terminal variables. There is a great deal of contingency built into this account: four divergent, six convergent and three nodal variables. With regard to the possible connections from systemism, the figure offers a more complete treatment. All four of the basic connections within a system – macro–macro, micro–micro, macro–micro and micro–macro – are included. So, too, are linkages from Northeast Asia back and forth with the international system. The only type of connection still missing is from the micro level of Northeast Asia into the international system.

Before moving ahead with specific connections in Figures 8.2a to 8.2bb, a few observations are in order. First, the points of elaboration over and beyond Figure 4.2 emphasize more recent years because events from a long time ago and especially before the new millennium have been in place long enough to obtain some degree of sustained consensus on interpretation. Second, the diagram is chronological, from left to right, in only an *approximate* way because of its internal complexity. The earliest of the initial variables appears at the far left and the two terminal variables appear at the extreme right, but it would be an act of false precision to say that all connections appear in exact order because the diagram is so intricate. As for the complexity itself, a point from Chapter 4 is worth raising again: While the figure conveys quite a bit of detail, this is because it is intellectually honest in conveying the data.

Figure 8.2a displays the region of Northeast Asia as the system and the international system as its environment. The micro and macro levels in Northeast Asia correspond, respectively, to individual actors and processes beyond them. For example, cross-Strait relations are macro, whereas public opinion in either the ROC or PRC is micro.

Figure 8.2b conveys a macro to micro linkage with 'KMT MIGRATION FROM MAINLAND' → 'promotion of Sinic identity for Taiwan'. These variables, respectively, are initial and divergent

A NEW VISION OF TAIWANESE IDENTITY

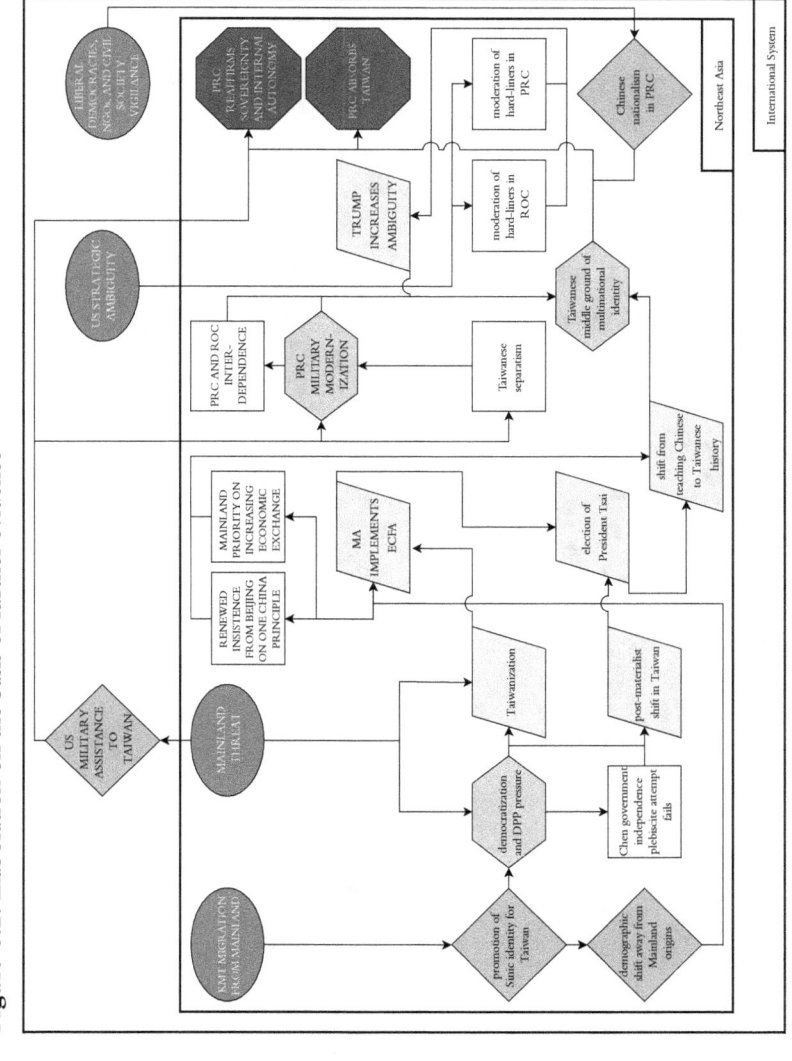

Figure 8.2: Elaboration on the basis of further evidence

Figure 8.2a: Elaboration on the basis of further evidence

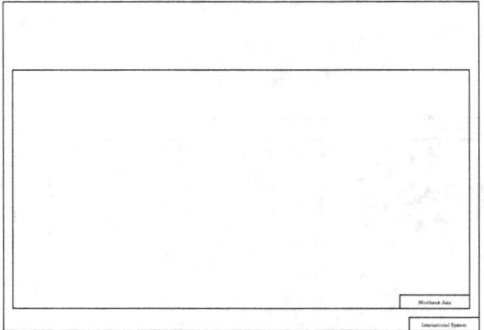

Figure 8.2b: Elaboration on the basis of further evidence

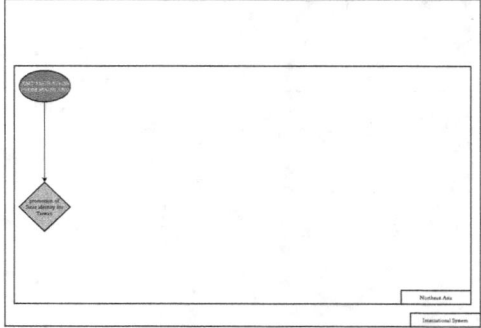

Figure 8.2c: Elaboration on the basis of further evidence

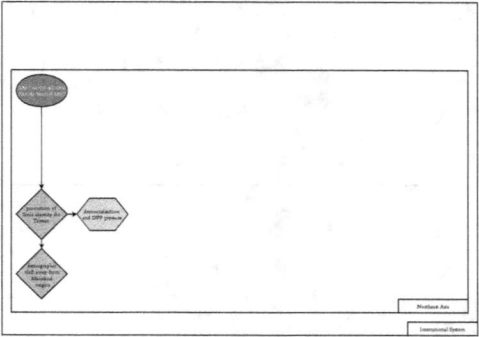

and therefore depicted as an oval and a diamond. With the massive migration to Formosa in the late stages of the Chinese Civil War, those who arrived from the Mainland attempted to sustain a Sinic identity through designation of events such as the National Day, along with parental influence and school indoctrination (Li, 2002: 107, 111).

This pathway continues with two branches at the micro level in Figure 8.2c. The first is 'promotion of Sinic identity for Taiwan' → 'demographic shift away from Mainland origins'. As a divergent variable, 'demographic shift away from Mainland origins' appears as a diamond. This demographic effect follows on as a form of resistance to Sinification that could have ensued in the population through further waves of migration after 1949. In spite of the attempt towards achieving a more uniform identification with Chinese culture, the demographics of Formosa moved in a different direction as a matter of choice towards a greater Taiwanese sense of self. The second branch in Figure 8.2c is 'promotion of Sinic identity for Taiwan' → 'democratization and DPP pressure'. As a nodal variable, 'democratization and DPP pressure' appears as a hexagon. A transforming event in this context is what became known as the 28 February incident, when protesters took over the Taiwan Radio building. Violent demonstrations in every major city, which reflected underlying grievances related to side effects of huge and ongoing KMT migration to Formosa, occurred in response to broadcasting of these events. In retrospect, the violent confrontations revealed serious divisions that became more intense with 'imposition of a Chinese nationalist discourse that rejected rather than incorporated Taiwanese local identity, language, culture, and perhaps most important, Taiwanese collective memory of the February 28 Incident' (Edmondson, 2002: 25, 28, 30). While the process itself took decades, the starting point for democratization can be traced to rejection of a one-party regime transplanted from the Mainland by a significant proportion of those already on the island of Formosa.

Figure 8.2d shows a connection from the micro to macro level: 'demographic shift away from Mainland origins' → 'MA IMPLEMENTS ECFA'. As a convergent variable, 'MA IMPLEMENTS ECFA' is depicted as a parallelogram. With a diminishing fraction of the population having lived through the Chinese Civil War on the Mainland, the KMT needed to pursue policies to keep the connection alive. Rapid development of the PRC provided an opening for Taiwan along the economic dimension, which Ma seized with ECFA. This policy reflected an effort to counteract the effects of Taiwanization and restore the electoral fortunes of the KMT.

Figure 8.2d: Elaboration on the basis of further evidence

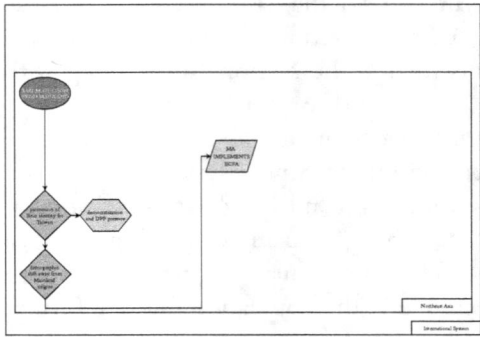

Figure 8.2e: Elaboration on the basis of further evidence

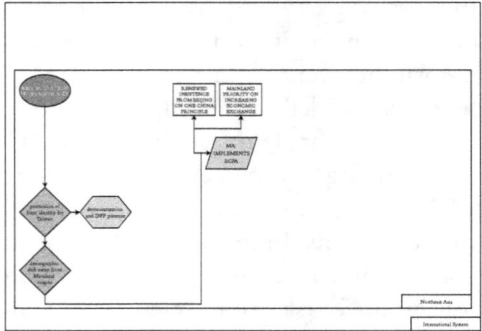

Figure 8.2f: Elaboration on the basis of further evidence

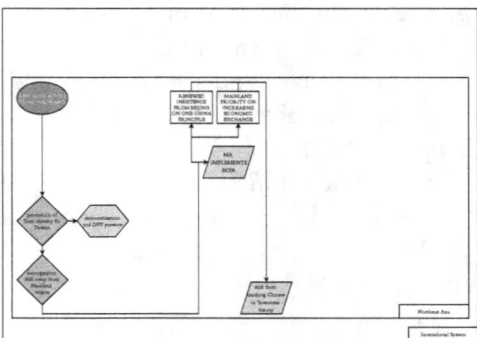

Figure 8.2e shows two further pathways that extend from the micro to the macro level. The first is 'demographic shift away from Mainland origins' → 'RENEWED INSISTENCE FROM BEIJING ON ONE CHINA PRINCIPLE'. The PRC also is able to see demographic change in Taiwan and the resultant weakening of the KMT. Take, for example, the protests from the losing KMT side after the 2000 election about what looked to them like the 'Taiwanization of politics' (Roy, 2003: 230–231). To counteract rising DPP influence, the Mainland increasingly emphasizes the existence of One China. While this is not understood in the same way on both sides of the Taiwan Strait, assertion of the principle pleases elite and mass opinion in the PRC because One China is taken to mean the existence of the PRC as a single state that incorporates adjacent territories such as Hong Kong and Taiwan. The other, and related, connection in Figure 8.2e is 'demographic shift away from Mainland origins' → 'MAINLAND PRIORITY ON INCREASING ECONOMIC EXCHANGE'. The straightforward linkage here is with pursuit of ECFA along with any number of miscellaneous economic exchanges with Taiwan. For example, the Mainland used 'fruit diplomacy' to connect with farmers in Taiwan and the first direct cargo flight between the ROC and PRC took place in July 2006 with the arrival of a flight into Shanghai (Shirk, 2007: 204). Like the KMT, the PRC hoped to counteract the weakening of Sinic identity in Taiwan as a by-product of the demographic change underway.

Pathways from the preceding diagram converge in Figure 8.2f with 'RENEWED INSISTENCE FROM BEIJING ON ONE CHINA PRINCIPLE' → 'shift from teaching Chinese to Taiwanese history' and 'MAINLAND PRIORITY ON INCREASING ECONOMIC EXCHANGE' → 'shift from teaching Chinese to Taiwanese history'. As a convergent variable, 'shift from teaching Chinese to Taiwanese history' appears as a parallelogram. The change in curriculum for Taiwanese schools constitutes a form of resistance against the political and economic pressures emanating from the Mainland. This approach, of course, is less confrontational and provocative than a direct attack on the principle of One China.

Figure 8.2g depicts movement from the macro to the micro level along two pathways. The first is 'MAINLAND THREAT' → 'democratization and DPP pressure'. As an initial variable, 'MAINLAND THREAT' is depicted as an oval. In an overall sense, observers for a long time have seen hostility to a democratizing Taiwan as causing, at least to some degree, mixed effects. A specific and nuanced example concerns the disposition of President Chen towards discussions

Figure 8.2g: Elaboration on the basis of further evidence

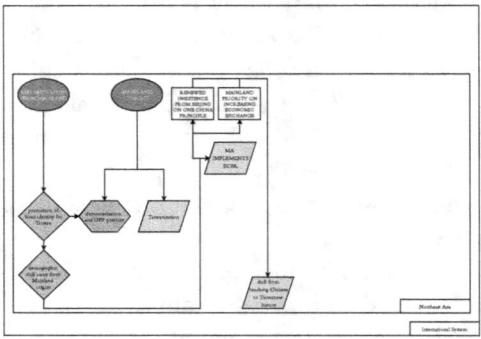

Figure 8.2h: Elaboration on the basis of further evidence

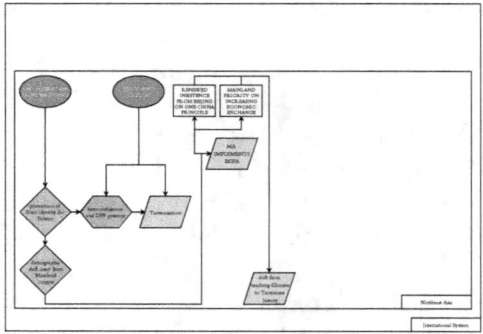

Figure 8.2i: Elaboration on the basis of further evidence

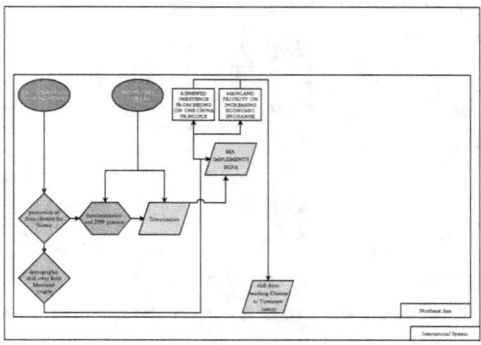

with the PRC. On the one hand, the president expressed a willingness to talk about the One China principle. On the other hand, Chen refused to accept, as a precondition for such discussions, the Mainland's version of the principle (Rigger, 2001: 213). The other connection in Figure 8.2g is 'MAINLAND THREAT' → 'Taiwanization'. As a convergent variable, 'Taiwanization' appears as a parallelogram. This shows a multifaceted set of effects from pursuit of intimidation tactics. Notably, the ascent of China is seen more negatively as a function of the rapidity in its military buildup (Chu and Chang, 2017: 106). This may even fully counteract whatever value the Mainland obtains from an aggressive-looking posture towards Taiwan.

Movement continues along a micro level pathway in Figure 8.2h with 'democratization and DPP pressure' → 'Taiwanization'. This is one of the most strongly confirmed connections with regard to the rise of Taiwanese identity. 'Accompanying democratization in Taiwan', observes Lin (2002: 219; see also Corcuff, 2002a: 92, 97; T. Lin, 2002: 127), 'are the awakening of a long-suppressed Taiwanese consciousness, the society's quest for international recognition, and the surfacing of domestic disputes between Taiwanese nationalists and Chinese nationalists on the statehood issue'. These words are just as true two decades on.

Figure 8.2i returns from the micro to the macro level: 'Taiwanization' → 'MA IMPLEMENTS ECFA'. Intuition about this is straightforward; the president attempted to counteract Taiwanization and resurrect the fortunes of the KMT by pointing towards greater prosperity via enhanced exchanges with the Mainland. This is followed by a closely related macro to micro connection in Figure 8.2j: 'MA IMPLEMENTS ECFA' → 'election of President Tsai'. Many on the island perceived ECFA to be beneficial only to a relatively narrow constituency, notably those already well off and in support of the KMT. Mounting economic grievances related to ECFA helped bring Tsai into office.

Figure 8.2k extends one of the pathways at the micro level: 'democratization and DPP pressure' → 'Chen government independence plebiscite fails'. This connection serves as an example of ongoing forces, on the island and beyond, which limit the prospects for achievement of status as an independent state. For example, factional conflict can be aggravated when the DPP moves assertively towards independence (Roy, 2003: 232). Even more obviously, any explicit movement in the direction of sovereignty is likely to produce an intense reaction from the PRC (O'Hanlon, 2000: 83). This could even include an invasion that many in the US might blame on Taiwan itself. Thus, it is not surprising that Chen's plebiscite looked like a 'bridge

Figure 8.2j: Elaboration on the basis of further evidence

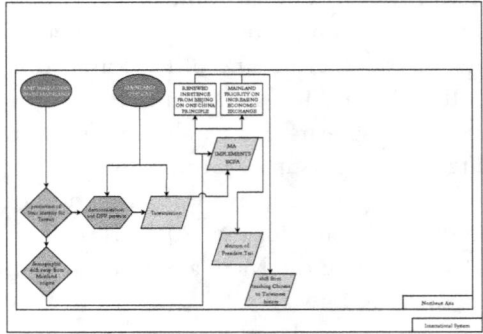

Figure 8.2k: Elaboration on the basis of further evidence

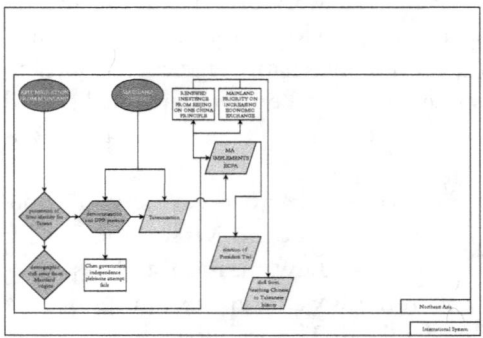

Figure 8.2l: Elaboration on the basis of further evidence

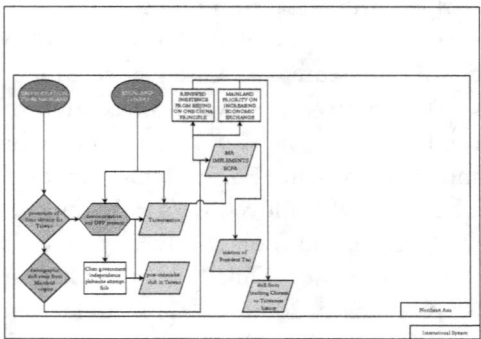

too far' even for a significant number of Pan-Green adherents while experiencing the DPP's ascent in politics on the island. Caution about signalling independence is likely to be even more entrenched today.

Figure 8.2l depicts two interrelated connections at the micro level: 'democratization and DPP pressure' → 'post-materialist shift in Taiwan' and 'Chen government independence plebiscite fails' → 'post-materialist shift in Taiwan'. Democratization and the political party associated with it point towards values that have been deemed post-materialism (Inglehart, 1981) – human rights, environmental quality and other items associated with the DPP agenda. These values are post-material in the sense that they do not pertain to the standard sense of political preference that leads to 'pocketbook' voting. In addition, the inability to move forward with an institutional change through a referendum process redirected energy even further in the direction of a transformed culture. All of this points towards greater post-materialism among the people of Taiwan. In light of this shift, the next step follows on quite easily in Figure 8.2m: 'post-materialist shift in Taiwan' → 'election of President Tsai'. The DPP candidate appealed to voters who supported post-materialist values that contrasted with the more business-oriented KMT.

Figure 8.2n extends the preceding pathway at the micro level: 'election of President Tsai' → 'shift from teaching Chinese to Taiwanese history'. This change reflected the value system of the new president and the DPP. In particular, the office of the president looked into 'historical truths concerning the era of single-party rule' (Gao, 2016: 15). This served as an obvious signal about a change in school curriculum to emphasize Taiwanese rather than Chinese history.

Figure 8.2o continues the preceding micro level route: 'shift from teaching Chinese to Taiwanese history' → 'Taiwanese middle ground

Figure 8.2m: Elaboration on the basis of further evidence

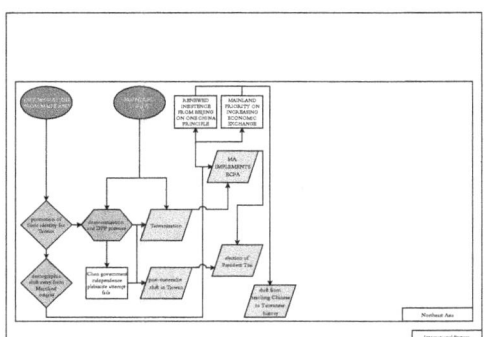

Figure 8.2n: Elaboration on the basis of further evidence

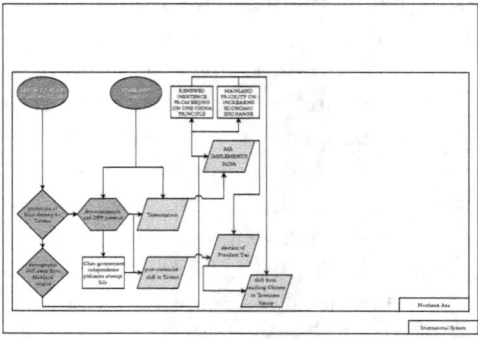

Figure 8.2o: Elaboration on the basis of further evidence

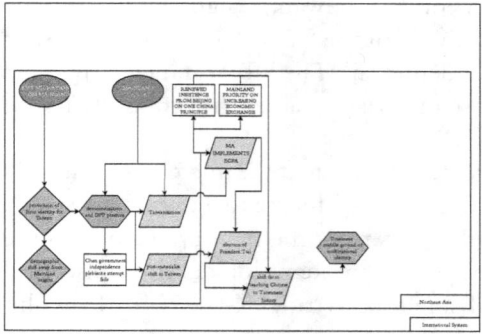

Figure 8.2p: Elaboration on the basis of further evidence

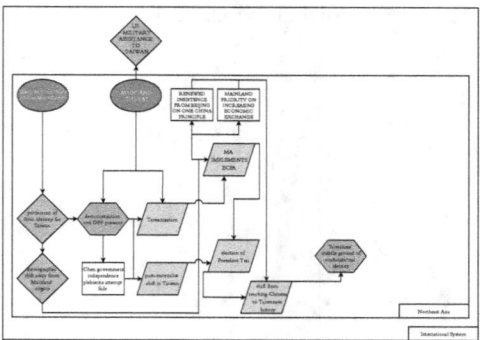

of multinational identity'. As a nodal variable, the latter appears as a hexagon. This connection is obvious because the history of Taiwan is far from purely Sinic and includes many aspects covered already in Chapter 2. The change in curriculum contributes to a more multifaceted and inclusive sense of self among those who live on Formosa.

Figure 8.2p shows a new pathway that ensues from the macro level to the international system: 'MAINLAND THREAT' → 'US MILITARY ASSISTANCE TO TAIWAN'. As a divergent variable, 'US MILITARY ASSISTANCE TO TAIWAN' appears as a diamond. This is a well-established connection, confirmed through various iterations of threat and response. For example, based on a Pentagon report at the end of the last millennium that referred to the possibility of the military balance tipping towards the PRC and away from Taiwan over time, one analyst argued that the US should help Taiwan 'upgrade its decaying submarine fleet' and grant Taipei its 'request for the P-3 Orion aircraft, which can drop buoys with sonar devices and fire torpedoes at any submarines the buoys detect' (O'Hanlon, 2000: 86, 85). A much more recent study echoed the same sentiments; Beijing's expanding military 'has fueled Taipei's counter-acquisition of new air and missile defenses, anti-submarine and anti-surface warfare systems, and counter-landing weapons' (Bitzinger, 2015: 47). The stimulus and response relationship for a Mainland threat and at least some military assistance from the US is unlikely to disappear.

Figure 8.2q completes a pathway with the following connection into the macro level of Northeast Asia: 'US MILITARY ASSISTANCE TO TAIWAN' → 'PRC REAFFIRMS SOVEREIGNTY AND INTERNAL AUTONOMY'. Sustained US support for Taiwan reinforces the status quo. However, a different possibility exists and Figure 8.2r finishes up this other route: 'US MILITARY ASSISTANCE TO TAIWAN' → 'PRC ABSORBS TAIWAN'. Instead of reinforcing the status quo, US military support for Taiwan could provoke an ascending PRC into a preemptive strike, if Beijing comes to believe that a unilateral declaration of independence is in the offing.

Figure 8.2s depicts two very different effects from the same variable. The first connection in that diagram, from the international system into the macro level of the region, is 'US MILITARY ASSISTANCE TO TAIWAN' → 'PRC MILITARY MODERNIZATION'. As a nodal variable, the latter appears as a hexagon. This might be summed up as a localized arms race. The other linkage in Figure 8.2s is from the international system to the micro level of the region: 'US MILITARY ASSISTANCE TO TAIWAN' → 'Taiwanese separatism'. This returns

Figure 8.2q: Elaboration on the basis of further evidence

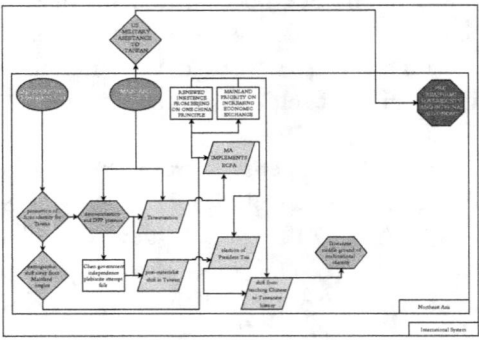

Figure 8.2r: Elaboration on the basis of further evidence

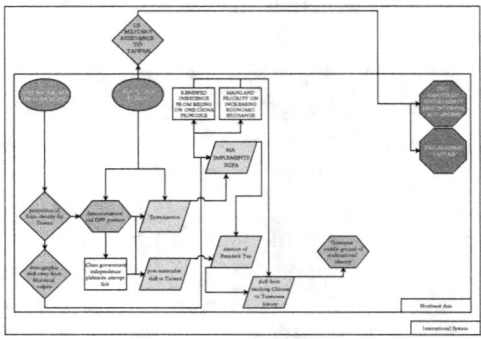

Figure 8.2s: Elaboration on the basis of further evidence

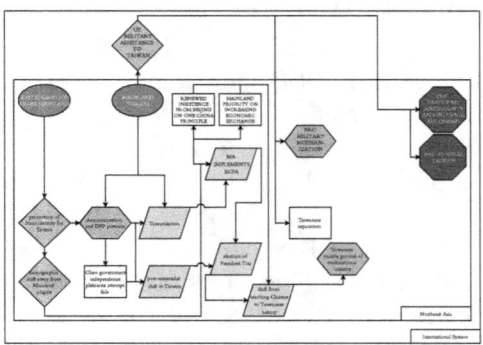

Figure 8.2t: Elaboration on the basis of further evidence

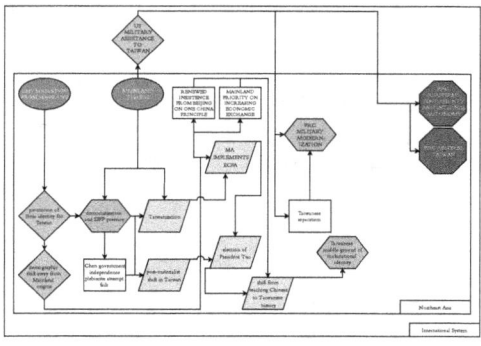

Figure 8.2u: Elaboration on the basis of further evidence

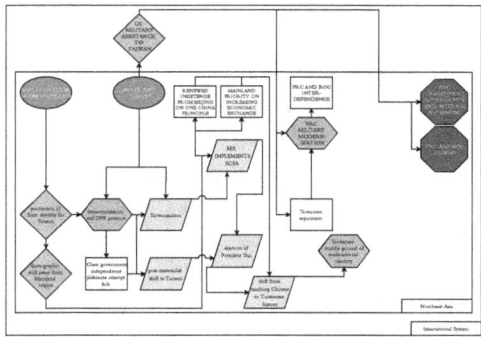

to the concept of a frenemy noted earlier on (Taliaferro, 2019); support from a patron could induce a higher level of risk acceptance for a client state and, in turn, result in reckless and highly unwelcome actions.

Figure 8.2t shows movement from the micro to the macro level: 'Taiwanese separatism' → 'PRC MILITARY MODERNIZATION'. This is one of the most intuitively obvious connections in the figure. When Taipei makes any gesture towards independence, this causes Beijing to seek a greater capacity to use force in order to prevent that process from moving forward.

Figure 8.2u extends the route at the macro level: 'PRC MILITARY MODERNIZATION'→ 'PRC AND ROC INTERDEPENDENCE'. This connection emphasizes a side effect of military enhancement for the Mainland. One reason for increased interdependence is that a more technologically advanced PRC *per se* would have more to offer in terms of potential for exchange with the ROC. The other force in motion would be pressure for greater interconnectedness if countervailing power from the US itself proves insufficient to balance an improved military capability on the Mainland.

From the macro to the micro level, further connections appear in Figure 8.2v. One is 'PRC AND ROC INTERDEPENDENCE' → 'Taiwanese middle ground of multinational identity'. This is a neo-Kantian type of inference. As interdependence increases for a dyad, it is reasonable to expect moderation of views – application of a 'carrot' in the language of bargaining models. The other connection, more like a 'stick' within that same terminology, is 'PRC MILITARY MODERNIZATION' → 'Taiwan middle ground of multinational identity'. Enhanced military capability on the Mainland creates an incentive to eschew movement towards an anti-Sinic form of Taiwanization in particular.

Figure 8.2w depicts two interrelated connections. The first is 'US STRATEGIC AMBIGUITY' → 'moderation of hard-liners in ROC'. As an initial variable, 'US STRATEGIC AMBIGUITY' appears as an oval. The second linkage is 'US STRATEGIC AMBIGUITY' → 'moderation of hard-liners in PRC'. In each instance the expectation is the same – uncertainty about the US position encourages risk aversion. While hard-liners in the ROC might want to declare independence, and hard-liners in the PRC would prefer an invasion, neither can act with impunity when reactions from the US remain difficult to gauge.

Figure 8.2x shows movement back up to the macro level through two interrelated linkages: 'moderation of hard-liners in ROC' → 'TRUMP INCREASES AMBIGUITY' and 'moderation of hard-liners in PRC' → 'TRUMP INCREASES AMBIGUITY'. As a convergent variable, 'TRUMP INCREASES AMBIGUITY' appears as a parallelogram. Note also that the variable appears at the macro level of Northeast Asia; rather than representing an action from the US, the metric corresponds to a *perception* held within the region. As their positions moderate, the hard-liners on either side of the Taiwan Strait become more likely to see the mixed policy positions from the Trump administration accurately. While Trump engaged in anti-PRC rhetoric about trade and other economic issues, he also tended towards isolationism. Thus, there is no obvious trend, but instead ambiguity, to see in the Trump era vis-à-vis Northeast Asia.

Figure 8.2y reveals a connection from the macro to the micro level: 'TRUMP INCREASES AMBIGUITY' → 'Taiwanese middle ground of multinational identity'. This effect is much the same as others already described. With no obvious trend in US policy either

Figure 8.2v: Elaboration on the basis of further evidence

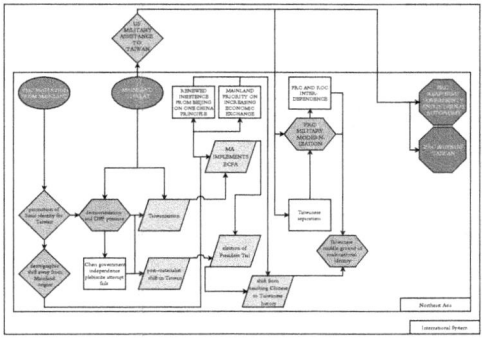

Figure 8.2w: Elaboration on the basis of further evidence

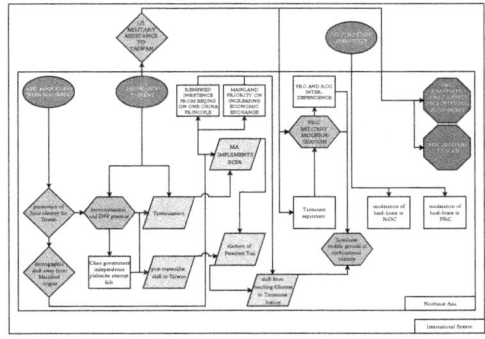

Figure 8.2x: Elaboration on the basis of further evidence

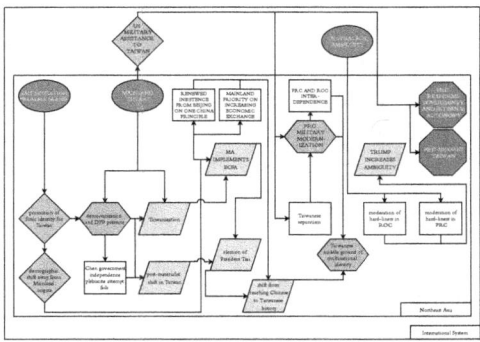

Figure 8.2y: Elaboration on the basis of further evidence

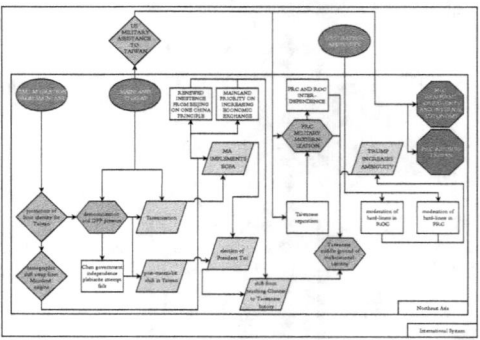

Figure 8.2z: Elaboration on the basis of further evidence

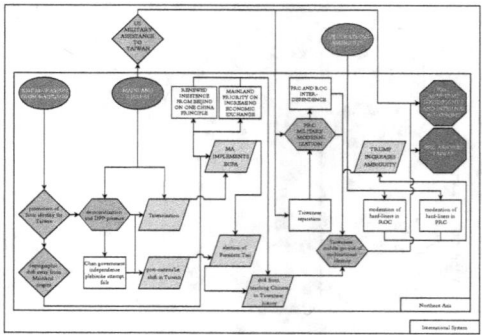

Figure 8.2aa: Elaboration on the basis of further evidence

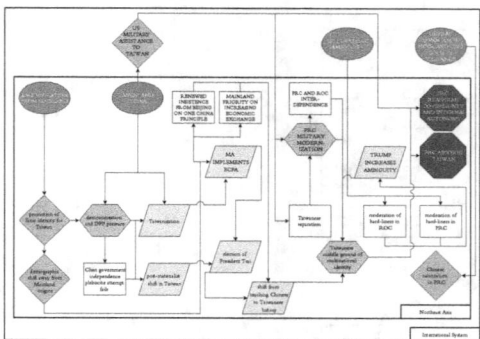

in favour of or against Taiwan, a middle ground, previously described as aquamarine in terms of identity, becomes more entrenched.

Figure 8.2z shows completion of two pathways. One is 'Taiwanese middle ground of multinational identity' → 'PRC ABSORBS TAIWAN'. As a terminal variable, 'PRC ABSORBS TAIWAN' is depicted as an octagon. The second route finishes up with 'Taiwanese middle ground of multinational identity' → 'PRC REAFFIRMS SOVEREIGNTY AND INTERNAL AUTONOMY'. These obviously very different outcomes remain in play because there are so many contingencies. The range of variables and connections leading up to these outcomes suggest a great deal of uncertainty going forward in terms of overall results, even as many specific processes have been identified and probed for significance.

Figure 8.2aa starts one final pathway: 'LIBERAL DEMOCRACIES, NGOs, AND CIVIL SOCIETY VIGIILANCE' → 'Chinese nationalism in PRC'. These variables are initial and divergent and therefore appear, respectively, as an oval and a diamond. Criticism from observers outside of the region is an ongoing irritation for both the elite and some of the mass public in the PRC. Two final connections appear in Figure 8.2bb. One is 'Chinese nationalism in PRC' → 'PRC ABSORBS TAIWAN'. The other connection in Figure 8.2bb is 'Chinese nationalism in PRC' → 'PRC REAFFIRMS SOVEREIGNTY AND INTERNAL AUTONOMY'. In line with earlier assertions, so many forces are in operation that either basic outcome – the status quo for Taiwan that includes *de facto* independence versus being absorbed into the PRC – seems quite possible.

Figure 8.2bb: Elaboration on the basis of further evidence

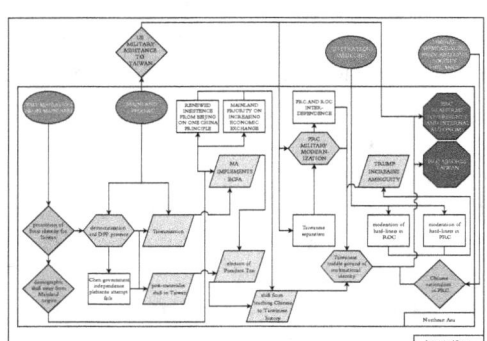

An elaborated vision

We have portrayed the complex system that we found influences the ideational process in Taiwan. 'What does it mean to be Taiwanese?' represents a multifaceted question. Figure 8.2 shows that explication of this complex question requires a multifaceted answer. However, rather than just say that ideation is a complex, interwoven tapestry, we tried to add structure to the process and highlight critical relationships and patterns that we found to be especially influential. Our approach attempts to navigate a path between those who (a) prefer answers to reflect clear cause and effect logics represented by equations and decision trees and (b) say 'it all depends', reject patterns and conditional arguments and view it all as a dialectical narrative. Yes, there are causes and effects, and yes, answers do very much depend on perspectives and narratives, but in between these two approaches lies our systemist visualization of a systematic, highly contingent, complex process.

Why is it so hard to answer the question: Who are you in Taiwan? As we have noted repeatedly, there is no consensus answer on what it means to be Taiwanese. In fact, within Taiwan, there is great variation on the meaning of Taiwanese identity, while China essentially sees the question as invalid, denying an independent Taiwanese persona.

Taiwanese identity reflects a complex array of factors that have shifted across time and vary in their ways of intersection. We have demonstrated that the ascent of China, cross-Strait relations and the role of the US strongly influence the identity formation process in Taiwan. Within these large conceptual bins, subfactors like democratization, the 1992 Consensus, internal politics in Taiwan, PRC and the US all contribute in varying ways to both elite and mass perceptions of Taiwanese identity.

Our study suggests that the answer to what it means to be Taiwanese does not converge on a single point estimate or simple response. Thus, we believe that a standard approach, such as that captured in a multivariate equation, only captures some of the underlying structure forming Taiwan's sense of self. Instead, using the graphic process of systemism, we lay out the complex, interwoven system of variables, relationships and interactive dynamics that shape the identity formation process in Taiwan. Like the multiple perspectives to the horrible crime of rape and murder in the Japanese movie *Rashômon*, each of the variables we identify provides a varied viewpoint to the identity formation process. Some factors have a direct influence, others mitigate the effects of variables, while others still only have indirect effects operating through additional factors.

None of the figures presented in this chapter individually captures the relational and shifting process of Taiwanese identity. Our systemist approach would ideally provide a dynamic, movie-like recording of the morphing system of influence suggested by our results. When translated into two-dimensional graphs, one can look through the sequence of figures presented to capture the fluid dynamics we envision forming ideational attitudes in Taiwan.

For literally thousands of years, international affairs observers have debated about whether countries balance or bandwagon against rising threats. This paradigm has often been applied to examining regional Asian relations that include Taiwan and China (Kang, 2004). Our focus here is not on international affairs *per se*, but on how international affairs influence peoples' identities. Using this approach as a metaphor, the question might be, how did people respond in terms of their identities to the ascension of China? Do they seek out personal opportunities created by this rise or does China's increased power reinforce ideological concerns about threats to Taiwan and strengthen the appeal of identifying as Taiwanese? We find that ideological factors that balance against rising China consistently have greater influence on individuals' decisions to view themselves as Taiwanese, especially as only Taiwanese, than bandwagoning on personal gain.

While it might seem quite distant from the agenda of this study, the long-standing three-body problem from physics provides a potentially helpful way of thinking about what has been discovered about the ROC, PRC and the US. The three-body problem goes all the way back to the origins of modern physics in the *Principia*, the *tour de force* from Isaac Newton in 1687. Unlike the case of two bodies in motion, with three, there is no closed form solution available. No elegant way exists, even centuries after *Principia*, to model three bodies in motion; the dynamics are chaotic and complex and thus numerical solutions are required.

In a sense, the ROC, PRC and US end up looking the same way as political actors; these entities combine to create their own challenging three-body problem for any would-be analyst. The trajectories of Taiwan, China and the US are complicated and not amenable to straightforward projection into the future. On the one hand, the complexity of Figure 8.2, with its 26 variables and many connections, might seem off-putting. On the other hand, the systemist visualization models the intellectual complexity of trilateral relations, and not least how they affect the politics of identity in Taiwan. Many different forces in and outside Taiwan are at work and a simple summation or prediction based upon it would not accurately depict actual identity formation on the ground.

Specifically, we have found the following:

1. Taiwanese identity is not fixed. It has always been and still represents an evolving process.
2. From the arrival of the Nationalists in 1949 to today, it is impossible to separate the history of Taiwan and the Mainland from the identity formation process in Taiwan. There is thus a powerful temporal component to Taiwanese identity.
3. At the same time, clear generational factors influence Taiwan's identity. Thus, on average, people today think differently about the question, 'who am I' than they did ten years ago. Today there is vast and seemingly growing variation between the young and the old.
4. We found minimal differences between the responses and thoughts of elites in our interviews and the survey results reflected in two different mass opinion surveys. While the elites in Taiwan obviously influence the views of the people in Taiwan, they seemingly do so with an authentic voice, encouraging people to follow their own ideational evolutionary path.
5. The impact of the rise of China is not straightforward. Put most simply, it changes the structure but not the values of the process. The growing economic success of China does not act as bait to draw people away from thinking of themselves as linked personally to Taiwan. If anything, it seems to create the opposite effect as people fear the leverage that China's growing power, especially economic power, provides the Mainland and thus its growing ability to sway outcomes.
6. The one country, two systems conceptualization is dying out. Those who viewed themselves exclusively as Taiwanese reject the 1992 Consensus and its compromise position. This compromise was largely built on the mutual acceptance of incompatible interpretations of the same document. Increasingly, Taiwanese are rejecting that acceptance and converging on a more homogenous interpretation.
7. The system has a feedback loop. The more likely the success of Taiwanese independence, the more likely people are to support independence and view themselves as exclusively Taiwanese.
8. Rather than bandwagon with ascending China and accrue personal gains, Taiwanese seem to balance against the rising Mainland and deepen their Taiwanese identity.

While these conclusions might have been reached in other ways, the traits of this pathway towards this new knowledge should be noted. These specific points have been reached through the application of multiple methods in tandem with systemist graphics to facilitate the understanding and retention of cause and effect.

After all of this, what can be said about Taiwanese identity in light of the ideal points from the ideational theoretical framework from Table 1.1: (a) Complementary (a product of ideology and self-interest); (b) Self-interested; (c) Ideological; and (d) Unmotivated (a product of neither ideology nor self-interest)? Evidence tilts towards ideology as the foundation for Taiwanese identity over the long term. While economic opportunities from the rise of the Mainland are attractive in one way, concerns about being absorbed by the gigantic autocratic neighbour are paramount for an increasing segment of opinion in Taiwan. A desire to preserve *de facto* independence, liberal values of a free and open society, and the democratic governance associated with it is very important in this context. Taken together the opposing gravitational forces of the US and PRC keep Taiwan somewhere in the middle, with an identity defined in ideological rather than self-interested terms.

Future research

While preceding chapters include a significant amount of new information about Taiwan, the rise of China, cross-Strait relations and the role of the US in Northeast Asia, so much more waits to be done. Several ideas for future research will be put forward at this point.

One possibility is to continue applying the methods of this book – a further review of academic literature, more elite interviews and additional public opinion surveys – to obtain updated data. Take, for example, a possible new wave of survey work. It would be interesting to apply this type of approach to another dataset to compare the relative impact of the support and opposition to the 1992 Consensus with attitudes towards the Sunflower Movement (Kwan, 2016; Au, 2017) and the ECFA (Lu, 2019).

The passing of the Hong Kong Security Law in June 2020 marks a significant change in Beijing's implementation of the one country, two systems model in Hong Kong. Beijing seems to be willing to sacrifice a great degree of Hong Kong's autonomy to preserve the country's overall stability. Hong Kong has always been considered as a model for the future of Taiwan. How will Beijing's firmer hand on the one country, two systems model affect how people in Taiwan perceive

China? More pointedly, how might it change Taiwan's identity even further? For instance, would recent political developments in Hong Kong further solidify the younger and future generations' sense of identifying only as Taiwanese? A series of new surveys and interviews could be implemented to obtain updated empirical data. Related studies show that people sometimes acquire information about more abstract issues, such as foreign policy, through personal ties and local experiences. For example, Americans' views on wars are greatly influenced by their personal ties and community experiences with military casualties from those conflicts (Gartner, 2008; Gartner and Segura, 2021). Thus, the distinction between personal interests that might influence variation in individuals' information and someone's ideological assessments might be more nuanced than portrayed here. Or put simply, individual interest might influence who you know and where you live, which in turn, might affect people's views on ideology.

Many consider the relationship of Taiwanese with Chinese culture as a critical factor in the ideational process, which in this volume we do not address (Liu, 2016). On a related point, there is growing recognition that the history of the island did not start in 1949 with the Nationalist arrival. Rather, there is more awareness of those individuals who lived on Formosa before 1949 and continue to live in Taiwan now and that these people have identities that need to be recognized and appreciated. But it seems unlikely from our results that widespread ideational change about what it means to be Taiwanese would be driven by recognition and deference to earlier settlers.

Rising tensions between China and the US after President Donald Trump came into power and the escalating trade wars between Beijing and Washington are rewriting the order of the international system. The unexpected COVID-19 pandemic has only accelerated this process. Can China continue its rise the way it has been in the last 30 years? *Has China Won*, as asked by Kishore Mahbubani in his 2020 book with the same title? Or has the US lost?

Moreover, 2020 marks an important year not only for US politics, but also for international politics as well, as Americans went to the polls in November for their general election. How will the administration of President Joseph Biden change the power balance between China and the US? How will the outcome of the US election and continued rise of China affect Taiwanese identity? It is predicted that the Biden administration will continue many of America's conflictual policies with China, especially regarding Taiwan (Hernandez and Chien, 2020). How will the continuation of the previous administration's policies and the adoption of new policies individually and interactively affect the US–China relationship? Attention needs to be given to several issues examined in this present project in the post-COVID and post-2020-US-election context to see how they shape relations between the US, China and, critically, Taiwan and the subsequent impact of these shifting dynamics on Taiwanese identity.

Another area for potential future research is to examine the Taiwan issue in the context of diversionary theory. Some limited work has been done previously. For example Li et al (2009) find clear evidence that the DPP has used Taiwan independence as a rhetorical diversion when faced with domestic political crisis. From both the perspectives of China and the US, evidence of diversion has been seen. For instance, did President Trump try to use China and the COVID-19 origin issue to divert attention away from his domestic challenges? Could President Xi, facing domestic pressures, such as the slowing down of China's economy and domestic tensions, also use the Taiwan issue as a scapegoat to quell China's rising nationalism? Moreover, how would this affect Taiwan's identity and cross-Strait relations?

Future work needs to revisit the concept of Taiwanese identity in and of itself. For example, it is interesting to assess whether a pro-Taiwan identity is the same as an anti-China identity in Taiwan (Kaeding, 2015). If being Taiwanese means rejecting political alliance with China, the question then is how would those who see themselves as supporters of a semi-sovereign entity, in which Taiwan is a part of the Mainland (that is, consistent with the 1992 Consensus and one country, two systems), identify themselves? Today they can identify as Taiwanese because, in their interpretation, Taiwanese does not always mean Taiwanese and not Chinese. As that dynamic shifts, however, which our research seems to support, does the statement 'I am Taiwanese' become not only a positive declaration of belonging but also a negative rejection of association with Mainland China? In addition, how will these identities and their meanings morph and change?

Interesting, but obviously also highly controversial, is one assessment to possibly draw from our results: It seems reasonable to think that in the future, those who identify as politically exclusively Taiwanese and culturally Chinese might refer to themselves with a hyphenated, dual identity as Chinese-Taiwanese. We recognize that such claims of identity, if widespread, would shock China and perhaps even disrupt the current Taiwanese national conceptualization of self. But such an identity seems consistent with the dynamics across and between generations that we observed. It is important, however, to differentiate between various potential hyphenated identity types. While the format might be similar to those, for example, who identify as Italian-Americans, the meaning would be quite different. By identifying as an Italian-American, someone is not only identifying with their past, but they are proclaiming dual support for both Italy and America. Instead, Chinese-Taiwanese would be more like Cuban-Americans, identifying a heritage but in doing so rejecting the status quo political system in their (or their parents' or increasingly grandparents') homeland. This hyphenated identity would thus be embraced not only by those who want to make clear the distinction between their cultural and political identities, but also by those who want to make a statement that their cultural affiliation is in opposition to their political affiliation.

Recall that Figure 8.2, the elaborated systemist graphic for cause and effect, still lacked one type of connection: micro level of the system out to the environment. With a significantly shifting identity in Taiwan, perhaps this exclusion – noteworthy in both prior literature, along with the present study's interviews and surveys – makes sense. Academe, elite and mass opinion have resembled each other in being reticent about how an evolving and increasingly ideology-based identity in Taiwan will project outward into Northeast Asia. This subject increasingly will come into play as the rise of China levels off and the overall strategic situation in Northeast Asia stabilizes into whatever constitutes a new status quo.

Consider any number of questions that beg for answers. Will the ideology-based Taiwanese identity constrain the policy space available to its leaders? Could all of this back the Mainland into a corner? What about a possible challenge to the seemingly established US policy of discouraging Taiwan from declaring *de jure* independence? Or, instead, will the rising identity of Taiwan turn out to be a quite peaceful by-product of democratization? These and other queries combine to set an interesting research agenda for years to come.

Comparative analysis offers a further pathway of interest. This study could be replicated for other three-way combinations that include a relatively small actor, a nearby threatening great power, and a more distant patron from possibly outside of the region. This could involve different roles for one or more states already under study or even go fully beyond the lineup of the PRC, Taiwan and US. Take, for example, Cuba, the US and USSR. This case would be different along two dimensions. One is that the US would be the nearby state that poses a threat, with the USSR as a sponsor of Cuba. The other obvious difference is that it stands as a completed case because the USSR disappeared and its principal successor, Russia, lacked the resources to continue as a patron for the Cuban client state.

Final thoughts

This book, in terms of an overall focus, takes on the complexity behind identity formation. Taiwan is a unique and especially relevant test case to apply the systemist approach, precisely because identities are dynamic, malleable and multidimensional in nature. Identities are shared between elites and masses, with an interactive process of change as events within state and society impact upon each other. Domestic politics, competition between the Pan-Green and Pan-Blue political parties, and continued democratization, for instance, combine to shape how the 23 million inhabitants on the island define their identity and what it means to be Taiwanese.

At the same time, there is an additional layer of regional and global uncertainty that affects identity formation in Taiwan. Sandwiched between a rapidly rising China and a dominant US hegemon keen to retain its global and regional primacy, Taiwan's identity is heavily influenced by these external developments well beyond its control. The elite interviews and survey research in this study capture how individuals respond to these exogenous dynamics differently, depending on their own personal characteristics, ideological views and relations with China and the US. Put simply, national identity is both influenced by, and influences, individual identities in non-linear ways. Taken together, the contents of the book show that changes outside of Taiwan, and internal developments within Taiwan, all impact upon identity and each other. Our study illustrates the cause and effect between and among China's rise, Taiwan's identity, cross-Strait relations and US activity under conditions of fast-paced and unpredictable multidimensional change in an increasingly important and nettlesome flashpoint in international security.

There are those around the world whose declaration of primary identity represents a strong, and considered by many, controversial, political statement: the Basques, the Kurds, and others. But neither the Basques, nor the Kurds, nor most of the other groups whose identity would incite these reactions have a sovereign government, powerful military, vibrant trading economy, global stock exchange, currency and support of the world's most powerful nation. For example, the Uighurs represent a people in China who incite repression through claiming their identity. But they lack everything that the Taiwanese have except for a connection to China. The juxtaposition between a fractured identity more akin to groups without a country with a powerful place whose economy and norms of democratic governance are growing rapidly captures the inherent tension infusing Taiwanese identity. That this tension reflects further cross-Strait, Northeast Asian and US–China competition, rivalry and power dynamics, makes it both more uncertain and complex. While 'I am Taiwanese' might be a relative straightforward response to a seemingly simple question of 'Who am I?' it belies the tangled layers of identity that represent the calculation and influence of a vast array of cultural, political, economic, sociological, anthropological and historical forces operating locally, regionally and globally. These three words, I am Taiwanese, arguably combine to represent among the most complex and contentious dynamics in our world today.

Note

[1] This quotation appears in Li (2006: 210).

APPENDIX A

Research Interview Questions, September–October 2015

1. To what degree is Taiwanese identity shaped and influenced by the rate of China's military modernization?
   a. To what degree is Taiwanese identity shaped and influenced by China's economic development?
   b. What implications does the change in the Beijing's capabilities have for political economy?
   c. For security?
2. How do these external factors (in Question 1) affect Taiwan's rate of democratization? Any specific examples?
3. Would cross-Strait economic and security policy be seen as constituency-driven or constituency-constrained?
4. What is the general public mood on cross-Strait relations?
   a. How will this mood determine the way presidential candidates present their policy towards Beijing?
5. How relevant is the '1992 Consensus' as the basis for future developments in cross-Strait relations?
   a. How does the evolving Taiwanese identity affect the continued relevance of the '1992 Consensus?'
6. Do you agree that there seems to be a diverging trend in cross-Strait relations, where there is increasing economic integration and interdependence all the while political fragmentation remains persistent?
7. Looking ahead, how might a DPP- or a KMT-government strike deals with Beijing without upsetting their domestic constituencies?
8. What are some of the emerging results – benefits and costs – of the Economic Cooperation Framework Agreement (ECFA)?
9. Is the government ensuring that the agreement's benefits are more widely diffused to a broader spectrum of Taiwanese society (eg

small and medium enterprises, labour unions, manufacturing and agriculture)?
    a. If so, how and if not, why not?
10. Have disadvantaged domestic constituents complicated the cross-Strait negotiation process?
11. What role might the United States play in the evolving situation in cross-Strait relations?
12. Under what conditions do you think the United States will more (or less) likely honour its security commitments under the Taiwan Relations Act?

APPENDIX B

Taiwanese Identity and the Rise of China: Survey Questions, 27 October 2015

1. What is the most appropriate name for our country? 您認為我們國家最正確的名稱是什麼?
   a. Republic of China 中華民國
   b. Taiwan 台灣
   c. Other (write in) 其它，（請寫入）
2. Do you agree or disagree that in our daily life we should speak more Taiwanese or Hakka than Mandarin Chinese? 您認為我們在日常生活中應該多說台語或客家語嗎?
   a. Yes 是
   b. No 不是
   c. Maybe 也許
   d. Don't know 不知道
3. Do you consider yourself Taiwanese, Chinese, both or neither (if neither, write in)? 您認為您是台灣人，中國人，即是台灣人也是中國人，兩者都是，還是兩者都不是? 如果您認為兩者都不是，請圈/寫最佳答案?
   a. Taiwanese 台灣人
   b. Chinese 中國人
   c. Both 兩者都是
   d. Neither (write in) 兩者都不是（請寫入）(text required)
   e. Others (text required)
4. In order of importance, rank what defines Taiwanese identity 請問什麼是台灣認同感最重要特點並請按最重要到最不重要的順序排序?
   a. Democratic system 民主体制
   b. Freedom of speech, assembly and religion 言論、結社及宗教自由

c. Creativity 鼓勵創新
   d. Loving peace 愛好和平
   e. Traditional culture 傳統文化
   f. Traditional Chinese 正體中文
   g. Economic achievement 經濟成就
   h. Party consensus 政黨認同
   i. Self-identity/ethnicity 自己的族群
   j. 其他 （text required）
5. Do you agree or disagree that traditional Chinese culture is essential for determining who you are?「我們的文化是正統的中華文化」請問您同意嗎？
   a. Yes 是
   b. No 不是
   c. Don't know 不知道
6. Have you travelled to Mainland China in the past five years (excluding Hong Kong and Macau)? 在過去五年裡您去過大陸嗎（不包括香港和澳門)？
   a. Yes 有
   b. No 沒有
7. What is the purpose of travel? 您為什麼去大陸？
   a. Business 工作
   b. Visiting in general 旅游
   c. Visiting relatives or friends 探親訪友
   d. Study 學習
   e. Other (write in) 其它，（請寫入）
8. Do you think standard of living is better in Taiwan or Mainland China now? 您覺得目前的生活水準是台灣高還是大陸高？
   a. Taiwan 台灣
   b. China 大陸
   c. Don't know 不知道
9. Do you think the standard of living will be better in Taiwan or Mainland China in ten years? 您覺得十年後台灣和大陸哪個地方會有更高的生活水準？
   a. Taiwan 台灣
   b. China 大陸
   c. Don't know 不知道
10. Would you ever consider working in Mainland China? 您會考慮去大陸工作嗎？
    a. Yes 是
    b. No 不是
    c. Maybe 也許
    d. Don't know 不知道

11. If you have children, would you consider letting them marrying someone from China? 如果您有孩子，您會考慮讓他們跟大陸人結婚嗎？
    a. Yes 是
    b. No 不是
    c. Maybe 也許
    d. Don't know 不知道
12. Do you see China's economic ascent as a threat or a benefit for Taiwan? 您覺得大陸的經濟崛起對台灣是個威脅還是機遇？
    a. Threat 威脅
    b. Opportunity 機遇
    c. Don't know 不知道
13. Do you support or oppose more mainlanders to visit Taiwan for tourism purposes? 您是否贊成開放更多陸客來台觀光旅遊？
    a. Support 贊成
    b. Oppose 不贊成
    c. Neutral 中立
    d. Don't know 不知道
14. Do you know what the '1992 Consensus' entails? 您知道"九二共識"的含義嗎？
    a. Yes 知道
    b. No 不知道
15. Do you agree or disagree that the '1992 Consensus' is the foundation for cross-Strait relations? 您同意"九二共識"是兩岸關係談判的基礎嗎？
    a. Yes 是
    b. No 不是
    c. Don't know 不知道
16. How much do you agree or disagree with the following statements? 您覺得以下的這些說法有多符合您的看法？(slider 0–10 for each option)
    a. Mainland China's political system will not change 大陸的政治體制不會改變
    b. Mainland China's political system will become more democratic 大陸政治將會變得更民主
    c. Mainland China's economy will be more prosperous 大陸經濟將會變得更繁榮
    d. Mainland China's society will be more free 大陸社會將會變得更自由

17. Do you think Taiwan and Mainland China will be politically united in the future? 您認為兩岸在未來政治上會統一嗎?
    a. Yes 會
    b. No 不會
    c. Maybe 也許
    d. Don't know 不知道
18. Do you agree or disagree that the US would come to Taiwan's rescue should cross-Strait relations escalate into armed conflict? 如果台海有衝突，您覺得美國會不會協助防衛台灣?
    a. Yes 會
    b. No 不會
    c. Maybe 也許
    d. Don't know 不知道
19. In what year were you born? 請問您是哪年出生的?
    a. _____年 (99)拒答
20. What's your gender? 請問您的性別是什麼?
    a. Female 女
    b. Male 男
21. What is your highest level of education? 請問您的教育程度是什麼?
    (01)不識字 (02)識字但未入學 (03)小學肄業 (04)小學畢業 (05)國、初中肄業
    (06)國、初中畢業 (07)高中、職肄業 (08)高中、職畢業 (09)專科肄業 (10)專科畢業 (11)大學肄業(含在學中) (12)大學畢業 (13)研究所(含在學、肄業、畢業)
    (90)其他_____
    (99)拒答
22. What city or county do you currently reside in? 請問您戶籍在台灣哪一個縣市?
    (01)台北市 (02)新北市 (03)基隆市 (04)桃園縣 (05)新竹市 (06)新竹縣
    (07)苗栗縣 (08)台中市 (09)彰化縣 (10)南投縣 (11)雲林縣 (12)嘉義市
    (13)嘉義縣 (14)台南市 (15)高雄市 (16)屏東縣 (17)台東縣 (18)花蓮縣
    (19)宜蘭縣 (20)澎湖縣 (21)金門縣 (99)不知道/拒答
23. Which of the following best describes your ethnic background? 請問以下哪項最能描述您的族群背景?
    a. 本省人 (包括客家)
    b. 外省人
    c. 原住民

APPENDIX B

24. Generally speaking, what political party do you support the most? 一般來說，請問您最支持哪一個政黨？
    a. KMT 國民黨
    b. DPP 民進黨
    c. Taiwan Solidarity Union 台灣團結聯盟
    d. People First Party 親民黨
    e. New Party 新黨
    f. Other (write in) 其它，（請寫入）
    g. Don't know 不知道

25. Would you call yourself a strong supporter of ___ or not a strong supporter of ___? 您認為您是____黨的忠實的支持者嗎？
    a. Yes 是
    b. No 不是
    c. Don't know 不知道

26. What political party does your father support the most? 請問您的父親最支持那一個政黨？
    a. KMT 國民黨
    b. DPP 民進黨
    c. Taiwan Solidarity Union 台灣團結聯盟
    d. People First Party 親民黨
    e. New Party 新黨
    f. Other (write in) 其它，（請寫入）
    g. Don't know 不知道

27. What political party does your mother support the most? 請問您的母親最支持那一個政黨？
    a. KMT 國民黨
    b. DPP 民進黨
    c. Taiwan Solidarity Union 台灣團結聯盟
    d. People First Party 親民黨
    e. New Party 新黨
    f. Other (write in) 其它，（請寫入）
    g. Don't know 不知道

APPENDIX C

Taiwan National Security Survey by Emerson Niou

Work group:____Seat number: ____Supervisor A:____
Supervisor B:____Interviewer number:____
Interviewer signature:____ Date: (mm) (dd)

PP1797B1
2017/11/29–12/05

Questionnaire number:_____Sample number:_____
(Interviewer please omit this blank.)

Select Survey Instrument Reflecting Variables Employed 2017 Cross-Strait Relations and National Security Public Opinion Questionnaire
Principle Investigator: Dr. Emerson Niou

(area code) – (telephone number)   Interviewee:____Male____Female
Interviewer signature:____

Hello, we are students from National Chengchi University. Our professor is conducting a telephone survey regarding <u>public opinion on cross-Strait relations</u>, and we have some questions to ask you. First, is there any adult over 20 years old in your household? Out of these_____adults, how many are male (_____)? Accordingly, would you please have_____come to the phone? We would like to ask him some questions, thank you!! (Interviewer should follow to the 'sampling rule out of a household' to select the interviewee.)

★★Please record appellation of the interviewee:_____★★
Before commencing the interview, please have the interviewers declaring the following statements:

As I am about to begin enquiring you some questions, should you feel like not responding to any of our questions, please do let me know, and I will skip the question; should there be any discomfort, you have the right to terminate the interview. All your personal information will be stored confidentially, and the future publication from this research will only be presented through summarized report.
(Interview begins. Please indicate the time right now:____ (mm)____ (dd),____ (day of the week)____, ____(hr)____(min))

工作區：座位號碼：督導A：督導B：
訪員編號：訪員簽名：日期：月日
（如因電腦當機而手動輸入者，請詳填以上資料，輸入完畢後勿再使用，逕交專任助理保存，謝謝）

PP1797B1
2017/11/29–12/05

問卷編號｜｜｜｜（訪員免填）樣本編號｜｜｜｜

2017年兩岸關係和國家安全民意調查
計畫主持人：牛銘實教授

｜｜｜—｜｜｜｜｜｜訪問對象：□男□女

（區域號碼）（電話號碼）
訪員簽名：_____

您好，我們是政治大學的學生，我們的老師正在做一項關於民眾對兩岸關係看法的電話訪問，有幾個問題想請教您。首先想請問：您家中年齡在二十歲以上的成年人有幾位？這____位當中男性有____位？那麼，麻煩請_____來聽電話好嗎？（訪員請按戶中抽樣原則抽出受訪者）我們想請教他一些問題，謝謝！

｜**請轉記受訪者的稱呼方式**｜
在開始訪問時，請訪員務必唸下列句子：

｜我想開始請教您一些問題，如果我們的問題您覺得不方便回答的話，請您告訴｜
｜我，我們就跳過去，或有任何感覺不愉快時，您都有權利終止訪問。您的個人｜
｜資料我們都會保密，未來研究報告也只用整體趨勢呈現。｜

（訪問開始，訪員請記下現在時間：____月____日，星期____,____時____分

APPENDIX C

Within our society, some people suggest that we should strengthen the economic and trade relations with the Mainland, while some suggest that we should diminish such relation. Which do you agree with more?

    01. Strengthen economic and trade relations with the Mainland
    02. Diminish economic and trade relations with the Mainland
    96. Depends
    97. Indifferent
    98. Don't know
    95. Decline to answer

我們社會上有人主張應該加強與大陸的經貿關係（臺：經濟貿易關係），有人主張應該降低與大陸的經貿關係，請問您比較同意那一種看法？

| 01. 加強與大陸的經貿關係 | | 02. 降低與大陸的經貿關係 |

| 96. 看情形 | | 97. 無意見 | | 98. 不知道 | | 95. 拒答 |

1. If someone says, 'If Taiwan overly rely its economy on the Mainland, in time the Mainland will use economy as a political leverage against Taiwan.' Do you agree or disagree with this statement?
   (The interviewer should enquire level of agreeance.)
       01. Completely disagree
       02. Disagree
       03. Agree
       04. Completely agree
   96. Depends
   97. Indifferent
   98. Don't know
   95. Decline to answer

有人說：「如果臺灣在經濟上太依賴大陸，將來大陸會利用經濟來要求臺灣做政治上的讓步。」請問您同不同意（臺：咁有同意）這種說法？【訪員請追問強弱程度】

| 01. 非常不同意 | | 02. 不同意 | | 03.同意 | | 04. 非常同意 |

| 96. 看情形 | | 97. 無意見 | | 98. 不知道 | | 95. 拒答 |

2. If cross-Strait relation becomes strained, do you think the economy in your household will become better, worse, or have no effect?
   01. Better
   02. Worse
   03. Have no effect
   96. Depends
   97. Indifferent
   98. Don't know
   95. Decline to answer

. 請問如果兩岸關係變得比較緊張，您覺得您家裡的經濟狀況會因此變得比較好(臺：卡好)、比較不好(臺：卡壞)，還是沒有影響？

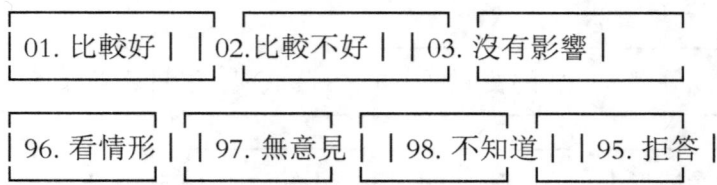

3. If the cross-Strait relation becomes strained, do you think Taiwanese economy will become better, worse, or have no effect?
   01. Better
   02. Worse
   03. Have no effect
   96. Depends
   97. Indifferent
   98. Don't know
   95. Decline to answer

. 請問如果兩岸關係變得比較緊張，您覺得臺灣的經濟狀況會因此變得比較好(臺：卡好)、比較不好(臺：卡壞)，還是沒有影響？

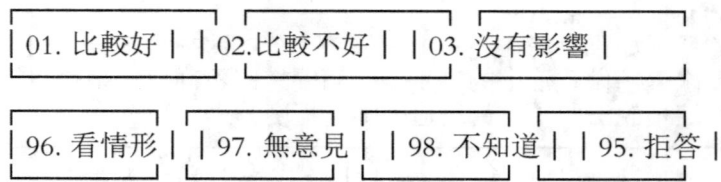

4. How satisfied are you towards Tsai Ing-Wen's overall performance since her presidency?
   (The interviewer should enquire level of agreeance.)
   01. Very satisfied

APPENDIX C

02. Satisfied
03. Dissatisfied
04. Very dissatisfied
96. Depends
97. Indifferent
98. Don't know
95. Decline to answer

8. 請問您對蔡英文擔任總統以來的整體表現滿不滿意（臺：咁唔滿意）？
【訪員追問強弱度】

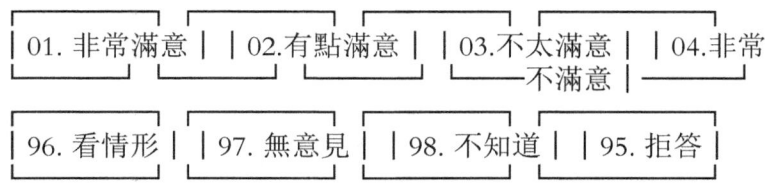

5. If *Taiwan declares independence unilaterally*, will the Mainland attack Taiwan?
   (The interviewer should enquire level of agreeance.)
   01. Absolutely not
   02. No
   03. Yes
   04. Absolutely yes
   96. Depends
   97. Indifferent
   98. Don't know
   95. Decline to answer

請問您是否擔心將來兩岸因為統獨問題發生戰爭？【訪員請追問強弱程度】

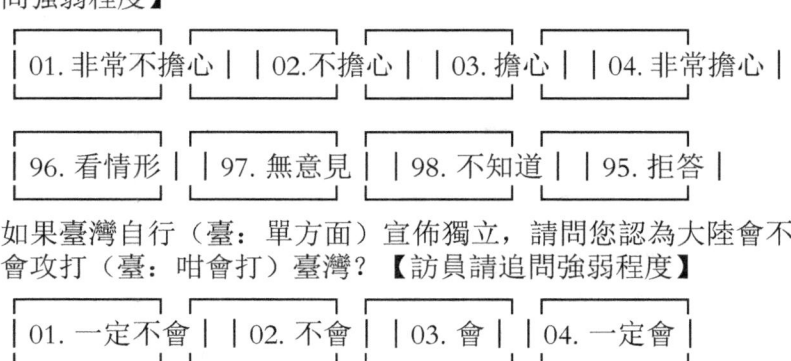

如果臺灣自行（臺：單方面）宣佈獨立，請問您認為大陸會不會攻打（臺：咁會打）臺灣？【訪員請追問強弱程度】

225

| 96. 看情形 | | 97. 無意見 | | 98. 不知道 | | 95. 拒答 |

6. On a scale of 0 to 10 to indicate the probability of *future success of Taiwanese independence*, with 0 being the least probable and 10 being the most probable, how would you rate the probability?
   95. Decline to answer
   96. Depends
   97. Indifferent
   98. Don't know

. 我們想請您用０到１０來表示將來臺灣獨立成功的可能性，０表示非常不可能，１０表示非常有可能，請問您覺得應該是多少？

_____ | 95. 拒答 | | 96. 看情形 | | 97. 無意見 | | 98. 不知道 |

7. Some argue that Taiwan and the Mainland should interact based on the principle of '1992 Consensus', do you support this claim? (The interviewer should enquire level of support.)
   01. Completely oppose
   02. Oppose
   03. Support
   04. Completely support
   96. Depends
   97. Indifferent
   98. Don't know
   95. Decline to answer

有些人主張臺灣和大陸應該在「一個中國、各自表述」（臺：一個中國，它的內容，臺灣甲中國，隨人講隨人ㄟ）的原則下進行（臺：來）交流，請問您支不支持（臺：咁有支持）這種主張？【訪員請追問強弱程度】

| 01. 非常不支持 | | 02. 不支持 | | 03. 支持 | | 04. 非常支持 |

| 96. 看情形 | | 97. 無意見 | | 98. 不知道 | | 95. 拒答 |

APPENDIX C

8. In our society, some call themselves as 'Taiwanese', and some call themselves as 'Chinese', while some say they are both. Do you consider yourself as Taiwanese, Chinese, or both?
   01. Taiwanese
   02. Both
   03. Chinese
   96. Hard to tell
   97. Indifferent
   98. Don't know
   95. Decline to answer

   在我們社會上，有人說自己是「臺灣人」，也有人說自己是「中國人」，也有人說都是。請問您認為您自己是「臺灣人」、「中國人」，或者都是？

   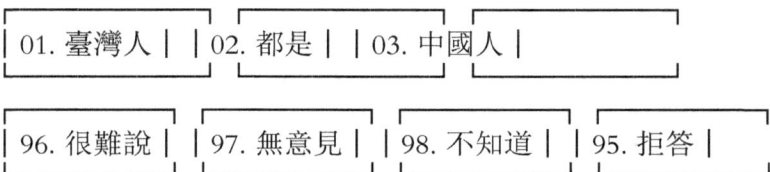

9. Which Republic Year were you born in?
   (For the respondents who are unsure, the interviewer may alternatively ask, 'How old are you?' Subsequently, the interviewer may convert the age to Republic Year at birth: 106 – age = Republic Year at birth.)
   Republic Year
   95. Decline to answer

   請問您是民國哪一年出生的？（說不出的改問：您今年幾歲？由訪員換算成出生年：106－歲數＝出生年次）

   _____ 年 | 95. 拒答 |

10. What is your highest degree of education attained (Taiwanese: Which level of education have you reached)?
    01. Illiterate or never enrolled
    02. Elementary school
    03. Junior high school
    04. Senior high school
    05. Junior college
    06. University
    07. Graduate school or above
    95. Decline to answer

請問您的最高學歷是什麼（臺：讀到什麼學校）？

| 01. 不識字及未入學 | | 02. 小學 | | 03. 國、初中 | | 04. 高中、職 |

| 05. 專科 | | 06. 大學 | | 07. 研究所及以上 | | 95. 拒答 |

★ ★ **Our interview has concluded. Your response is of great help to us, and we appreciate you agreeing with our interview. Thank you! Goodbye!** ★ ★

11. Sex:
    01. Male
    02. Female
性別：

| 01. 男性 | | 02. 女性 |

Interview concluded: <u>(hr) (min)</u>, minutes in total.

References

Aberbach, Joel D. and Bert A. Rockman. 2002. 'Conducting and Coding Elite Interviews', *PS: Political Science and Politics* 35: 673–676.

Allison, Graham T. 2017. *Destined for War: Can America and China Escape Thucydides's Trap?* Boston, MA: Houghton Mifflin Harcourt.

Almond, Gabriel A. 1956. 'Comparative Political Systems', *The Journal of Politics* 18: 391–409.

Au, Anson. 2017. 'The Sunflower Movement and the Taiwanese National Identity: Building an Anti-Sinoist Civic Nationalism', *Berkeley Journal of Sociology*. http://berkeleyjournal.org/2017/04/the-sunflower-movement-and-the-taiwanese-national-identity-building-an-anti-sinoist-civic-nationalism/.

Baron, James. 2016. 'Looking Back, Moving Forward: Foreign Policy Challenges for Taiwan's New Leader', *Global Asia* 11: 64–69.

Batto, Nathan F. 2019. 'Cleavage Structure and the Demise of a Dominant Party: The Role of National Identity in the Fall of the KMT in Taiwan', *Asian Journal of Comparative Politics* 4: 81–101.

BBC. 2019. 'China Renews Vow to Reunite with Taiwan'. www.bbc.com/news/world-asia-china-46733174.

Bechhofer, Frank and David McCrone. 2010. 'Choosing National Identity', *Sociological Research Online* 15(3): 1–13.

Beckley, Michael. 2011/2012. 'China's Century? Why America's Edge Will Endure', *International Security* 36: 41–78.

Bedford, Olwen and Kwang-Kuo Hwang. 2006. *Taiwanese Identity and Democracy: The Social Psychology of Taiwan's 2004 Elections*. New York: Palgrave Macmillan.

Bertucci, Mariano E., Jarrod Hayes and Patrick James, eds. 2018. *Constructivism Reconsidered: Past, Present and Future*. Ann Arbor, MI: University of Michigan Press.

Bitzinger, Richard A. 2015. 'China's Military Buildup: Regional Repercussions', in Mingjiang Li and Kalyan M. Kemburi, eds. *China's Power and Asian Security*. New York: Routledge, pp 42–61.

Blanchard, Ben and Jessica M. Yu. 2017. 'China Says Taiwan Not a Country, Taiwan Says China Needs Reality Check', *Reuters*. www.reuters.com/article/us-china-taiwan/china-says-taiwan-not-a-country-taiwan-says-china-needs-reality-check-idUSKCN1C20YF.

Bliuc, Ana Maria, Craig McGarty, Katherine Reynolds and Daniela Muntele. 2007. 'Opinion-Based Group Membership as a Predictor of Commitment to Political Action', *European Journal of Social Psychology* 37(1): 19–32.

Bobrow, Davis B., Steve Chan and John Kringen. 1979. *Understanding Foreign Policy Decisions: The Chinese Case*. New York: Free Press.

Bortolini, Tiago, Martha Newson, Jean Carlos Natividade, Alexandra Vázquez and Angel Gómez. 2018. 'Identity Fusion Predicts Endorsement of Pro-Group Behaviors Targeting Nationality, Religion, or Football in Brazilian Samples', *British Journal of Social Psychology* 57: 346–366.

Brooks, Stephen G. and William C. Wohlforth. 2015. 'The Rise and Fall of the Great Powers in the Twenty-first Century', *International Security* 40: 7–53.

Brown, Melissa J. 2004. *Is Taiwan Chinese? The Impact of Culture, Power, and Migration on Changing Identities*. Berkeley, CA: University of California Press.

Brzezinski, Zbigniew and John Mearsheimer. 2005. 'Clash of the Titans', *Foreign Policy* 146: 46–50.

Buckley, Chris and Keith Bradsher. 2020. 'Brushing Aside Opponents, Beijing Imposes Security Law on Hong Kong', *New York Times*. www.nytimes.com/2020/06/30/world/asia/china-critics-security-law-hong-kong.html?action=click&module=Top%20Stories&pgtype=Homepage.

Bunge, Mario. 1996. *Finding Philosophy in Social Science*. New Haven, CT: Yale University Press.

Bush, Richard C. 2005. *Untying the Knot: Making Peace in the Taiwan Strait*. Washington, DC: The Brookings Institution.

Bush, Richard C. 2019. '8 Key Things to Notice from Xi Jinping's New Year Speech on Taiwan', Order from Chaos (blog). The Brookings Institution, last modified 7 January 2019. https://search.proquest.com/docview/2164326938.

Callahan, William A. 2010. *China: The Pessoptimist Nation*. Oxford: Oxford University Press.

Carpenter, Ted Galen. 2006. *America's Coming War with China: A Collision Course over Taiwan*. New York: Palgrave.

Chambers, Michael R. 2002. 'Rising China: A Threat to Its Neighbors?' in Carolyn W. Pumphrey, ed. *The Rise of China in Asia: Security Implications*. Carlisle Barracks, PA: Storming Media.

Chan, Steve. 2004. 'Extended Deterrence in the Taiwan Strait: Learning from Rationalist Explanations in International Relations', *Asian Affairs: An American Review* 31: 166–191.

Chan, Steve. 2005. 'Taiwan in 2004: Electoral Contests and Political Stasis', *Asian Survey* 45: 54–58.

Chan, Steve. 2017. *Trust and Distrust in Sino-American Relation: Challenge and Opportunity*. Amherst, NY: Cambria Press.

Chan, Steve. 2019. 'More than One Trap: Problematic Interpretations and Overlooked Lessons from Thucydides', *Journal of Chinese Political Science* 24(1): 11–24.

Chen, Dean P. 2017. *US-China Rivalry and Taiwan's Mainland Policy: Security, Nationalism and the 1992 Consensus*. New York: Palgrave Macmillan.

Chen, Fang Yu, Wei-ting Yen, Austin Horng-en Wang and Brian Hioe. 2017. 'The Taiwanese See Themselves as Taiwanese, Not as Chinese', *Washington Post*. www.washingtonpost.com/news/monkey-cage/wp/2017/01/02/yes-taiwan-wants-one-china-but-which-china-does-it-want/.

Chen, Guo-Ming and William J. Starosta. 1997. 'Chinese Conflict Management and Resolution: Overview and Implications', *Intercultural Communication Studies* 7: 1–16.

Chen, Rou-Lan. 2014. 'Reconstructed Nationalism in Taiwan: A Politicized and Economically Driven Identity', *Nations and Nationalism* 20: 523–545.

Chen, Zhuo, Chris Chao Su and Anfan Chen. 2019. 'Top-down or Bottom-up? A Network Agenda-setting Study of Chinese Nationalism on Social Media', *Journal of Broadcasting and Electronic Media* 63(3): 512–533.

Chiang, Chun-Fang, Jin-Tan Liu and Tsai-Wei Wen. 2014. 'Economic Integration and National Identity', *Journal of Population Economics* 32(2): 351-367.

Chiang, Chun-Fang, Jin-Tan Liu and Tsai-Wei Wen. 2019. 'National Identity under Economic Integration', *Journal of Population Economics* 32: 351–367.

Chilton, Stephen. 1988. 'Defining Political Culture', *Western Political Quarterly* 41: 419–445.

Chiung, Wi-vun Taiffalo. 2018. 'Languages Under Colonization', in J.B. Jacobs and P. Kang (eds), *Changing Taiwanese Identities*. New York: Routledge, pp 39–63.

Chu, Yun-han. 2016. 'How Do Millennials See It? The Future of Democracy, Legitimacy and Governance in Asia', *Global Asia* 11: 46–51.

Chu, Yun-han and Yu-tzung Chang. 2017. 'Xi's Foreign-Policy Turn and Asia Perceptions of a Rising China', *Global Asia* 12: 104–111.

Chu, Yun-han and Jih-wen Lin. 2001. 'Political Development in 20th-Century Taiwan: State-Building, Regime Transformation and the Construction of National Identity', *The China Quarterly (London)* 165(165): 102–129.

Clark, Cal. 2007. 'Taiwan Enters Troubled Waters: The Elective Presidencies of Lee Teng-hui and Chen Shui-bian', in Murray A. Rubenstein, ed. *Taiwan: A New History*. Expanded edn. Armonk, NY: M.E. Sharpe, pp 496–535.

Clough, Ralph N. 2003. 'Growing Cross-Strait Cooperation Despite Political Impasse', in Donald S. Zagoria, with the assistance of Chris Fugarino, ed. *Breaking the China-Taiwan Impasse*. Westport, CT: Praeger, pp 115–125.

Coker, Christopher. 2015. *The Improbable War: China, the United States and the Logic of Great Power Conflict*. Oxford: Oxford University Press.

Copper, John F. 1990. *Nation-State or Province*. Boulder, CO: Westview Press.

Corcuff, Stéphane. 2002a. 'The Symbolic Dimension of Democratization and the Transition of National Identity Under Lee Teng-hui', in Stéphane Corcuff, ed. *Memories of the Future: National Identity Issues and the Search for a New Taiwan*. New York: M.E. Sharpe, pp 73–101.

Corcuff, Stéphane. 2002b. 'Taiwan's "Mainlanders," New Taiwanese?' in Stéphane Corcuff, ed. *Memories of the Future: National Identity Issues and the Search for a New Taiwan*. New York: M.E. Sharpe, pp 163–195.

de Vries, Catherine and Kees van Kersbergen. 2007. 'Interests, Identity and Political Allegiance in the European Union', *Acta Politica* 42(2–3): 307–328.

Dellios, Rosita. 2005. 'The Rise of China as a Global Power', *Culture Mandala: The Bulletin of the Centre for East-West Cultural and Economic Studies* 6(2): Article 3.

Dittmer, Lowell 2004. 'Taiwan and the Issue of National Identity', *Asian Survey* 44(4): 475–483.

Doubek, James. 2018. 'China Removes Presidential Term Limits, Enabling Xi Jinping to Rule Indefinitely', The Two-Way (blog). NPR, last modified 11 March 2018. https://search.proquest.com/docview/2012798356.

Edmondson, Robert. 2002. 'The February 28 Incident and National Identity', in Stéphane Corcuff, ed. *Memories of the Future: National Identity Issues and the Search for a New Taiwan*. New York: M.E. Sharpe, pp 25–46.

Election Study Center, NCCU. 2020. 'Changes in the Taiwanese/ Chinese Identity of Taiwanese', last modified 3 July 2020. https:// esc.nccu.edu.tw/course/news.php?Sn=166.

Ellemers, Naomi, Russell Spears and Bertjan Doosje. 2002. 'Self and Social Identity', *Annual Review of Psychology* 53(1): 161–186.

Fenby, Jonathan. 2008. *Modern China: The Fall and Rise of a Great Power, 1850 to the Present*. New York: HarperCollins.

Foot, Rosemary. 2013. 'Introduction: China Across the Divide', in Rosemary Foot, ed. *China Across the Divide: The Domestic and Global in Politics and Society*. Oxford: Oxford University Press, pp 1–15.

Fravel, M. Taylor. 2005. 'Regime Insecurity and International Cooperation: Explaining China's Compromises in Territorial Disputes', *International Security* 30(2): 46–83.

Freedman, Samuel G. 2000. *Jew vs. Jew: The Struggle for the Soul of American Jewry*. New York: Simon and Schuster.

Friedberg, Aaron. 1994. 'Ripe for Rivalry: Prospects for Peace in a Multipolar Asia', *International Security* 18: 5–33.

Friedberg, Aaron L. 2005. 'The Future of U.S.-China Relations: Is Conflict Inevitable?' *International Security* 30: 7–45.

Friedberg, Aaron. 2010. *Contest for Supremacy: China, America, and the Struggle for Mastery in Asia*. New York: Norton.

Frisch, Nick. 2016. 'How China Lost Taiwan', *New York Times*. www.nytimes.com/2016/01/28/opinion/how-china-lost-taiwan.html.

Funnell, Antony. 2018. '"One China" Means Different Things to Different People: It Also Might Mean War', Australian Broadcasting Corporation. www.abc.net.au/news/2018-11-08/one-china-policy-history-and-relevance-explained/10465740.

Gao, Pat. 2016. 'Progressive Leadership', *Taiwan Review* May/ June: 12–15.

Garrison, Jean A. 2005. *Making China Policy: From Nixon to G.W. Bush*. Boulder, CO: Lynne Rienner.

Gartner, Scott Sigmund. 2008. 'Ties to the Dead: Connections to Iraq War and 9/11 Casualties and Presidential Approval', *American Sociological Review* 73(4): 690–695.

Gartner, Scott Sigmund. 2011. 'On Behalf of a Grateful Nation: Conventionalized Images of Loss and Individual Public Opinion Change in War', *International Studies Quarterly* 55: 545–561.

Gartner, Scott Sigmund and Gary M. Segura. 1997. 'Appearances can be Deceptive: Self-selection, Social Group Identification, and Political Mobilization', *Rationality and Society* 9(2): 131–161.

Gartner, Scott Sigmund and Gary M. Segura. 2021. *Costly Calculations: A Theory of War, Casualties and Politics*. Cambridge: Cambridge University Press.

Gartner, Scott Sigmund and Aimee Tannehill. 2008. 'Negotiating w/the Dragon: The People's Republic of China and International Dispute Settlement Duration', *Tamkang Journal of International Affairs* 12(1): 69–99.

Glaser, Bonnie S. 2004. " 'U.S.-China Relations: A Familiar Pattern: Cooperation with a Dash of Friction', *Comparative Connections* 6: 196–207.

Glaser, Charles. 2011. 'Will China's Rise Lead to War? Why Realism Does Not Mean Pessimism', *Foreign Affairs* 90: 80–91.

Glaser, Charles. 2015. 'A U.S.-China Grand Bargain: The Hard Choice between Military Competition and Accommodation', *International Security* 39: 49–90.

Goh, Evelyn. 2016. 'Is a "Grand Bargain" the Way Forward in Northeast Asia?' *Global Asia* 11: 58–65.

Goldstein, Avery. 2013. 'First Things First: The Present (If Not Clear) Danger of Crisis Instability in U.S.-China Relations', *International Security* 37: 49–89.

Goldstein, Kenneth. 2002. 'Getting in the Door: Sampling and Completing Elite Interviews', *PS: Political Science and Politics* 35: 669–672.

Gong, Gerrit W. 2000. *Taiwan Strait Dilemmas: China-Taiwan-US Policies in the New Century*. Washington, DC: Center for International and Strategic Studies.

Gourevitch, Peter. 1978. 'The Second Image Reversed: The International Sources of Domestic Politics', *International Organization* 32: 881–912.

Green, Frederik H. 2017. 'All under Heaven KANO: The Politics of Nostalgia and the Making of a New Taiwanese Identity in Wei Te-Sheng's Taiwan-Japan Trilogy', *East Asian Journal of Popular Culture* 3: 169–182.

Gries, Peter Hays and Kaiping Peng. 2002. 'Culture Clash? Apologies East and West', *The Journal of Contemporary China* 11(30): 173–178.

Gries, Peter Hays and Jenny Su. 2013. 'Taiwanese Views of China and the World: Party Identification, Ethnicity, and Cross-Strait Relations', *Japanese Journal of Political Science* 14: 73–96.

Guibernau, Montserrat. 2011. 'The Birth of a United Europe: On Why the EU Has Generated a "Non-Emotional" Identity', *Nations and Nationalism* 17: 302–315.

Gurr, Ted Robert. 1970. *Why Men Rebel*. Princeton, NJ: Princeton University Press.

Han, Zhen and T.V. Paul. 2020. 'China's Rise and Balance of Power Politics', *The Chinese Journal of International Politics* 13(1): 1–26.

He, Yinan. 2014. 'Identity Politics and Foreign Policy: Taiwan's Relations with China and Japan, 1895–2012', *Political Science Quarterly* 129: 469–500.

Hernandez, Javier C. and Camy Chang Chien. 2020. 'After Trump, Biden Faces Pressure to Stand Up to China by Embracing Taiwan', *New York Times*, 24 November. www.nytimes.com/2020/11/24/world/asia/taiwan-china-trump-biden.html?searchResultPosition=1.

Hickey, Dennis V. 2001. *The Armies of East Asia: China, Taiwan, Japan and the Koreas*. Boulder, CO: Lynne Rienner.

Hickey, Dennis V. 2015. 'Time to Review US Policy on Taiwan', *The Diplomat*, 15 August.

Hickey, Dennis V. and Yitan Li. 2002. 'Cross-Strait Relations in the Aftermath of the Election of Chen Shui-bian', *Asian Affairs: An American Review* 28: 201–216.

Hong, Seok-Hyun. 2016. 'Bring the Tigers into the Trees: The Rise of China and the Future American Role in Asia', *Global Asia* 11: 63–69.

Horowitz, Julia. 2018. 'Huawei CFO Meng Wanzhou Arrested in Canada, Faces Extradition to United States', *CNN Business*. www.cnn.com/2018/12/05/tech/huawei-cfo-arrested-canada/index.html.

Hsu, Chien-Jung. 2018. 'Cyberspace and the Rise of Taiwanese Identity', in *Changing Taiwanese Identities*. 1st edn. Abingdon: Routledge, pp 93–110.

Huang, Chi. 2005. 'Dimensions of Taiwanese/Chinese Identity and National Identity in Taiwan: A Latent Class Analysis', *Journal of Asian and African Studies* 40(1–2): 51–70.

Huang, Chin-Hao and Patrick James. 2014. 'Blue, Green or Aquamarine? Taiwan and the Status Quo Preference in Cross-Strait Relations', *The China Quarterly* 219: 670–692.

Huang, Min-Hua and Mark Weatherall. 2017. 'Democratic Distance and Asian Views of Chinese and American Influence', *Global Asia* 12: 118–123.

Huntington, Samuel P. 1991. *The Third Wave: Democratization in the Late Twentieth Century*. Norman, OK and London: University of Oklahoma Press.

Inglehart, Ronald F. 1981. 'Post-Materialism in an Environment of Insecurity', *The American Political Science Review* 75: 880–900.

Inglehart, Ronald F. 1990. *Culture Shift in Advanced Industrial Society*. Princeton, NJ: Princeton University Press.

Inglehart, Ronald F. 2016. 'After Postmaterialism: An Essay on China, Russia and the United States: A Comment', *Canadian Journal of Sociology* 41(2): 213–222.

Inglehart, Ronald F. and Christian Welzel. 2001. *Modernization, Cultural Change, and Democracy: The Human Development Sequence*. Cambridge: Cambridge University Press.

Jacobs, Bruce J. and Peter Kang. 2018. *Changing Taiwanese Identities*. New York: Routledge.

Jacques, Martin. 2012. *When China Rules the World*. 2nd edn. London and New York: Penguin Books.

James, Patrick. 2012. 'Deterrence and Systemism: A Diagrammatic Exposition of Deterrence-Related Processes Leading to the War in Iraq', *St. Antony's International Review* 7: 139–163.

James, Patrick. 2019a. 'What Do We Know About Crisis, Escalation and War? A Visual Assessment of the International Crisis Behavior Project', *Conflict Management and Peace Science* 36: 3–19.

James, Patrick. 2019b. 'Systemist International Relations', *International Studies Quarterly* 63: 781–804.

Jentleson, Bruce W. 2016. 'The Post-Trump World in Context: The US and the Northeast Asian Strategic Order', *Global Asia* 11: 50–57.

Jerdén, Björn. 2014. 'The Assertive China Narrative: Why It Is Wrong and How So Many Still Bought into It', *The Chinese Journal of International Politics* 7: 47–88.

Johnston, Alastair Iain. 2003. 'Is China a Status Quo Power?' *International Security* 27: 5–56.

Johnston, Alastair Iain. 2013. 'How New and Assertive Is China's New Assertiveness?' *International Security* 37: 7–48.

Kaeding, Malte P. 2015. 'Resisting Chinese Influence: Social Movements in Hong Kong and Taiwan', *Current History* 114: 210–216.

Kan, Shirley. 2014. 'China/Taiwan: Evolution of the "One China" Policy—Key Statements from Washington, Beijing, and Taipei', *Congressional Research Service* 90, 10 October.

Kang, David C. 2004. 'Hierarchy, Balancing, and Empirical Puzzles in Asian International Relations', *International Security* 28(3): 165–180.

Kang, David C. 2007. *China Rising: Peace, Power, and Order in East Asia*. New York: Columbia University Press.

Kastner, Scott L. 2009. *Political Conflict and Economic Interdependence Across the Taiwan Strait and Beyond*. Stanford, CA: Stanford University Press.

Kastner, Scott L. 2015. 'Economic Interdependence and the Prospects for Peace in the Taiwan Strait', paper presented at the 5th Annual EAP Conference, November, Singapore.

Kastner, Scott L. 2016. 'Is the Taiwan Strait Still a Flash Point? Rethinking the Prospects for Armed Conflict between China and Taiwan', *International Security* 40: 54–92.

Keller, William and Thomas Rawski. 2007. *China's Rise and the Balance of Influence in Asia: Asia's Shifting Strategic and Economic Landscape*. Pittsburgh, PA: University of Pittsburgh Press.

Kerr, George H. 1965. *Formosa Betrayed*. Boston, MA: Houghton Mifflin.

King, Amy. 2016. 'Taiwan's Place in Northeast Asia's Memory Contests: Can Strategic Diplomacy Help?' *Global Asia* 11: 42–49.

King, Gary, Jennifer Pan and Margaret E. Roberts. 2014. 'Reverse-Engineering Censorship in China: Randomized Experimentation and Participant Observation', *Science* 345(6199): 1–10.

Knapp, Ronald G. 1999. *China's Living Houses: Folk Beliefs, Symbols, and Household Ornamentation*. Honolulu, HI: University of Hawaii Press.

Knapp, Ronald G. 2007. 'The Shaping of Taiwan's Landscapes', in Murray A. Rubenstein, ed. *Taiwan: A New History*. Expanded edn. Armonk, NY: M.E. Sharpe, pp 3–26.

Kou, Ying and Ying Huang. 2015. 'A Study on Ethnic Identity Status and its Contextual Factors Among College Students of Bai Nationality in Yunnan', *Journal of Language Teaching and Research* 6(3): 595–602.

Kwan, Justin P. 2016. 'The Rise of Civic Nationalism: Shifting Identities in Hong Kong and Taiwan', *Contemporary Chinese Political Economy and Strategic Relations: An International Journal* 2: 941–973.

Lamley, Harry J. 2007. 'Taiwan Under Japanese Rule, 1895–1945', in Murray A. Rubenstein, ed. *Taiwan: A New History*. Expanded edn. Armonk, NY: M.E. Sharpe, pp 201–260.

Lasswell, Harold D. 1941. 'The Garrison State', *American Journal of Sociology* 46: 455–468.

Layne, Christopher. 2008. 'China's Challenge to US Hegemony', *Current History* 107(705): 13–18.

Lee, Kuan-Chen, Wei-feng Tzeng, Karl Ho and Harold Clarke. 2018. 'Against Everything Involving China? Two Types of Sinophobia in Taiwan', *Journal of Asian and African Studies* 53(6): 830–851.

Lee, Yimou and James Pomfret. 2019. 'Pro-China Groups Step Up Offensive to Win over Taiwan', *Reuters*. www.reuters.com/article/us-taiwan-china-campaign-insight-idUSKCN1TR01H.

Leech, Beth L. 2002. 'Asking Questions: Techniques for Semistructured Interviews', *PS: Political Science and Politics* 35: 665–668.

Legro, Jeffrey W. 2007. 'What China Will Want: The Future Intentions of a Rising Power', *International Security* 5: 515–534.

Lepesant, Tanguy. 2018. 'Taiwanese Youth and National Identity Under Ma Ying-Jeou', in J.B. Jacobs and P. Kang (eds), *Changing Taiwanese Identities*. New York: Routledge, pp 64–86

Levy, Jack S. 1989. 'The Diversionary Theory of War: A Critique', in Manus I. Midlarsky, ed. *Handbook of War Studies*. Boston, MA: Unwin Hyman, pp 259–288.

Li, Kuang-chün. 2002. 'Mirrors and Masks: An Interpretative Study of Mainlanders' Identity Dilemma', in Stéphane Corcuff, ed. *Memories of the Future: National Identity Issues and the Search for a New Taiwan*. New York: M.E. Sharpe, pp 102–122.

Li, Ruru. 2006. '"Who Is It That Can Tell Me Who I Am?"/"Lear's Shadow": A Taiwanese Actor's Personal Response to King Lear', *Shakespeare Quarterly* 57(2): 195–215.

Li, Yitan. 2014a. 'Constructing Peace in the Taiwan Strait: A Constructivist Analysis of the Changing Dynamics of Identities and Nationalisms', *Journal of Contemporary China* 29: 119–142.

Li, Yitan. 2014b. 'At the Nexus of New Challenges: China's Leadership Change and Cross-Strait Relations', *Fudan Journal of Humanities and Social Sciences* 7: 57–76.

Li, Yitan and Enyu Zhang. 2017. 'Changing Taiwanese Identity and Cross-Strait Relations: A Post 2016 Taiwan Presidential Election Analysis', *Journal of Chinese Political Science* 22: 17–35.

Li, Yitan, Patrick James and A. Cooper Drury. 2009. 'Diversionary Dragons, Or "Talking Tough in Taipei": Cross-Strait Relations in the New Millennium', *Journal of East Asian Studies* 9(3): 369–398.

Lin, Cheng-Yi. 2007. 'The Rise of China and Taiwan's Response: The Anti-Secession Law as a Case Study', *Issues and Studies* 43: 159–188.

Lin, Chia-lung. 2002. 'The Political Formation of Taiwanese Nationalism', in Stéphane Corcuff, ed. *Memories of the Future: National Identity Issues and the Search for a New Taiwan*. New York: M.E. Sharpe, pp 219–241.

Lin, Gang. 2019. 'Politics of Identity in Taiwan', in Gang Lin, ed. *Taiwan's Party Politics and Cross-Strait Relations in Evolution (2008–2018)*. Singapore: Palgrave Macmillan, pp 69–96.

Lin, Syaru Shirley. 2016. *Taiwan's China Dilemma: Contested Identities and Multiple Interests in Taiwan's Cross-Strait Economic Policy*. Stanford, CA: Stanford University Press.

Lin, Tse-Min, Chin-En Wu and Feng-Yu Lee. 2006. '"Neighborhood" Influence on the Formation of National Identity in Taiwan: Spatial Regression with Disjoint Neighborhoods', *Political Research Quarterly* 59(1): 35–46.

Lin, Tsong-jyi. 2002. 'The Evolution of National Identity Issues in Democratizing Taiwan: An Investigation of the Elite-Mass Linkage', in Stéphane Corcuff, ed. *Memories of the Future: National Identity Issues and the Search for a New Taiwan.* New York: M.E. Sharpe, pp 123–143.

Lin, Wen-Cheng. 2016. 'Taiwan Enters the Tsai Ing-Wen Era and the Impact on Cross-Strait Relations', *ISPI Analysis* 293: 1–12.

Liu, Frank Cheng-Shan. 2015. 'Views about Cross-Strait Relations', Institute of Political Science at the National Sun Yat-Sen University, 20 November–14 December.

Liu, Frank Cheng-Shan. 2016. 'Taiwanese Voters Political Identification Profile, 2013–2014: Becoming One China or Creating a New Country?' *Asian Survey* 56: 931–957.

Liu, Frank Cheng-Shan and Yitan Li. 2017. 'Generation Matters: Taiwan's Perceptions of Mainland China and Attitudes Towards Cross-Strait Trade Talks', *Journal of Contemporary China* 26: 263–279.

Lipset, Seymour Martin. 1959. 'Some Social Requisites of Democracy: Economic Development and Political Legitimacy', *The American Political Science Review* 53(1): 69–105.

Lu, Chieh Ju. 2019. 'The Role of ECFA in Taiwanese/Chinese Identity of Taiwanese', University of Oregon Scholars' Bank. https://scholarsbank.uoregon.edu/xmlui/handle/1794/24916.

Lynch, Daniel C. 2006. *Rising China and Asian Democratization.* Stanford, CA: Stanford University Press.

Maehara, Shiho. 2018. 'Lee Teng-Hui and the Formation of Taiwanese Identity', in J.B. Jacobs and P. Kang (eds), *Changing Taiwanese Identities*. New York: Routledge, pp 87–92.

Mahbubani, Kishore. 2020. *Has China Won? The Chinese Challenge to American Primacy.* New York: Public Affairs.

Marsh, Robert. 2002. 'National Identity and Ethnicity in Taiwan: Some Trends in the 1990s', in Stéphane Corcuff, ed. *Memories of the Future: National Identity Issues and the Search for a New Taiwan.* New York: M.E. Sharpe, pp 144–159.

Mearsheimer, John J. 2014a. 'Say Goodbye to Taiwan', *The National Interest*, March–April.

Mearsheimer, John J. 2014b. *The Tragedy of Great Power Politics.* Updated edn. New York: W.W. Norton.

Mearsheimer, John J. 2019. *The Great Delusion: Liberal Dreams and International Realities*. New Haven, CT: Yale University Press.

Mengin, Françoise. 1998. *Trajectoires Chinoises*. Paris: Éd. Karthala

Mitrany, David. 1975. *The Functional Theory of Politics*. London: Robertson.

Momesso, Lara and Chun-Yi Lee. 2019. 'Nation, Migration, Identity: Learning from the Cross-Strait Context', *International Migration* 57: 218–231.

Money, Jeannette and Sarah P. Lockhart. 2019. *Migration Crises and the Structure of International Cooperation*. Athens, GA: University of Georgia Press.

Mosca, Matthew W. 2013. *From Frontier Policy to Foreign Policy: The Question of India and the Transformation of Geopolitics in Qing China*. Stanford, CA: Stanford University Press.

Muyard, Frank. 2018. 'The Role of Democracy in the Rise of the Taiwanese National Identity', in Jonathan Sullivan and Chun-Yi Lee, eds. *A New Era in Democratic Taiwan: Trajectories and Turning Points in Politics and Cross-Strait Relations*. New York: Routledge, pp 36–62.

Narozhna, Tanya and W. Andy Knight. 2016. *Female Suicide Bombings: A Critical Gender Approach*. Toronto: University of Toronto Press.

Navarro, Peter and Greg Autry. 2011. *Death by China*. Upper Saddle River, NJ: Prentice Hall.

Newsweek. 2016. 'Trump Says "One China" Policy Should be Part of Broader Deal'. www.newsweek.com/trump-china-taiwan-one-china-trade-tariffs-economy-fox-530673.

Niou, Emerson. 2017. 'The Taiwan National Security Survey'. Collected by the Election Study Center of the National Chengchi University, Taipei, Taiwan under the auspices of the Program in Asian Security Studies (PASS) at Duke University.

O'Hanlon, Michael. 2000. 'Why China Cannot Conquer Taiwan', *International Security* 25: 51–86.

Organski, A.F.K. 1958. *World Politics*. New York: Alfred A. Knopf.

Organski, A.F.K. and Jacek Kugler. 1980. *The War Ledger*. Chicago, IL: University of Chicago Press.

Pan, Hejun. 2007. 'Taiwan is Not, Nor Has It Ever Been, an Independent Country', *The Guardian*. www.theguardian.com/commentisfree/2007/sep/07/comment.china.

Pan, Shiyin Rung. 2015. 'Changing Civil Society and National Identity after the Sunflower Movement', *Procedia: Social and Behavioral Sciences* 202: 456–461.

Pfonner, Michael R. and Patrick James. 2020. 'The Visual International Relations Project', *International Studies Review* 22: 192–213.

Pillsbury, Michael. 2016. *The Hundred-Year Marathon: China's Secret Strategy to Replace America as the Global Superpower*. New York: St. Martin's Griffin.

Przeworski, Adam and Fernando Limongi. 1997. 'Modernization: Theories and Facts', *World Politics* 49(2): 155–183.

Putnam, Robert D., Robert Leonardi and Raffaella Y. Nanetti. 1994. *Making Democracy Work*. Princeton, NJ: Princeton University Press.

Pye, Lucian Wilmot. 1968. *The Spirit of Chinese Politics*. Cambridge, MA: MIT Press.

Rigger, Shelley. 2001. *From Opposition to Power: Taiwan's Democratic Progressive Party*. Boulder, CO: Lynne Rienner.

Rob, Schmitz. 2018. 'What It Means to be Taiwanese and Why It's Different Depending on Generation', National Public Radio. www.npr.org/2018/05/28/615010184/what-it-means-to-be-taiwanese-and-why-its-different-depending-on-generation.

Romberg, Alan D. 2007. 'Election 2008 and the Future of Cross-Strait Relations', *China Leadership Monitor*. 1–29.

Ross, Robert S. 2012. 'The Domestic Sources of China's "Assertive Diplomacy"', in Rosemary Foot, ed. *China Across the Divide: The Domestic and Global in Politics and Society*. Oxford: Oxford University Press, pp 72–93.

Ross, Robert S. and Zhu Feng. 2008. 'The Rise of China: Theoretical and Policy Perspectives', in Robert S. Ross and Zhu Feng, eds. *China's Ascent: Power, Security, and the Future of International Politics*. Ithaca, NY: Cornell University Press, pp 293–315.

Roy, Dennis. 2003. *Taiwan: A Political History*. Ithaca, NY: Cornell University Press.

Rubenstein, Murray A. 2007a. 'Taiwan's Socioeconomic Modernization, 1971–1996', in Murray A. Rubenstein, ed. *Taiwan: A New History*. Expanded edn. Armonk, NY: M.E. Sharpe, pp 366–402.

Rubenstein, Murray A. 2007b. 'Political Taiwanization and Pragmatic Diplomacy: The Eras of Chiang Ching-koo and Lee Teng-hui, 1971–1994', in Murray A. Rubenstein, ed. *Taiwan: A New History*. Expanded edn. Armonk, NY: M.E. Sharpe, pp 436–495.

Schafferer, Christian. 2016. 'The Dialectic of Nationalism and Democratic Governance in Taiwan', *Asian International Studies Review* 17: 159–176.

Schelling, Thomas C. 1960. *The Strategy of Conflict*. Cambridge, MA: Harvard University Press.

Shambaugh, David. 2004. 'China Engages Asia: Reshaping the Regional Order', *International Security* 29: 64–99.

Sheng, Lijun. 2001. *China's Dilemma: The Taiwan Issue*. New York: Taurus.

Shirk, Susan L. 2007. *China: Fragile Superpower*. Oxford: Oxford University Press.

Sil, Rudra and Peter J. Katzenstein. 2010a. 'Analytic Eclecticism in the Study of World Politics: Reconfiguring Problems and Mechanisms across Research Traditions', *Perspectives on Politics* 8: 411–431.

Sil, Rudra and Peter J. Katzenstein. 2010b. *Beyond Paradigms: Analytic Eclecticism in the Study of World Politics*. New York: Palgrave.

Spence, Jonathan D. 1999. *The Search for Modern China*. 2nd edn. New York: Norton.

Stainton, Michael. 2007. 'Aboriginal Self-Government: Taiwan's Uncompleted Agenda', in Murray A. Rubenstein, ed. *Taiwan: A New History*. Expanded edn. Armonk, NY: M.E. Sharpe, pp 419–435.

Stockton, Hans. 2002. 'National Identity on Taiwan: Causes and Consequences for Political Reunification', *American Journal of Chinese Studies* 9: 155–178.

Su, Chi and An-Kuo Cheng. 2002. *One China, with Respective Interpretations: A Historical Account of the Consensus of 1992*. Taipei: National Policy Foundation.

Sutter, Robert. 2004. 'China's Good Neighbor Policy and Its Implications for Taiwan', *Journal of Contemporary China* 13: 717–731.

Swaine, Michael D. 2015. 'China: The Influence of History', *The Diplomat*, 14 January.

Taiwan Foundation for Democracy. 2019. Press Release: 2019 TFD Survey on Taiwanese View of Democratic Values and Governance, 19 July. www.taiwandemocracy.org.tw/export/sites/tfd/files/news/pressRelease/0719_press-release_web.pdf.

Taiwan Relations Act. 1979. Public Law 96–8, *U.S. Code 22*. Washington, DC: Government of the United States of America.

Taliaferro, Jeffrey W. 2019. *Defending Frenemies: Alliance Politics and Nuclear Nonproliferation in US Foreign Policy*. Oxford: Oxford University Press.

Tan, Alexander, Steve Chan and Calvin Jillson. 2001. *Taiwan's National Security: Dilemmas and Opportunities*. Burlington, VT: Ashgate.

Tansey, Oisin. 2007. 'Process Tracing and Elite Interviewing: A Case for Non-Probability Sampling', *PS: Political Science and Politics* 40: 765–772.

Thrush, Glenn, Kate Kelly and Maggie Haberman. 2017. 'Trump to Ask for Sharp Increases in Military Spending, Officials Say', *New York Times*. www.nytimes.com/2017/02/26/us/politics/trump-budget.html?_r=0.

Tsai, Chang-Yen. 2007. *National Identity, Ethnic Identity, and Party Identity in Taiwan*. Baltimore, MD: University of Maryland.

Tucker, Nancy Bernkopf. 1998–1999. 'China-Taiwan: US Debates and Policy Choices', *Survival* 40: 150–167.

Tung, Chen-Yuan. 2016. 'Prospects of Taiwan-China Relations after the 2016 Elections', *American Journal of Chinese Studies* 23: 1–6.

van der Horst, Linda. 2016. 'The Evolution of Taiwanese Identity', *The Diplomat*. https://thediplomat.com/2016/06/the-evolution-of-taiwanese-identity/.

Van Vugt, Mark and Claire Hart. 2004. 'Social Identity as Social Glue: The Origins of Group Loyalty', *Journal of Personality and Social Psychology* 86(4): 585–598.

Verba, Sidney and Gabriel A. Almond. 1965. In Sidney Verba, ed. *The Civic Culture: Political Attitudes and Democracy in Five Nations, an Analytic Study*. Boston, MA: Little, Brown.

Vogel, Ezra F. 2011. *Deng Xiaoping and the Transformation of China*. Cambridge, MA: The Belknap Press of Harvard University Press.

Waltz, Kenneth N. 1979. *Theory of International Politics*. Reading, MA: Addison-Wesley.

Wang, Austin. 2017. 'The Waning Effect of China's Carrot and Stick Policies on Taiwanese People', *Asian Survey* 57: 475–503.

Wang, Austin, Charles K.S. Wu, Yao-Yuan Yeh and Fang-Yu Chen. 2018. 'What Does the 1992 Consensus Mean to Citizens in Taiwan?' *The Diplomat*. https://thediplomat.com/2018/11/what-does-the-1992-consensus-mean-to-citizens-in-taiwan/.

Wang, Chi. 2018. 'China's Reunification Dream Will Remain Out of Reach as Long As Taiwanese Feel They Don't Belong', *South China Morning Post*. www.scmp.com/comment/insight-opinion/article/2134091/chinas-reunification-dream-will-remain-out-reach-long.

Wang, Fu-chang. 2005. 'Why Bother about School Textbooks? An Analysis of the Origin of the Disputes Over Renshi Taiwan Textbooks in 1997', in J. Makeham and A. Hsiau (eds), *Cultural, Ethnic, and Political Nationalism in Contemporary Taiwan*. New York: Palgrave Macmillan, pp 55–102.

Wang, Peter Chen-main. 2007. 'A Bastion Created, a Regime Reformed, an Economy Reengineered, 1949–1970', in Murray A. Rubenstein, ed. *Taiwan: A New History*. Expanded edn. Armonk, NY: M.E. Sharpe, pp 320–338.

Wang, Te-Yu and I-Chou Liu. 2004. 'Contending Identities in Taiwan: Implications for Cross-Strait Relations', *Asian Survey* 44: 568–590.

Wang, Yuan-Kang. 2004. 'Taiwan's Democratization and Cross-Strait Security', *Orbis* 48: 293–304.

Weiss, Jessica Chen. 2019. 'How Hawkish is the Chinese Public? Another Look at "Rising Nationalism" and Chinese Foreign Policy', *Journal of Contemporary China* 28(119): 679–695.

Wendt, Alexander. 1992. 'Anarchy is What States Make of It: The Social Construction of Power Politics', *International Organization* 46: 391–425.

White, Hugh. 2013. *The China Choice: Why We Should Share Power*. Oxford: Oxford University Press.

White, Ismail, Chryl Laird and Troy Allen. 2014. 'Selling Out? The Politics of Navigating Conflicts Between Racial Group Interest and Self-Interest', *The American Political Science Review* 108(4): 783–800.

Wu, Chung-Li, Xiaochen Su and Hsiao-Chien Tsui. 2014. 'Threats, Acceptance, and Ambivalence in Cooperation: The Image of China in Taiwan', *East Asia* 31: 305–322.

Wu, Hsin-hsing. 1994. *Bridging the Strait: Taiwan, China, and the Prospects for Reunification*. New York: Oxford University Press.

Wu, Yu-Shan. 2016. 'Heading Towards Troubled Waters? The Impact of Taiwan's 2016 Elections on Cross-Strait Relations', *American Journal of Chinese Studies* 23: 59–75.

Xu, Shiquan. 2001. 'The 1992 Consensus: A Review and Assessment of Consultations Between the Association for Relations Across the Taiwan Strait and the Straits Exchange Foundation', *American Foreign Policy Interests* 23: 121–140.

Yang, Jiechi. 2014. 'Innovations in China's Diplomatic Theory and Practice under New Circumstances', *Qiushi* 6. http://english.qstheory.cn/magazine/201401/201401/t20140121_315115.htm

Yang, Philip. 2005. 'Rise of China and the Cross-Strait Relations', 5th Europe Northeast Asia Forum, Berlin, 15–17 December.

Yang, Xiangfeng. 2017. 'The Anachronism of a China Socialized: Why Engagement Is Not All It's Cracked Up to Be', *The Chinese Journal of International Politics* 10: 67–94.

Yeh, Hsin-Yi. 2014. 'A Sacred Bastion? A Nation in Itself? An Economic Partner of Rising China? Three Waves of Nation-Building in Taiwan after 1949', *Studies in Ethnicity and Nationalism* 14: 207–228.

Yeh, Su-ping, Yu Hsiang and Chung Yu-chen. 2019. 'Terry Gou Supports Cellphone Polling for KMT Primary' *Focus Taiwan*. https://focustaiwan.tw/politics/201905130022.

Yu, Peter Kien-hong. 2017. *Reinventing the Methodology of Studying Contemporary China*. Singapore: Springer.

Yuan, Jingdong. 2015. 'The Rise of China and the Emerging Order in Asia', in Mingjiang Li and Kalyan M. Kemburi, eds. *China's Power and Asian Security*. New York: Routledge, pp 25–37.

Zagoria, Donald S. 2003. 'Conclusion', in Donald S. Zagoria, with the assistance of Chris Fugarino, ed. *Breaking the China-Taiwan Impasse*. Westport, CT: Praeger, pp 207–212.

Zhai, Yida. 2019. 'A Peaceful Prospect or a Threat to Global Order: How Asian Youth View a Rising China', *International Studies Review* 21: 38–56.

Zhao, Suisheng and Xiong Qi. 2016. 'Hedging and Geostrategic Balance of East Asian Countries Toward China', *Journal of Contemporary China* 25: 485–499.

Zhong, Yang. 2016. 'Explaining National Identity Shift in Taiwan', *The Journal of Contemporary China* 25(99): 336–352.

Index

Note: Page numbers for figures are shown in **bold** and those for tables appear in *italics*.

1992 Consensus
  adoption and nature of agreement
     30–31, 95–96, 119, 165–166
  and China
    interpretation of 31, 166–167
    perceived value of 96
  and Taiwan
    elite views on 96–98
    as factor in Taiwanese identity
     157–177, 158–173, *159*, *164*,
     168–169, *171*, *173*
    interpretation of 31, 49, 95, 166–167
    political positions on 2–3, 97,
     112, 116
    popular opinion on 134–135,
     134, 139, **139**, **140**
  see also 'one country, two systems' model
228 Incident (also 28 February
    incident) 24, 31, 36, 189

A
Aboriginals (Austronesians) 28, 47–48, 120
age, as factor in Taiwanese identity
    45–46, 94–95, 97, 102–103, 112,
    126, 129–130
  survey data 158–177, *159*, *164*,
    168–169, *171*, *173*
Alliance of Taiwan Aboriginals 28
Allison, Graham T. 9
Almond, Gabriel A. 143
analytic eclecticism 65–66, 71–72
Association for Relations Across the
    Taiwan Strait (ARATS) 31,
    165–167
Austronesians (Aboriginals) 28, 47–48, 120
Autry, Greg 9

B
banknotes, reform of 33–34
Baron, James 39
Beckley, Michael 39, 50, 51
Benshengren 28, 47
Biden, Joseph 4, 208–209
Bobrow, Davis B. 20n1
Bonaparte, Napoleon 6
Brexit 140
Brooks, Stephen G. 50–51
Brown, Melissa J. 47–48, 147
Brzezinski, Zbigniew 67
Bunge, Mario 72–73, 89n6
Bush, George W. 35–36
Bush, Richard C. 5

C
Callahan, William A. 36, 53–54
Canada, comparisons with 110, 153n3
Carpenter, Ted Galen 51
causal mechanisms
  baseline from academic literature
    76–88, **79–81**, **83–84**, **86–88**
  elaboration based on further
    evidence 184–207, **185**, **187–188**,
    190, **192**, **194–196**, **198–199**,
    201–203
Chan, Steve 10
Chen, Dean P. 8
Chen Li-hung 173
Chen Shui-bian
  China's view of 114
  election victory 2000 35, 116–117
  policy positions and decisions 7,
    36–37, 94, 96, 101–102, 119, 148,
    191–193, 193–195
Chiang Ching-kuo 29

Chiang Kai-shek 24, 25, 104, 148
Chilton, Stephen 143
China
  Chinese economy
    as factor in Taiwanese identity 121, 130, **131**, 145–146, 157–178, *159, 164, 168–169, 171, 173*
    economic rise 50–53, 70–71
    ties with Taiwan 7, 60, 98–102, 106, 111, 170, 189, 191
  and Hong Kong 5–6, 13, 121, 147, 151, 207–208
  impact of people-to-people exchanges 150–151
  importance of Taiwan to Chinese identity 58–59, 70
  influence of students educated abroad 107
  and Japan 22–23, 35, 38–39
  migration to Taiwan 23–24, 45
  military buildup 58, 59, 84, 105–106
  military exercises and incidents 32, 36, 105, 152
  and nationalism 33, 38–39, 53–56, 59–60, 63n1, 153n6
  One China principle 60, 166, **187**
  'one country, two systems' model 5–6, 13, 121, 134
  rule of Taiwan during Qing Dynasty 22, 44
  strategies to promote unification 174
  and Taiwanese identity 16, 140
  terminology used 19–20
  tourism and travel
    Chinese visits to Taiwan 37, 111, 136–139, **138**, 152
    Taiwanese visits to China 127–128, **128**, *128*, 135, **136**
  and Tsai presidency 113–114
  United Nations recognition 25–26
  and United States
    1970s initiative and normalization 26, 27, 113
    ongoing relationship 51–53, 61–63, 67–68, 89n2, 122–123, 152, 178, 200
    past tensions 9–10, 31–36, 39, 67–68
    recent literature on 8–9, 13
    views on KLM and DPP leaders 114, 153n7
Chu, Eric 3, 124n4
Chu, Yun-han 52–53
civil liberties 5–6, 13, 120–121, 151
Coker, Christopher 56, 61
computer industry 27–28
constructivism 69, 89n3
Corcuff, Stéphane 29, 34, 47

COVID-19 152, 177, 209
cross-Strait relations, recent literature 7–8, 13
Cross-Strait Service Trade Agreement (CSSTA) 100–101, 103–104, 110
currency, reform of 26, 33–34

D

Dangwai movement 26
Democratic Progressive Party (DPP)
  Chen administration 2000–2008
    China's view of 114
    election victory 2000 35, 116–117, 191
    policy positions and decisions 7, 36–37, 94, 96, 101–102, 119, 148, 191–193, 193–195
  development during 1980s 29, 30
  in opposition 38
  origins and formation 26, 29, 104
  and Pan-Green coalition 48
  and Sunflower Movement 103
  Tsai administration from 2016
    election victory 2016 3, 105, 115, 119–120, 172
    election victory 2020 6, 105, 151
    policy positions and priorities 3–6, 96–97, 98, 111–114, 172–173, 195
    public satisfaction with 3–4, *159*, 160, 172–173, *173*, 175–176
  use of diversionary tactics 209
democratization
  growth of 29, 30, 97, 189
  and national identity 11, 70, 120–121, 135–136, *137*, 146–148, 150
Deng Xiaoping 4, 27, 50, 54, 60
Dole, Bob 115
DPP *see* Democratic Progressive Party
Dutch colonial settlement 22

E

Economic Cooperation Framework Agreement (ECFA) 98–102, 111, 170, 189
Edmondson, Robert 24
education level, whether factor in Taiwanese identity 157–177, *159, 164, 168–169, 171, 173*
education system
  school curriculum 37–38, 45, 148, 195
  school textbooks 29–30, 32–33, 103–105, 147
  teaching of history 29–30
    Japanese colonial legacy 103–105
    Sinicization 37–38, 45
    Taiwanization 29–30, 32–33, 147, 148, 195
  universities 32

INDEX

Era of Change 103
ethnic identities 28, 47–48, 120

F

Feng, Zhu 59
Foot, Rosemary 50
Formosa Incident *see* Kaohsiung Incident
Fravel, M. Taylor 59
fruit diplomacy 191

G

gender, whether factor in Taiwanese identity 157–177, *159*, *164*, *168–169*, *171*, *173*
Germany, value priorities 144
Glaser, Charles 50
Goh, Evelyn 27
Gong, Gerrit W. 8
Gourevitch, Peter 77
Gries, Peter Hays 10, 145
Gurr, Ted Robert 76

H

Hakka 47–48, 120
Han, Zhen 123
Han Chinese 44, 47–48, 120
Han Kuo-yu 6
Holo 47–48, 120
Hong Kong 5–6, 13, 121, 147, 151, 207–208
Hsu, Chien-Jung 127, 132
Huang, Chin-Hao 49, 92
Huawei 39
human rights 5–6, 13, 120–121, 151
Hung Hsiu-chu 115–116, 124n4
Huntington, Samuel P. 124n1

I

ideation
  and national identity 13–17
  theoretical framework *14*
independence *see* Taiwanese independence
industrialization 23–24, 26
Inglehart, Ronald F. 17, 143–145, 146
International Civil Aviation Organization 152

J

Jacobs, Bruce J. 8, 155
Jacques, Martin 9
James, Patrick 49, 78, 92
Japan 22–24, 28, 35, 38–39, 70, 103–105
Jerdén, Björn 57
Jiang Zemin 32
Johnston, Alastair Iain 13, 57, 84

K

Kang, David C. 56
Kang, Peter 8, 155
Kaohsiung Incident (also Formosa Incident) 26–27
Kastner, Scott L. 7–8
Katzenstein, Peter J. 72
Kennedy, John F. 115
  While England Slept 112, 124n3
Kenya 39
Kerry, John 109
KMT *see* Kuomintang
Ko Wen-je 48
Korea 23
Kuomintang (KMT)
  China's views and positions on 153n7
  loss of 2000 election 35, 191
  loss of 2016 election 2–3, 115–117, 124n4
  loss of 2020 election 6
  Ma administration 2008–2016
    election victory 2008 98–99
    deepening of cross-Strait ties and 1992 Consensus 96
    bilateral summit 2015 2–3
    ECFA 98–102, 111, 170, 189
    halting arms deals with US 112
    reactions to and protests against 102–103, 110, 118, 119, 145–146
    intraparty politics 116
    and native Taiwanese 104
    and Pan-Blue coalition 48, 116
    persona of Ma 116, 132
  rule 1949-1979 24–27, 45, 104, 186–189
  rule during 1980s 27–30
  rule during 1990s 30–34
  and Sinicization 37–38

L

language use 130–132, **132**
  see also Taiwanization
Lasswell, Harold D. 82
Layne, Christopher 51, 62
Lee Teng-hui 25, 30, 31–32, 33, 104, 105, 114, 148
Lepesant, Tanguy 130, 132–133
Levy, Jack S. 77
Li, Kuang-chün 58
Li, Yitan 45–46, 50, 59–60, 209
liberalism 69
Lien Chan 37, 99
Lin, Chia-lung 46
Lin, Syaru Shirley 7, 145
Lipset, Seymour Martin 144

Liu, Frank Cheng-Shan 45–46, 50, 126
Liu, I-Chou 10, 145

M

Ma Ying-jeou
  deepening of cross-Strait ties and 1992 Consensus 96
  bilateral summit 2015 2–3
  ECFA 98–102, 111, 170, 189
  halting arms deals with US 112
  reactions to and protests against 102–103, 110, 118, 119, 145–146
  election victory 2008 98–99
  intraparty politics 116
  persona 116, 132
  and Sinicization 37–38
Mahbubani, Kishore 9, 55, 208
Mainland *see* China
Mainland Economic Ties *see* Taiwanese economy
Mainlanders (*Waishengren*) 23, 28, 47–48, 94, 120
Malaysia 39
Mandarinization (Sinicization) 24, 29–30, 37–38, 45
Mao Zedong 44
Marsh, Robert 48–49, 77
martial law 24, 29
Mearsheimer, John J. 52, 66–67
Meng Wanzhou 39
Mosca, Matthew W. 22

N

National Day (Taiwan) 112, 189
National Humiliation Day (China) 35
National Unification Council 30, 37, 166
Nationalist Party *see* Kuomintang
Navarro, Peter 9
New Party 46, 48
New People's Society 23
New Power Party 48
New Zealand 111
Newton, Isaac 205
Niou, Emerson 127, 158, 179n1
Nixon, Richard 113–114

O

Obama, Barack 109
Olympic Games 33, 36, 37
'one country, two systems' model 5–6, 13, 97, 121, 134
opinion polls 45–47, 94, 126–127
Organski, A.F.K. 20n2

P

Pan-Blue and Pan-Green coalitions 48–49
Paul, T.V. 123
People First Party 48, 115, 116
Pfonner, Michael R. 78
Pillsbury, Michael 9, 51–52, 58
pocketbook *see* self-interest
PRC *see* China

R

realism 69
relational mechanisms *see* causal mechanisms
research methodology 92–93, 126–127, 158–173, *159*, *164*, *168–169*, *171*
reunification *see* unification
Rigger, Shelley 34, 48
Rob, Schmitz 157
Ross, Robert S. 57–58, 59
Roy, Dennis 59

S

same-sex marriage 121
Schelling, Thomas C. 61
school curriculum 37–38, 45, 148, 195
school textbooks 29–30, 32–33, 103–105, 147
Second World War, commemoration of 38
self-interest, influence on identity 14–15, *14*, 16–17, 101, 207
  survey data 157–178, *159*, *164*, *168–169*, *171*, *173*
Shakespeare, William 181
Sheng, Lijun 32
Shirk, Susan L. 13, 35, 36, 44, 54, 59, 60, 77
Sil, Rudra 72
Singapore 111
Sinicization (Mandarinization) 24, 29–30, 37–38, 45
Sino-Japanese war 22–23
Snow, Edgar 44
socialization hypothesis 17, 144–145, 146–148
Soong, James 37, 116, 132
standard of living 128–130, **129**
  see also self-interest
status quo
  elite views on 111–113
  popular opinion on 132–133, **133**, **134**
  position of Tsai administration 94–95, 119–120
Straits Exchange Foundation (SEF) 31, 165–167

INDEX

Su, Chi 166
Su, Jenny 10, 145
Sun Yat-sen 29, 34, 148
Sunflower Movement 102–103, 110
Swaine, Michael D. 56, 57
systemism 9, 65–66, 72–76, **73–75**, *76*, 156
see also causal mechanisms

T

Taiwan People's Party 48
Taiwan Relations Act (TRA) 27, 107–108, 113
Taiwan Solidarity Union 48
Taiwanese culture
 influence on identity 135–136, **137**
 relation to Chinese culture 143–144, **143**
Taiwanese economy
 economic challenges 114
 as factor in Taiwanese identity 121, 130, **131**, 145–146, 157–178, *159*, *164*, *168–169*, *171*, *173*
 Free Trade Agreements 103, 109–110, 111
 growth of 25, 26, 27–28
 reform of banknotes 33–34
 ties with China 7, 60, 98–102, 106, 111, 170, 189, 191
 impact of people-to-people exchanges 150–151
Taiwanese history
 1949-1979 24–27, 45, 104, 186–189
 1980s and 1990s 27–34
 2000 onwards 35–40
 early history 21–22, 44
 Japanese rule 22–24, 28, 103–105
 overview 21, 40–41
 teaching of
  Japanese colonial legacy 103–105
  Sinicization 37–38, 45
  Taiwanization 29–30, 32–33, 147, 148, 195
Taiwanese identity
 ideas for future research 207–210
 introduction and overview 6–17, **12**, 45–49
 significance of 173–174
 summary of conclusions 206–207
Taiwanese independence
 elite views on 112
 as factor in Taiwanese identity 157–178, *159*, *164*, *168–169*, *171*, *173*
 and politics 48–49, 209
 popular opinion on 132–133, 132–135, **133**, **133–134**

and referendums 36–37, 112, 119, 193–195
Taiwanization 30, 49, 120–121, 147, 191
Taliaferro, Jeffrey W. 62
theoretical approaches *see* analytic eclecticism; systemism
Thucydides Trap 9, 10, 40
tourism and travel
 Chinese visits to Taiwan 37, 111, 136–139, **138**, 152
 impact of people-to-people exchanges 150–151
 Taiwanese visits to China 127–128, **128**, *128*, 135, **136**
Trans-Pacific Partnership 103, 109–110
Travel Agency Association 111
travel permits 106–107, 152
tridemism 29
Trump, Donald 3, 4, 39–40, 67–68, 89n2, 200, 209
Tsai, Chang-Yen 27, 28, 47, 49
Tsai Ing-wen
 China's view of 114
 election victory 2016 3, 105, 115, 119–120, 172
 election victory 2020 6, 105, 151
 policy positions and priorities 3–6, 96–97, 98, 111–114, 172–173, 195
 public satisfaction with 3–4, *159*, 160, 172–173, *173*, 175–176

U

unification
 Chinese strategies to promote 174
 importance to China 55, 58, 59
 and Pan-Blue coalition 48–49
 popular opinion on 132–135, **133–134**, 139–140, **141**
 see also 1992 Consensus; 'one country, two systems' model
United Daily, The 47
United Nations 25–26
United States
 'America First' rhetoric 39–40
 American identity xiv, 16, 157, 174
 and China
  1970s initiative and normalization 26, 27, 113
  ongoing relationship 51–53, 61–63, 67–68, 89n2, 122–123, 152, 178, 200
  past tensions 9–10, 31–36, 39, 67–68
  recent literature on 8–9, 13
 and Taiwan
  aid under Nationalist rule 25
  direct dialogue with Taiwan 3–4

effect of support on identity formation 62–63, 121–123
military assistance 61–62, 84, 108–109, 140–143, **142**, 197–198
arms sales 27, 57, 112–113
official visits 31–32
Taiwan Relations Act 27, 107–108, 113
during Trump era 39–40, 67–68, 200
universities 32
see also Sunflower Movement

V
Verba, Sidney 143

W
Waishengren (Mainlanders) 23, 28, 47–48, 94, 120
Waltz, Kenneth N. 76
Wang, Grace 37
Wang Jin-pyng 116
Wang, Te-Yu 10, 145
Welzel, Christian 17, 144–145, 146
Wendt, Alexander 153n7
White, Hugh 122–123
White Terror 24
Wohlforth, William C. 50–51
World Health Assembly 152
World Trade Organization (WTO) 40
Wu Hsing-Kuo 181

X
Xi Jinping 2, 4, 5, 58–59, 105–106, 113, 147

Y
Yu, Peter Kien-hong 66
Yuan, Jingdong 51

Z
Zhang, Enyu 59–60
Zheng Chenggong (Koxinga) 22
Zhong, Yang 147
Zhongli Incident 26

www.ingramcontent.com/pod-product-compliance
Lightning Source LLC
Chambersburg PA
CBHW071153070526
44584CB00019B/2778